Working women and the law

Scarcely a week goes by without a news item highlighting the problems facing working women in Britain, from sexual harassment to lack of child care facilities. *Working Women and the Law* investigates why the law, and in particular the anti-discrimination laws, have failed women in the workplace.

The authors, drawing on their considerable teaching and research experience, explore the practical and theoretical barriers that limit the law's ability to achieve change. As well as looking at specific legislative measures, they consider how the law works in practice, with chapters on wages, social security and taxation, and access to work. They identify three main strands in the law's treatment of working women – protection through paternalism, equality of treatment, and the granting of additional rights – and, setting the law in its social context, they discuss women's patterns of employment and the practices which can adversely affect women's working lives.

A unique overview of law, theory and practice, *Working Women and the Law* deals with issues which are central to the lives of women at work. It presents the law in a way which, while dealing with the legal complexities, remains accessible to non-lawyers, and will be particularly useful to students on courses in Women and the Law, Employment Law, and Women's Studies. It will also appeal to anyone with an interest in the law's treatment of working women, including practitioners in the law and in management.

Working women and the law

Equality and discrimination in theory and practice

Anne E. Morris
and
Susan M. Nott

Routledge/Sweet & Maxwell
London and New York

For Hannah

First published in 1991
by Routledge, in association with Sweet & Maxwell, London
11 New Fetter Lane, London EC4P 4EE

Simultaneously published in the USA and Canada
by Routledge
a division of Routledge, Chapman and Hall Inc.
29 West 35th Street, New York, NY 10001

© 1991 Anne E. Morris and Susan M. Nott

Typeset by LaserScript Limited, Mitcham, Surrey.
Printed and bound in Great Britain by Mackays of Chatham PLC, Kent

British Library Cataloguing in Publication Data

Morris, Anne E. *1952–*
    Working women and the law : equality and discrimination in theory and practice.
    1. Great Britain. Women. Employment. Law.
    I. Title II. Nott, Susan M.
    344.10414

Library of Congress Cataloging in Publication Data

Morris, Anne E., 1952–
    Working women and the law : equality and discrimination in theory and practice / by Anne E. Morris and Susan M. Nott.
    p. cm.
    1. Sex discrimination in employment—Law and legislation—United States. 2. Women—Employment—Law and legislation—United States. 3. Sex discrimination against women—Law and legislation—United States. I. Nott, Susan M., . II. Title.
    KF3467.M67   1990
    344.73'014133—dc20
    [347.30414133]   90–8483
                                                                          CIP

ISBN 0-415-05739-6
     0-415-00937-5 (pbk)

Contents

Statutes

Trade Boards Act 1909

Wages Act 1986
    section 12
    section 13
    section 14
    section 14(6)(a)

Wages Councils Acts 1945–1979

Cases

Commission for Racial Equality v Amari Plastics Ltd [1982]
Community Task Force v Rimmer [1986]
Coomes (Holdings) Ltd v Shields [1978]
Coyne v Export Credits Guarantee Department [1981]
Curl v Air UK Ltd (1988)

Defrenne v Sabena 43/74 [1976]
Dennehy v Sealink UK Ltd [1987]
De Souza v The Automobile Association [1986]
Dugdale v Kraft Foods Ltd [1977]
Duke v Reliance Systems Ltd [1988]

Eaton Ltd v Nuttall [1977]
Electrolux Ltd v Hutchinson [1976]
Elegbede v The Wellcome Foundation Ltd [1977]
Enderby v Frenchay Health Authority and Secretary of State for Health
    (1989)

Forex Neptune (Overseas) Ltd v Miller [1987]
Foster v British Gas plc [1988]
FTATU v Modgill [1980]; PEL v Modgill

Garland v British Rail Engineering Ltd 12/81 [1982]
Gates v Wirral Borough Council (unreported)
Green v Broxtowe District Council [1977]
Grimsby Carpet Company v Bedford [1987]
Gregory v Tudsbury [1982]

Hammersmith & Queen Charlotte's Special Health Authority v Cato
    [1988]
Hampson v Department of Education and Science [1989], [1990]
Handels-og Kontorfunktionaererernes Forbund I Danmark v Dansk
    Arbejdsgiverforening (acting for Danfoss) 109/88 [1989]
Handley v Mono Ltd [1979]
Hayes v Malleable Working Men's Club and Institute [1985]
Hayward v Cammell Laird Shipbuilders Ltd (No. 2) [1988]
Home Office v Commission for Racial Equality [1982]
Home Office v Holmes [1985]
Horsey v Dyfed County Council [1982]
Hugh-Jones v St John's College, Cambridge [1979]
Hurley v Mustoe [1981]
Hurley v Mustoe (No. 2) [1983]

James v Eastleigh Borough Council [1989], [1990]
Jenkins v Kingsgate (Clothing Productions) Ltd 96/80 [1981]
Jenkins v Kingsgate (Clothing Productions) Ltd (No. 2) [1981]
Jex-Blake v Senatus of Edinburgh University (1873)

R v Birmingham City Council ex parte Equal Opportunities
   Commission [1989]
R v Commission for Racial Equality ex parte London Borough of
   Hillingdon [1982]
R v Commission for Racial Equality ex parte Prestige Group plc [1984]
R v London Borough of Islington ex parte Building Employers
   Confederation [1989]
Rainey v Greater Glasgow Health Board [1987]
Redland Roof Tiles Ltd v Harper [1977]
Reed Packaging Ltd v Boozer [1988]
Rinner-Kühn v FWW Spezial-Gebaudereinigung GmbH & Co KG
   171/88 [1989]
Roberts v Hopwood [1925]
Roberts v Tate & Lyle Food Distribution Ltd [1983]
Rookes v Barnard [1964]
Rummler v Dato-Druck GmbH 237/85 [1987]

Saunders v Richmond upon Thames BC [1977]
Science Research Council v Nasse [1978], [1980]
Secretary of State for Employment v Levy [1989]
Short v Poole Corporation [1926]
Snowball v Gardner Merchant [1987]
Snoxell and Davies v Vauxhall Motors Ltd [1978]
Southampton and South-West Hampshire Area Health Authority
   (Teaching) v Marshall (No. 2) [1989]
Steel v Union of Post Office Workers [1978]
Strathclyde Regional Council v Porcelli [1986]

Tennants Textiles Colours Ltd v Todd [1989]
Thomas v NCB [1987]
Turley v Allders Department Stores Ltd [1980]
Turner v Labour Party and Labour Party Superannuation Society [1987]

United Biscuits v Young [1978]

Van Duyn v Home Office 41/74 [1975]
Vaux & Associated Breweries v Ward (1968)
Von Colson and Kamann v Land Nordrhein-Westfalen 14/83 (1984)

Waddington v Leicester Council for Voluntary Services [1977]
Wallace v South Eastern Education and Library Board [1980]
Watches of Switzerland v Savell [1983]
West Midlands Passenger Transport Executive v Singh [1988]
Wileman v Minilec Engineering [1988]
Williams v Thomas and Dyfed County Council (1986)
Wilsons & Clyde Coal Ltd v English [1938]
Worringham and Humphreys v Lloyds Bank Ltd 69/80 [1981]

Tables

Preface

The initial inspiration for this book sprang from our experiences teaching 'Women and the Law' at the University of Liverpool and we were spurred on by discussion and debate within the University's Women's Studies Group, whose membership is drawn from a variety of disciplines. To the members of that group, to our own students and especially to our colleague and fellow teacher on the 'Women and the Law' course, Kate Williams, we are grateful for the stimulation and enthusiasm which encouraged us to write this text.

We have not attempted to defend the law, though we do believe that it should not be dismissed as futile or even damaging to the improvement of the situation of women in paid employment. Even whilst writing we have been constantly updating and amending as the law has changed. Many of these changes, though sadly not all, have been positive and constructive and have convinced us of the need to have a text which, while it acknowledges the limits of the law, has faith in its potential to improve matters for women. We have endeavoured throughout to write a book which presents the law in a way which deals with the legal complexities but which we hope remains accessible to non-lawyers.

We are indebted to many people for their help, support and encouragement during the process of writing. It is always difficult to single out particular individuals, but we must mention the assistance and infinite patience offered by our colleagues Bernadette Walsh and Tim Evans in their efforts, ultimately successful, to familiarise us with the intricacies of the word processor, and also in Bernadette's case with those of the social security system. We are grateful too to Gill Davies at Routledge for her help and encouragement. Lastly, we wish to thank Peter Morgan and Michael Jones whose unfailing willingness to offer constructive criticism and practical help have contributed in large part to the completion of this book. Responsibility for the contents and any shortcomings is, of course, entirely ours. The law is stated as at 31 January 1990 although the publishers have kindly allowed us to take into account certain important developments, including *Barber* v *Guardian Royal Exchange Assurance Group* and *James* v *Eastleigh Borough Council.*

Anne E. Morris
Susan M. Nott

Chapter one

Women in work
Law in a social context

Traditional legal scholarship concentrates on the content of legal rules and the manner in which those rules are interpreted by the courts. Consequently there are numerous books and papers on the general theme of 'workers and the law' which set out to define the worker's legal position.[1] Where women have been singled out, it is because areas of law with particular relevance for women, such as the law relating to equal pay, are the centre of attention rather than women themselves. Women are indisputably the focus of this book which is intended as a critique of the law as it affects working women. Some explanation and justification may be required for taking such an approach.

In the first place, the subject matter of this book is working women, that is women who are in paid employment. The decision to focus on laws that affect them in the course of their working lives is deliberate and has positive advantages. Primarily it allows a judgement to be made on the impact that a homogeneous body of law has on a specific group of individuals. This impact is rarely experienced directly. Instead, most women's contact with the law is through intermediaries (who may well be male), such as solicitors, social security officials or chairmen of industrial tribunals, applying their interpretation of legal rules to the circumstances of a particular woman.[2] Legal research which concentrates on textual analysis makes little or no attempt to assess the practical impact of legal rules. The guiding principle of this book is that it is not only desirable but also essential to appreciate the human dimension within which legal rules function. This includes acknowledging that laws can and do bear differently upon men and women. Conventionally, the law has been regarded as being largely gender-neutral, affecting men and women equally. This notion is now being questioned as is evidenced by the growth of 'Women and the Law' courses, the publication of books written from the perspective of women as subjects of law and the establishment of organisations designed to focus on women's issues, such as the Women's Legal Defence Fund.[3] The decision to explore the impact of the law on the lives of working women is, therefore, defen-

1

sible from a theoretical as well as a practical perspective. Currently there are approximately ten million women in paid employment and most women work for a considerable portion of their lives between leaving education and retirement. Given that these women form a substantial part of the working population as a whole, it is legitimate to enquire to what extent the law recognises this fact. As will become apparent, the law is a far from subtle device with which to advance the interests of a particular group. That could be an argument for saying that the law should be used only to respond to the needs of the greatest number, but even on the uncertain philosophical basis of sheer weight of numbers, working women have a claim that the law should take account of their needs. On the stronger grounds of what justice demands, their case would seem a compelling one.

Obviously, there are other groups in society – the disabled or ethnic minorities for example – from whose perspective it might prove valuable to examine the law. Within these groups, however, there is still a divide between working men and working women. The adverse response that individuals may receive because they are coloured or disabled does not, by definition, depend on their sex, but a black or disabled worker who also happens to be female may face an additional form of discrimination which sets her apart from her male counterparts. This makes it imperative to give priority to analysing the law's treatment of working women, since it is only once this is appreciated that other 'disabilities' can be considered in their correct context.

Just as the decision to concentrate on women in paid employment has to be justified, so too does the decision to focus not on some particular aspect of the law but on all laws that have a bearing on the lives of those women who work. Whilst a study of a specific piece of legislation can prove valuable, it can give a distorted impression of the impact of the law since it ignores the cumulative effect of laws. A critique of the statutory definition of discrimination might make no mention of the law relating to social security and yet the concept of the family employed in the social security legislation may effectively reduce the benefits to be extracted from any anti-discrimination legislation.[4] In addition, as one commentator has most cogently remarked:

> That a law is gender-specific in its formulation need not, however, mean that it is significant for women's position in law or society. The same applies to the directives found in sex discrimination legislation. Even though its express objective gives it an automatic relevance to women's law, and even though the act's enforcement measures are many and comprehensive, this in itself is not tantamount to the law's consequences having special significance for women's lives and rights, either generally or in decisions in individual cases.[5]

Whilst clearly not ignoring anti-discrimination legislation or those laws specifically designed to safeguard the position of the pregnant employee, it seems wise also to consider the variety of laws that can affect a particular aspect of a woman's life. For some commentators this has the added advantage of abandoning traditional subject divisions, such as employment law, revenue law or social security law, and reorganising legal rules on a basis that is of greater relevance to women. Tove Stang Dahl in her book, *Women's Law*, makes this point. 'Women's law is built in part upon *new* concepts: birth law, equal status law, housewives' law, paid work law.'[6] It is, therefore, essential to appreciate the range of laws that can have a bearing upon a woman in employment.

Analyses of specific areas of the law can also be misleading in other respects. When discussing the law relating to sex discrimination or equal pay it is essential to consider the machinery available for rectifying breaches of the law. In this context criticisms might be directed at the way such claims are handled by industrial tribunals. The problem here is that a perspective which is too narrow can ignore certain important questions. If, for example, industrial tribunals handle sex discrimination cases badly, it may be that the fault lies specifically in over-complex anti-discrimination laws. Alternatively, as recent research seems to suggest,[7] the problem may be much wider than this, exposing lack of sympathy with or appreciation of the policy behind the anti-discrimination legislation. Still other failings, such as the non-availability of legal aid, may be experienced by all those who wish to utilise the tribunal system.

The approach taken in the course of the chapters which follow is intended to reflect the theme of this book. There is no shortage of data regarding the patterns of working women's lives. Figures are produced by government and by other researchers on the hours women work, the wages which they earn and the employment which they favour. By relating the law to the pattern of working women's lives, an insight can be gained into how women are affected by the law. For example, if it becomes apparent that legal rules are in the main designed to benefit full-time employees, then their impact will be negligible on that sizeable portion of women who work part-time. As well as these straightforward statistics, however, there is reference to research which has highlighted those occasions and circumstances when women are likely to be treated less favourably than men. Various writers have remarked that lawyers cannot afford to ignore the empirical data generated in the course of sociological research and, in this context, such research helps to measure how successfully the law is meeting the needs of working women.

By analysing the content as well as the practical impact of the law, the intention is to make this book accessible to lawyers and non-lawyers alike. On the one hand it will provide lawyers with a breadth of information that sadly tends to be lacking in conventional legal texts. On the other hand it will include details of the law for those non-lawyers who may be too disposed to dismiss legal rules as if they were of little significance. One writer commenting on the lack of reference to equality legislation in her book justified the omission in the following terms:

> equality legislation is peripheral, for two broad reasons: the restrictive application of the legislation in its own terms and the small scope of legislation around 'equality' in relation to the profound character of gender divisions. None of this is to argue the irrelevance of equality legislation; rather that the real dynamic of change lies elsewhere.[8]

This perception of law as peripheral or symbolic requires careful consideration since it raises the fundamental issue of what exactly may be expected of the law. Carol Smart, in *Feminism and the Power of Law*, asserts that her purpose is to 'construct a warning to feminism to avoid the siren call of law'.[9] To this end, she presents a picture of law as a power within society which has little that is positive to offer women. Attempts at law reform are seen as fruitless since the law's basic values remain inimical to the interests of women. Any experiment in constructing a feminist alternative to those basic values, that is a feminist jurisprudence, is rejected since it is said to preserve 'law's place in the hierarchy of discourses which maintains that law has access to truth and justice'.[10] As an alternative to these activities feminists are encouraged to challenge the power of law.

Whilst avoiding the issue of whether this book can claim to be written from a feminist perspective, it is impossible to ignore those arguments which either marginalise the law or condemn it as a negative force. The following chapters will provide countless examples of the law failing to satisfy the aspirations of working women. It is a fundamental issue whether the nature of law is such that its use can never substantially improve the situation of women. Therefore, the opening chapters of this book will explore the limits of the law in the sense of what it may be possible to achieve when employing legal rules. It is all too tempting when writing about the law to pay close attention to the content of rules whilst neglecting the characteristics of the system of which those rules are part. There is a long-standing tradition of legal philosophy which has devoted much thought to how judicial decisions are made, to developing a coherent concept of justice and to exploring the nature of law. It is to those traditional theories, as well as the more radical views of feminist jurisprudence, that reference will be made in Chapter 2 in order to determine how readily the law can transform an ideal – a dramatic improvement in women's standing in society – into reality.

Using this assessment of the limitations of the law as its basis, Chapter 3 continues the theoretical approach by advancing the notion that the law as it affects working women does not have a single objective, but rather has a number of policy goals. Since these policy goals are not compatible but contradictory, the law is not as effective as it might be. In subsequent chapters which analyse the relevant legal rules, an attempt is made to determine which of the various policy goals is being pursued. This should allow some conclusion to be reached on where policy changes are necessary.

Chapter 4 provides a contrast to the opening chapters by presenting statistical information on the patterns of working women's lives. In the course of this introduction reference has continually been made to working women as if they formed a homogeneous group with common needs and aspirations. What Chapter 4 demonstrates is that this is far from the truth. There is a diversity about the working lives of women which is not true of working men. The interesting question is whether this diversity is born of choice or necessity. Would, for example, as many women work part-time as currently do, if the state were to provide adequate child care facilities? Alternatively, is that decision influenced by the liability to make national insurance contributions and pay income tax?[11] Some commentators have argued that, as increasing numbers of women enter a particular profession, it is possible to ask whether 'feminisation' of that profession or occupation will occur. In other words, will different qualities come to be valued and will working practices adjust to take account of women's needs? Information which indicates how women organise their working lives poses a similar question in relation to the law. Is there any evidence of its 'feminisation'? Does the law as it currently stands take account of the interests of working women and, if not, is it possible for it to do so?

The remaining chapters consider various aspects of employment including access to jobs, wages, tax, pensions and the enforcement of employment rights. This gives scope to consider relevant laws, relevant research and any other relevant issue raised in the opening chapters. In the chapter concerned with wages, for example, the law relating to equal pay, social security and low wages is examined in the light of current figures on women's earnings, and these practical matters are set against the earlier theoretical discussions. In this manner a more complete understanding of the situation is possible than if the debate focused on a single piece of legislation such as the Equal Pay Act 1970.

This introduction is intended to give some indication of the themes that will be pursued in the following chapters. The book is a product of the dissatisfaction felt with existing books on this topic which do little to demonstrate that the law is an inherently complex discipline with limited powers to transform the face of society. Yet, however limited the law may be, there is no comparable substitute. Early authors on women's rights placed a good deal of faith in the power of the law to change society. Clearly, it is unrealistic to expect the law to act as if by magic to transform human nature and human behaviour overnight, but that does not detract from the importance of attempting to construct the best possible legal framework in pursuit of such change.

Chapter two

Theory and practice
The realisation of an ideal

The White Paper, *Equality for Women*,[1] published prior to the passage of the Sex Discrimination Act 1975, reflected upon the role of the law in eliminating discrimination and cautioned against expecting too much:

> It is important to recognise the inevitable restraints on what can be achieved by legislation, so that it is seen in proper perspective, without arousing false expectations or encouraging a sense of complacency. An anti-discrimination law is relevant only to the extent that economic and social conditions enable people to develop their individual potential and to compete for opportunities on more or less equal terms. A woman will obtain little benefit from equal employment opportunity if she is denied adequate education and training because economic necessity or social pressures have induced her to enter the labour market at an early age. Some mothers will derive as little benefit if there is inadequate provision for part-time work or flexible working hours, or for day nurseries....Legislation is a necessary pre-condition for an effective equal opportunity policy but it is not a sufficient condition. A wide range of administrative and voluntary measures will be needed to translate the ideal of equal opportunity into practical reality. The responsibility for these wider measures does not rest with Government alone. It must be accepted by employers and trade unions, by commercial undertakings and the professions, by universities, colleges and schools, and by the community as a whole.[2]

The emphasis on the law's limited scope to influence individual behaviour is underlined by the reference elsewhere in the White Paper to law as 'an unequivocal declaration of public policy'. The implication is that a measure such as the Sex Discrimination Act 1975 functions as a declaration of intent rather than a radical means of coercing individuals into modifying their behaviour. If this is correct, it may in part account for the criticism levelled at the Sex Discrimination Act and other anti-discrimination legislation by certain commentators. On

7

various occasions this body of legislation has been described as 'peripheral',[3] as creating a climate rather than an infrastructure[4] and as making 'no significant material change to women's lives'.[5] The fairness of these comments and others like them depends, however, on whether their authors appreciated the constraints on the law's facility to secure change. It is hardly appropriate to condemn the anti-discrimination legislation if it represents the best possible solution in the circumstances.

Legislation can be viewed and appraised from two very distinct perspectives. On the one hand the content of legislation can be analysed, the concepts it employs can be reviewed, uncertainties may be highlighted and inconsistencies with other legislative measures pinpointed. On the other hand legislation can be judged as a response to a particular predicament. This requires not only a clear understanding of the circumstances giving rise to the predicament, but an appreciation of what it is possible for the law to achieve, since, undeniably, there are both practical and theoretical limits on the law and its power to set change in motion. A practical limitation is represented by the problem regarding the enforcement of legislation. No law will be observed by all of the people for all of the time. At best, enforcement involves compromises between efficiency and available resources. Theoretical limits are based on certain hypotheses concerning the nature of law. Some of those dealt with in the course of this chapter are best described as traditional. They reflect orthodox views on issues such as the concept of justice. Their inclusion is deliberate since they represent the line of thought that lawyers are most likely to be exposed to during the academic stage of their training. Other more radical views do exist and these too are analysed. In short, the range of opinions canvassed here is intended to emphasise how an individual's perception of the uses to which law can be put is fundamentally affected by views as to its very nature.

By taking account of both theoretical and practical limits, it is possible to evaluate the law from an informed perspective. A critical framework emerges which enables the identification, even before the legislation is drafted, of the barriers that prevent an ideal – such as the elimination of discrimination – from becoming a reality.

Theoretical limitations

The nature of law

Over the centuries legal theorists have speculated upon the nature of law and the role which law performs within the state. The answers vary with the standpoint of the particular theorist. Although this is not a book devoted to reviewing legal philosophies,[6] the existence of that continuing debate and, in particular, the issues to which legal theorists address themselves are crucial, since such fundamental questions can shed some light upon the nature of law and its limitations.

Remarkable unanimity exists over the necessity for every society[7] to be regulated by laws. It is claimed that even the most rudimentary societies will have rules concerning what is regarded as acceptable or unacceptable behaviour, though whether such rules can accurately be described as laws and their whole as constituting a legal system is open to argument.[8] As a society becomes larger and more sophisticated, it develops those features and institutions which are commonly associated with a legal system, such as a legislature and a law enforcement agency.[9] The political organisation within a given society will, of course, influence the form that such institutions take.

There is, however, an important exception to this general line of thinking about law and legal systems. This is represented by Marxist theory, which maintains that law, far from being a social necessity, is a product of the economic relations within a particular society. Marx drew a distinction between the economic base of society and its social superstructure. It was his contention that the economic base shaped the form and content of the superstructure, though exactly how was not clear. Law, according to Marx, is part of the social superstructure and its content must presumably be determined by the economic base.[10] What has intrigued legal theorists is exactly how this process of 'cause and effect' works. Two explanations have been advanced. The first, 'crude materialism',[11] suggests that the law reacts to whatever constitutes the means of producing wealth in a society at any particular time. Hence, when land represented the prime source of wealth in England, elaborate laws evolved to protect ownership and prevent alienation of land. As, however, the emphasis shifted from agriculture to industry, the law responded and it became easier to buy and sell land since this was what the industrial economy required. As an explanation 'crude materialism' leaves much to be desired. In a very general sense it must be true to say that the law takes account of shifts in economic activity, but Marx seemed to imply that the link was much closer than this. 'Crude materialism' fails, however, to explain the mechanism by which this process occurs. In addition, since the law is concerned with the whole range of human activity, it is difficult to see how legal rules concerning issues such as child abuse are directly related to the economic base.

'Class instrumentalism'[12] is a second and arguably more convincing explanation of how the content of law is determined by the existing economic order. It portrays the law as an instrument of class oppression. The individuals who at any particular time control the means of producing wealth in society use the law to maintain their dominant

9

position and safeguard their particular interests. Thus the emphasis on safeguarding private property in English law works to the benefit of the dominant class, though the law is always spoken of as if it were to everyone's advantage and treats everyone equally. The 'mystique' that surrounds the law legitimises this oppressive situation and prevents it being recognised for what it is. Plausible though this theory may appear, it still fails to explain adequately the logistics of the process. The dominant class are deemed to know who they are, to have a common purpose and to be capable of translating that purpose into law.

Marxist theory represents a singular approach towards the nature of law and legal systems. In general, legal theorists argue over the uses to which law may be put, the taxonomy of law and whether the law's content has to conform to certain abstract standards.[13] What those individuals do not dispute is the need for law. Marxist commentators set little store by these matters since to discuss them is to accept the ideology that is part of the law. Indeed Engels, in a much quoted remark, asserted that once a communist state was established the institutions of the bourgeois state including law would 'wither away' since they would no longer be required.[14] Though subsequently this position has been refined,[15] it is still contended that 'law' in a communist society would be very different from law in a capitalist society since the whole basis on which communist and capitalist societies are organised is different.[16]

The Marxist perception of law, if correct, demands a particular attitude towards the law as it affects working women. The content of the anti-discrimination legislation, for example, would have to be analysed on the basis that it advanced the interests of the capitalist economy. Though there are commentators investigating the treatment of women who find the Marxist approach an illuminating one,[17] some women have criticised the theory as making no attempt to distinguish those forms of oppression experienced by women as opposed to those experienced by men.[18] Indeed, it may be possible to argue that the oppression of women predates capitalist oppression and that the latter has simply taken full advantage of the former.

An alternative thesis is that the law represents a means of oppressing women and entrenching men's power over them. In one sense this proposition seems easier to substantiate than its Marxist counterpart. It is a matter of historical fact that men have used the law in order to assert their dominance over women. The way in which this was achieved was straightforward since men alone had access to the political process and were responsible for administering the law. Over the past one hundred years, however, the position of women has altered radically as discriminatory laws were repealed and equality of opportunity became an accepted political aim. The continuing assertion that the law represents a means of oppressing women therefore appears problematic. Nevertheless, as the contents of later chapters will show, women are still a considerable way from achieving that elusive goal of equality.

Faced with these facts various responses are possible. The most extreme would be to emulate Marxist theory and repudiate the law as a means of securing fundamental change.[19] Carol Smart in *Feminism and the Power of Law*[20] seems to advocate such a strategy. She challenges law's claim to represent some abiding truth within society and argues that it should cease to be a focus of attention. Her message is to repudiate the power of law. This essentially negative viewpoint rests on the belief that society needs to undergo some radical readjustment, in this case an acknowledgement of women's interests. Smart is, however, trapped by her own logic: if the law is so powerful, it should be possible to harness that power to the cause of women and thus use the law as a positive force. No one would suggest that this is an easy task, but understanding the law is the first step in the process of using it.

One of the ways in which women might attempt to exploit the law is by constructing a female perspective on the law, that is a feminist jurisprudence. Traditional legal theory may emphasise masculine as opposed to feminine values. Hence a traditional axiom of justice – to treat like cases alike – could be seen as having a masculine bias. For example, the need to work for two years before qualifying for certain employment rights applies equally to all workers, male or female.[21] Yet, because of family commitments, a woman can find it much harder to satisfy the condition than a man and treating like cases alike means women workers suffer discrimination. Women may therefore find it productive to construct their own critical framework for law.[22] Since the law cannot be assumed to be an embodiment of the truth, a woman's perspective on justice arguably has no more intrinsic validity than that of a man or a representative of a racial minority. This, of course, presupposes in turn that there are no abiding truths to be discovered, and that it is possible merely to construct alternative standards.

The final response to the proposition that the law represents a device for female oppression – and the one adopted in this book – is to acknowledge the law's precedents grounded in male domination and its current shortcomings. Undeniably these shortcomings are real and deep-rooted, yet pressure must still be maintained for changes in the law, and not only for changes that benefit women. As the account of Marxism should make plain, women are not the only group who are or believe themselves to be exploited by the law. The aim should not be to replace the dominance of men with that of another group. An insight into the limits of law and how it can be manipulated by powerful interests should make women aware that others can and do suffer in similar ways.

Justice

There is often assumed, incorrectly, to be a correlation between law and justice. There are instances of laws, and indeed legal systems, which condone behaviour that is cruel, divisive and 'unjust'.[23] As a general rule, however, most states commit themselves in theory, if not in practice, to the cause of justice and claim that their laws, and in particular their written constitutions with their guarantees of fundamental rights and freedoms, serve to promote that end. But a state's commitment to abstract notions of rights and freedoms may or may not be reflected in the detail of its substantive laws. Indeed, it is possible to conceive of a state whose laws are beyond reproach in terms of content, but which administers those laws in a way which negates any guarantees of rights and freedoms.[24]

Any analysis of the notion of justice involves considering a number of complex issues. Most importantly, it entails asking whether a discoverable set of principles exists which can accurately be said to represent 'justice'. Justice has so far been referred to as if it were simply a question of guaranteeing individuals certain fundamental rights or freedoms. Arguably, much more than this is involved. When individuals live together in a society, besides wishing to enjoy as much freedom as is compatible with the freedom of others, those individuals must agree on the distribution of finite resources within that society. Justice involves decisions on the allocation of material as well as abstract resources.

As long ago as Aristotle,[25] the distinction was made between distributive and corrective justice. Distributive justice acknowledges that in the allocation of resources equals should receive equal treatment. It is the business of corrective justice to restore this equality when the balance has been upset, perhaps by the commission of a crime. The correlation made between justice and equality is significant, particularly in the context of the anti-discrimination legislation. The exhortation to treat equals alike must not be allowed to obscure the fact that individuals who appear to be equals are, by reason of their education, their position in society, their colour or their sex, far from equal. Neither should it be regarded as pre-empting treatment designed to acknowledge and compensate for this fact.

What should be apparent is that the role of law can alter dramatically depending on the way in which justice is conceived. If the law sanctions a distribution of resources on the basis of allowing those with strength or talent to keep whatever 'fortune' they amass, then laws designed to reallocate goods to those in need will be regarded as unacceptable. In addition, any guarantee of equality of opportunity may become worthless as the unequal distribution of resources distorts the impact of that undertaking.

The diversity of views advanced on the question of what constitutes justice makes it possible to mention only a few of the more influential. According to traditional Marxist theory there is no objective standard of justice.[26] A capitalist society might well use the law to promote and guarantee certain fundamental political rights and freedoms, including equality before the law, yet their existence may simply serve to disguise and legitimate the real inequalities of that society, which arise as a direct result of economic relations within it. To speak of equality and equality of opportunity is a nonsense when the majority of people lack the means fully to exploit what is available. Education may be free and entrance to university may be on merit alone, yet the need for a young person to leave school and, if possible, contribute to the family budget may make that freedom an illusion. If this reasoning is correct then it makes no sense to ask whether a particular society is just or not, since justice is a relative and not an absolute concept. Communist societies will put into practice their own concept of justice which is a product of the way in which that society is organised and not derived from some ultimate and overriding standard. Indeed, the communist state as conceived of by Marx may have no need of justice. Freedoms require protection only when there are individuals prepared to violate them. The need for justice is a product of inequality and conflict. Since the communist state conceives of individuals living in harmony it may be 'beyond' justice.[27]

The Marxist approach has been criticised and it may express no more than a half-truth. The Marxist premise is that law is used to impose the will of one section of society (the bourgeoisie) on another (the proletariat). When, therefore, the law is used to guarantee 'fundamental rights and freedoms', this may in effect result in those self-same 'rights and freedoms' oppressing those who are without economic power. Admittedly, the effectiveness of rights and freedoms can be diminished by economic circumstances, but this does not mean that they cannot and do not represent objective standards. Any view of law which assigns it a single role in society neglects the possibility that it could have a range of functions, including an educative and moral function, and this could explain why these statements of rights and freedoms often appear no more than empty gestures: the law is being put to a variety of uses not all of which are compatible.

The Marxist view of justice represents only one aspect of what is a very broad spectrum of opinion. Justice has attracted the interest of writers from Aristotle onwards, making it invidious in one sense to concentrate on the views of one or two selected writers, but the opinions expressed by John Rawls in *A Theory of Justice*[28] provide a contrast to Marxist views and another illustration of how theoretical limits may be imposed on the use of law. Indeed, his views are regarded by some as expressing the theoretical rationale that underpins Western liberal democracies. Rawls repudiates an earlier approach to the question of what constitutes justice, namely utilitarianism. The guiding principle of the utilitarian argument is, according to Rawls, 'that society is rightly ordered, and therefore just, when its major institutions are arranged so as to achieve the greatest net balance of satisfaction summed over all the individuals belonging to it'.[29]

Although in the nineteenth century utilitarianism provided the impetus for major law reform,[30] it has become discredited in the twentieth century. There are various reasons for this, including its neglect of the individual, who is relegated to the role of someone experiencing either satisfaction or dissatisfaction. Moreover, as Rawls himself points out, there is no guarantee that whatever action promotes the greatest satisfaction is 'good'. Hence the majority of individuals in society might derive great pleasure or satisfaction from the use of torture, yet this is no argument for saying that torture is good. In place of utilitarianism, Rawls offers his own conception of justice which consists of two principles[31] designed to govern the allocation of primary social goods, namely basic liberties, opportunity, power and a minimum of wealth. The first principle states:

> each person is to have an equal right to the most extensive total system of equal basic liberties compatible with a similar system of liberty for all.

The second principle states:

> social and economic inequalities are to be arranged so that they are both:
> (a) to the greatest benefit of the least advantaged, consistent with the just savings principle, and
> (b) attached to offices and positions open to all under conditions of fair equality of opportunity.

Rawls arrives at these principles using what he terms 'the original position'.[32] This involves a hypothetical group of individuals who, not knowing their standing in society, their sex, what talents they possess, or the period in which they are living, endeavour to agree upon a set of principles to govern their association together. The suggestion is that in this state of ignorance these individuals, guided by self-interest, will agree upon a set of principles which will work to their advantage, or more accurately will involve the least disadvantage, whatever position they might ultimately find themselves in. In the first place, Rawls suggests, they will wish to ensure that they have as much freedom as possible and give this priority over any other goal. Attempts to restrict or compromise basic liberties will, Rawls argues, be rejected even though this could work to the advantage of some, since no one knows whether he or she will be the one to benefit or to suffer. As for the second principle, that requires further explanation since it countenances inequalities in the distribution of material resources. The major restriction on this principle is that such inequalities must be to the benefit of the least advantaged in society.[33] This means that individuals can increase their share of wealth only if in the process of doing so everyone gains. Therefore, to take a simple example, three people could run a business and divide any profits equally. If, however, one person were to assume the position of 'manager' because that person was more astute, then that person could receive more – say half the profits – and the other two share the remaining profits, provided that this arrangement was an improvement on the earlier situation when smaller profits were shared equally. Besides stipulating that any inequality must work to the benefit of the least advantaged, Rawls is forced further to qualify his second principle since it would appear possible for individuals to observe it but still produce an inherently unjust society. In the first place the 'just savings' principle must be observed.[34] This requires each generation to take account of the needs of succeeding generations. To quote Rawls:

> Each generation must not only preserve the gains of culture and civilization, and maintain intact those just institutions that have been established, but it must also put aside in each period of time a suitable amount of real capital accumulation.[35]

In other words, the current generation cannot fritter away the resources at its disposal without a thought for what will happen in the future. Finally Rawls insists that positions and offices must be open to all. He justifies this 'principle of open position'[36] in the following manner:

> It expresses the conviction that if some places were not open on a basis fair to all, those kept out would be right in feeling unjustly treated even though they benefited from the greater efforts of those who were allowed to hold them. They would be justified in their complaint not only because they were excluded from certain external rewards of office such as wealth and privilege, but because they were debarred from experiencing the realization of self which comes from a skilful and devoted exercise of social duties. They would be deprived of one of the main forms of human good.[37]

It should be apparent that Rawls's theory of justice is diametrically at odds with the views of Marx. Indeed one commentator has said that it:

> provides the nearest thing we have to a rational assessment of why the poor should allow the wealthy to keep most of that wealth and not, as in Marxist ideology, seek to expropriate it without so much as a thank you.[38]

One feature which Rawls's theory shares with Marx is the scant attention paid to law and legal systems, on the basis that legal rules are relevant only to the extent to which they either help or hinder the implementation of a particular theory. Judged as an exposition of the nature of justice, Rawls's theory has attracted its share of criticism. This has centred on the principles adopted by his persons in the original position.[39] It has been argued that they might prefer to opt for a 'winner takes all' stance or a completely equitable distribution of resources. Despite Rawls's claims to the contrary, there appears to be no categorical reason why the principles formulated in *A Theory of Justice* are not two possibilities out of a whole range of equally acceptable alternatives. Other critics have expressed doubts over whether the first and second principles are compatible. 'Is it not the case that inequalities in wealth and power always produce inequalities in basic liberty?'[40]

This theory of justice also imposes limits on the way in which legal rules can be used, incidentally raising interesting questions about the law as it affects working women. Is it possible, for example, to justify sex discrimination on the basis of Rawls's theory? In the first place it is not clear whether non-discrimination is one of the basic political liberties. What is certain is Rawls's insistence that offices should be open to all which would seem to guarantee equality of opportunity. Yet he also sanctions economic inequalities provided this is to the benefit of the least advantaged. Women, therefore, must be allowed to compete for the same jobs as men. If, however, the highly paid posts come to be occupied solely by men whilst women perform low-paid work, then this still seems to accord with Rawls's second principle, provided it can be shown that overall women 'benefit', or are least disadvantaged in these circumstances. The problem is who should judge whether this is so.

References are frequently made to the unjust way in which the law treats women, but in order for this to have any meaning, the standard of justice by which the law is judged must be defined. Justice may act as a limiting factor not only on the uses to which the law is put but also on its content. Hence, if justice is seen as demanding equal treatment of individual citizens, laws aimed at eliminating discrimination, that is outlawing the inferior treatment of one group of individuals, will be acceptable. By the same criterion, however, laws requiring positive discrimination, that is preferential treatment for what was a previously disadvantaged group, may be labelled unjust.[41] As one writer on the subject has said, 'We cannot think about positive discrimination without thinking about justice.'[42]

It has also been suggested that certain concepts of justice, such as that of Rawls, are flawed since they do not take specific account of women's interests. This ignores the fact that it might be possible to construct a model of justice which is applicable to men and women alike. Be that as it may, some women have attempted to frame a women's concept of justice. Tove Stang Dahl, for example, in *Women's Law*[43] suggests the following way of proceeding.

> Considerations of justice in women's law start by identifying the needs and wants of women in general, and particularly their opinions about what is just. Out of this matrix of needs and opinions we may develop a series of hypotheses about values on the basis of which we wish to study and examine the law.[44]

It is beyond the scope of this book to determine whether an objective and discoverable standard of justice exists, but these various alternative concepts demonstrate the influence they may exert in imposing limits on what the law can achieve. In that sense women are correct in questioning current wisdom on what is just, lest flawed concepts are being used as an excuse to resist change.

The content of law

A discussion of the ways in which different theorists have chosen to analyse justice shows how different conceptions of what is just can influence the content of law. That content is no random matter but is shaped by various forces at work within society. To economic forces can be added religious and moral ideals, as well as political ideologies. It is obvious that the way in which a society chooses to organise itself politically will influence the content of its laws. A single party state may have very different laws on freedom of speech, freedom of assembly and trade unions from a liberal democracy. The strength of a society's moral convictions must also be taken into account. Although, therefore, slavery may be economically advantageous, the moral revulsion that it generates may render it totally unacceptable.

Although these forces influence the content of law, it should not be imagined that every clause of every bill is scrutinised in order to determine whether it accords with the political beliefs and economic strategy of government, as well as reflecting society's concept of justice. Political dogma can be abandoned for the sake of expediency, economic strategy can be sacrificed for electoral gain and justice has a constant meaning only at a theoretical level. Nor do these forces exert a uniform pull in a single direction. Justice may indicate one course of action, economics another. For this reason alone it is unwise to take a single piece of legislation and attempt to make general statements about the law on the basis of its content. That legislation may be atypical. It may represent the end of a particular legislative phase or the beginning of another. It is far wiser to look at legislative 'trends'. There are a number of clearly defined features, for example, in the laws affecting working

17

women in the nineteenth and twentieth centuries. There were those laws, such as the criminal law, which on the whole applied equally to men and women. In contrast, areas of law existed which either took no account of women or allowed a husband to make decisions on his wife's behalf. In the nineteenth century women were unable to vote,[45] were excluded from the professions[46] and ownership of their property passed to their husbands on marriage.[47] Yet another feature of the law was its 'paternalistic' treatment of women, with laws designed to restrict women's freedom 'for their own good'.[48] More recently the emphasis has shifted to the promotion of equality and the elimination of discrimination.

A detailed discussion of these trends in the law over the past two centuries will feature in Chapter 3, but it is apparent that those forces which are at work shaping the law act as limiting factors on possible courses of action. It would have been impossible to have contemplated outlawing sex discrimination in the nineteenth century since it would have been incompatible with the economics, the politics and moral conceptions of the day. In particular it would have been incompatible with the perception of women that existed at the time. If contemporary judicial decisions are any indication, women were regarded as the 'weaker sex', whose proper place was in the home and whose role in life was to be wife and mother.[49] The literature and reports whose publication preceded the passage of legislation which was to have a major effect on the lives of women present a similar picture.[50] The factors which contributed to the growth of that image were, it has been suggested, in part religious as well as, in part, related to the separation between home and workplace in post-Industrial Revolution Britain. Add to this a woman's inability to control her own fertility and the statement that 'a woman's place is in the home' took on the air of a self-fulfilling prophecy. To refer to how women were perceived at any particular time is, of course, to ignore those women who did not conform to a particular stereotype. Women were no more a homogeneous group one hundred or two hundred years ago than they are now. Whilst acknowledging those women who defied tradition, who organised resistance to measures such as the Factories Acts[51] and were forced, for whatever reason, to combine work and family, theirs was not the accepted view of how a woman should behave. It was that alternative image of a woman as wife and mother that the law reinforced and in so doing gave it a reality that was exceedingly hard to change. Needless to say, the idealised image of hearth, home and children was not extended to those for whom economic necessity entailed paid labour as a means of survival.

Whilst discussing the way in which the law underlined this perception of women as homemakers, it is appropriate to consider the thesis put forward by O'Donovan in *Sexual Divisions in Law*.[52] She argues that there has been a deliberate policy to avoid legal intervention in what she terms the 'private sphere' of the family. Where such intervention is un-avoidable, the law, in general, emphasises the man's role as head of household and breadwinner, at the same time neglecting the tasks that a wife/mother performs for her family. In contrast, according to O'Donovan, the 'public sphere', that is the workplace, has been the object of a sustained programme of legal regulation. However, that intervention is characterised by the fact that it takes no account of a woman's responsibilities in the private sphere. Instead, the workplace is geared to the needs of those who have no domestic or child care responsibilities, putting the majority of women at an immediate disadvantage.

The proposition that the law's reluctance to regulate the private sphere puts women at a disadvantage when they compete with men in the public sphere requires careful thought. It is offered as a key to understanding why women have suffered so badly at the hands of the law and undoubtedly there is a great deal of truth in what O'Donovan has to say. The argument is at its weakest, however, in its perception of the private sphere, that is the family. The 'traditional' nuclear family may be fast becoming the exception rather than the rule as single-parent families, for example, proliferate. Far from being beyond the reach of the law, single-parent families, in common with other individuals in need, may find themselves with no alternative but to rely on state benefits and to attempt to make sense of the complex rules governing their availability. It has become fashionable and, moreover, accurate to refer to the feminisation of poverty, meaning that more often than not it is women who find themselves in this unenviable position. An equally accurate description would refer to the legalisation of poverty, underlining the increasingly complex legal provisions which govern the availability of state benefits, such as income support. With increasing legal intervention there comes a formal acknowledgement of equality between the sexes, since within the family either partner may claim.[53] In practical terms, however, conditions may have to be satisfied, such as availability for work, that women will find it difficult to satisfy and which reassert traditional perceptions of women.

The law is therefore taking an increasing interest in the family, not directly by regulating the ongoing relationship between husband and wife, but tangentially. Over the years, for example, greater emphasis has been placed on monitoring the relationship between parent and child. This desire to regulate the way in which children are treated has far-reaching consequences for the partner who assumes major responsibility for child care. In the majority of cases this will be the woman. The law's insistence that children are properly cared for[54] and the powers given to officials, such as social workers,[55] to ensure that these standards are met can put a woman seeking paid employment in a disadvantageous position.

Despite the attractiveness of O'Donovan's thesis, there is evidence of the law taking a closer interest in the family, even if it is to emphasise a woman's traditional role. Nor does her theory offer an explanation for the fate of those women who, unencumbered by partner or children, still discover that they are not treated as men's equals in the workplace. The cause may lie not in a lack of legal regulation, but rather in the image of women as homemakers that the law still reinforces in the public and private spheres.[56]

Even if O'Donovan's argument is accepted, the problem remains of how matters can be changed. The law is restricted in its ability to influence behaviour. That power is at its greatest when it is possible to impose a sanction on those who refuse to modify their behaviour, as commonly happens in the criminal law. Merely requiring behaviour or providing conditions which encourage such behaviour is no guarantee of compliance. Hence it would be possible to regulate the family, to share a couple's assets equitably between them and to give them equal power so that neither is acknowledged as head of the household. It would be possible to amend the law so that employers had to take account of their employees' domestic responsibilities. Yet, even in the face of all these changes, it would be impossible for the law to force a man to take his fair share of household tasks or to rid society of the belief that a woman should take major responsibility for caring.

One is thus forced to return to the initial proposition that the way in which women are perceived in society has a powerful influence on the way in which the law treats them. Consequently, laws which fly in the face of that 'image' are likely to prove singularly unhelpful unless they are backed by an effective sanction.

A final point regarding the influences on the content of law concerns two conflicting processes: those of regulation and of deregulation. Many think of the law solely in terms of its power to regulate. In their minds, the content of legal rules will be positive in its effect, controlling behaviour or activities that were previously uncontrolled or, alternatively, modifying already existing rules. Yet on occasions the aim of legislation is the complete opposite, namely to remove rather than impose controls. The process of deregulation is not that uncommon. For example, during the 1980s the legislation restricting the hours women might work and preventing them, in certain circumstances, from undertaking night work was repealed.[57] Also under threat are the Wages Councils whose task it is to set minimum wages for certain industries.[58] Since women make up a substantial portion of the workforce in those industries, the disappearance of the Wages Councils would be of particular significance for them.

The implications of deregulation can vary. On some occasions it is a sign that the activity in question is so rare or the efficacy of the legislation so doubtful that deregulation seems the only sensible course of action. On other occasions deregulation can mark a shift in moral attitudes. Where some justification exists for retaining legislation, then deregulation may be more in the nature of a political gesture, and those affected may take it as a sign that behaviour which was once illegal is now acceptable. Indeed, a contrast may be drawn, unlikely though it may sound, between removing the criminal sanction from attempted suicide and abolishing Wages Councils. The first act of deregulation will neither encourage suicide nor render it more or less acceptable. The second act of deregulation, should it occur, could be taken as proof that whatever level of wages a worker is prepared to accept is tolerable.

Privatisation is sometimes linked with deregulation and can take different forms. On the one hand it can signify the decision to sell what was previously a nationalised industry in public ownership, such as British Gas, to the private sector. Control of that industry then passes from government into the hands of individual shareholders. Alternatively, a public concern such as the National Health Service may be encouraged to privatise some of its activities – for example cleaning – in order to save money. Cleaners will cease to be employed by the health authority and instead a private company will be engaged and it will use its own employees. This form of privatisation can have serious consequences for employees.[59] In the case of cleaners, since women comprise a substantial proportion of those employed, they will suffer disproportionately. In particular, privatisation may result in reduced hours and cuts in wages as firms make competitive tenders for contracts.

Privatisation is largely a political and economic phenomenon, but, in order to achieve it, a government may have to countenance a degree of deregulation. Hence the Fair Wages Resolution,[60] which was designed to ensure that contractors engaged by government paid wages equivalent to those in the public sector for identical work, has fallen victim to the latest round of privatisation. Privatisation may therefore be accompanied by both deregulation and a subsequent deterioration in working conditions.

Judicial decision making

Legislation constitutes a large portion of the body of legal rules, but there are areas of the law where rules are derived either in whole or in part from common law principles. The law relating to contracts of employment is one such example.[61] In these circumstances the law is built up on a case by case basis as and when situations arise. The law relating to working women is largely found in statutes but occasionally a situation will be governed by the common law. In the case of safety at work, for example, employers owe a common law duty of care to their

21

employees.[62] In comparison with legislation, the common law rules can appear very imprecise. It may take a whole series of cases to gain a clear idea of what a rule may or may not permit. Once established, it may be necessary to consider whether the rule can apply only to situations which exactly resemble those where the rule was first employed. Can the rule be extended? What factual element is so essential that its absence will render the rule inoperative? It may take a decade or more before the exact ramifications of a common law rule are apparent.

Judges have a key role to play in developing common law rules as well as in interpreting legislation and there are a variety of views as to how they approach this task. Those views on the subject can be neither proved nor disproved and, in the context of this chapter, that is not the central issue. More relevant by far are the consequences of a particular view on the process of judicial decision making. There would appear to be two extremes. On the one hand there are the views of Ronald Dworkin which have been expressed most recently and most comprehensively in *Law's Empire*.[63] Dworkin's analysis of how judges decide 'hard cases', which he regards as cases to which no settled rule applies, is simply a part of a more extensive exploration of law and legal systems. The emphasis he places on judicial decision making, however, arises from the importance he attaches to rights and his contention that rights cannot be sacrificed for the greater wealth or happiness of the community as a whole.[64] In Dworkin's scheme of things, judges have the task of interpreting the law so as to safeguard rights. This is not to suggest that judges have a 'strong' discretion, so that they can interpret the law according to their own personal desires and feelings. Instead, by reflecting on the legal system and the political institutions within the community, a judge should, in theory, be able to construct 'a scheme of abstract and concrete principles that provides a coherent justification for all common law precedents and, so far as these are to be justified on principle, constitutional and statutory principles as well'.[65] When faced with a 'hard case', a judge can then arrive at the right decison by resolving that case in a manner which best fits with that theory of law he or she has determined upon. In *Law's Empire*, Dworkin develops the notions of 'law as literature'[66] and 'law as integrity'.[67] His aim is to stress that a comprehensive knowledge and understanding of the law produces what can best be described as a state of empathy. This will enable a judge to do what is right rather than reach a decision that strikes a discordant note and places a potential gain to the community above individual rights.

Dworkin's theory has been criticised on various counts. Perhaps the most pertinent criticism in this context relates to his use of the judge 'Hercules' to illustrate his argument. Dworkin describes Hercules as 'an imaginary judge of superhuman intellectual power and patience who accepts law as an integrity'.[68] Since Hercules is far superior to any real life judge, critics argue that in practice a judge's chance of arriving at the right answer by adopting Hercules' comprehensive approach are very slim indeed.[69] Only Dworkin's word with his examples of a fictitious judge make it possible to construct a 'scheme of abstract and concrete principles'. Dworkin's reply to this criticism is to concede that Hercules is 'more reflective and self-conscious than any real judge need be or, given the press of work, could be'.[70] But, in other respects Hercules is said to resemble real life judges:

> he has no vision into transcendental mysteries opaque to them. His judgments of fit and political morality are made on the same material and have the same character as theirs. He does what they would do if they had a career to devote to a single decision; they need, not a different conception of law from his, but skills of craft husbandry and efficiency he has never had to cultivate.[71]

It is a matter of opinion whether Dworkin's reasoning is convincing, particularly in light of the fact that many of the hard cases that will be encountered in later chapters were decided in industrial tribunals where two of the three adjudicators are lay persons. Whether they are capable of constructing a scheme of principles for themselves may be open to question, particularly in view of their lack of legal training.

Providing a complete contrast to Dworkin is the proposition that interpretation of the law involves a judge in the exercise of discretion and that, objectively speaking, no right answer exists. Many commentators, including some judges, adopt variations on this theme. One of the best-known versions must be that of Professor H. L. A. Hart.[72] Professor Hart conceives of a legal system which consists of rules. He concedes that, however precise one seeks to make a rule, there will always be what he terms a penumbra of uncertainty regarding what is or is not included, since that is a consequence of the imprecision of language. Faced with a novel set of circumstances, a judge is forced to exercise discretion. On this occasion the term 'discretion' is used in a 'strong' sense indicating that the judge is free to make up his or her own mind on the issue.[73]

The notion that judges are exercising a personal discretion when they interpret the law leaves judicial decisions open to wide-ranging criticism. Judges, the majority of whom are male, still share a predominantly similar background – public school, Oxbridge and the Bar. This background is likely to give them a particular set of personal values and views which will in turn colour the exercise of their discretion.[74] When, therefore, a judge is called upon to interpret a legislative provision which is significant for working women, he may show himself ignorant of their needs and prejudiced in his attitude towards them.[75] He may see it as his task to pursue a particular policy which he regards as in society's best interests and to ride rough-shod over the rights of the individual.

If, however, Dworkin is correct – and it should be apparent that his views are the antithesis of Professor Hart's – then are judicial decisions to be treated as above reproach? Even Dworkin is prepared to concede that judges can make mistakes.[76] There are numerous factors which can cause an 'incorrect' decision to be reached. They include lack of familiarity with the area of the law that is under discussion. For example, research that has been undertaken into the work of industrial tribunals has demonstrated a lack of comprehension over the scope of the anti-discrimination legislation. This has inevitably led to wrong decisions being made. In the light of this, Dworkin's theory is best treated as a device against which judicial decisions may be evaluated rather than as an assertion of their 'rightness'. He is perhaps emphasising that in a perfect world judicial decisions would take account of everyone's rights or interests.

Clearly one's approach to the issue of judicial decision making has a radical influence upon one's treatment of judicial decisions. To those disturbed by the degree of discretion a judge may possess, it is possible to offer some apparent consolation by suggesting that the law may have its own system of checks and balances to act as a counterweight to personal prejudice. In short, the experience of the law that an individual may have before becoming a judge may counteract personal prejudices.[77] A legal education emphasises the importance of logic and the need for impartiality. Therefore, those who eventually become judges are likely to have a feel for 'fit'. This means that a judge is likely to develop the law along lines that are in accordance with past decisions rather than radically at odds with them. The doctrine of precedent[78] which requires inferior courts to follow the judgments of superior courts, such as the House of Lords, is but one guarantee of this fact. Whether women can take much consolation from an emphasis on tradition, precedent and training is problematic. Many of the judicial decisions analysed in subsequent chapters bear witness to stereotypical attitudes to a women's role in society. There are, however, encouraging exceptions where the courts were prepared to put their full weight behind the policy of the anti-discrimination legislation and ignore arguments over potential disruption to employers. In practice, therefore, it is impossible either wholeheartedly to trust the judges or to dismiss them as prejudiced against women. As for those theoretical perspectives on judicial decision making, these simply provide a framework within which the process can be better understood and criticised.

Practical limitations

Theoretical limits on the use of law arise out of the analysis of law and legal concepts. Legal systems are, however, limited in their effectiveness by shortcomings which are in the main a product of the machinery through which the law is administered. Much of the law that relates to working women is to be found in legislation. As a device for conveying legal rules, legislation has its advantages and disadvantages. On the one hand, it can be precise and detailed. On the other hand, it can take a considerable time to mobilise the political will to secure the passage of legislation. In addition, once that legislation is in place it may be difficult to secure its amendment or repeal, since this can be achieved only by further legislation. Another characteristic of legislation is that, however detailed its terms, there will always be doubts over the precise meanings of words and whether or not a particular situation is covered by the legislation in question. The simple prohibition 'no motor vehicles in the park', even though it might be accompanied by a definition of the key terms 'motor vehicle' and 'park', can be open to interpretation. There may be doubts over whether invalid cars, motorised wheelchairs or a child's motorised toy car are included in the prohibition.

Apart from uncertainty, one piece of legislation may appear to be at odds with another. In *Page* v *Freight Hire (Tank Haulage) Ltd* [79] an employer was judged to be in breach of the Sex Discrimination Act 1975 when he prevented a female employee, but not her male counterparts, from driving a tanker lorry containing an embryotoxic chemical. The employer did, however, have a defence, based on the requirement in the Health and Safety at Work Act 1974 that an employer ensure as far as is practicable the health, safety and welfare at work of his employees. The apparent inconsistency between the two pieces of legislation was dealt with by section 51(1) [80] of the Sex Discrimination Act 1975, which stated:

> Nothing in Parts II to IV shall render unlawful any act done by a person if it was necessary for him to do it in order to comply with a requirement – (a) of an Act passed before this Act....

This was taken by the Employment Appeal Tribunal as indicating that the duty imposed on an employer by the 1974 Act could allow a breach of the 1975 Act. It is questionable whether the exception in section 51(1) was intended to include the Health and Safety at Work Act, but the problem was that, since it was not categorically excluded, there seemed no reason not to include it, apart that is from the impression it gives that the law was taking away with one hand what it gave with another.

Another shortcoming of legislation is that it may omit to mention a particular matter. When an unforeseen situation arises, therefore, a decision has to be taken on whether this point is covered by existing legislation. A good example is sexual harassment.[81] The legal concept of a female employee being sexually harassed by her male colleagues is a relatively new notion in this country, though not in the United States. The harassment consists in the female employee being subjected to sexual remarks or behaviour of a sexual nature. Indeed, matters can reach such a pitch that a woman may be forced to accept a transfer or even to leave her job. Until recently, English law was unfamiliar with the term 'sexual harassment'. The criminal offences of assault and rape exist but it is unusual for the conduct in question to be so serious as to amount to rape, and women may be reluctant to bring criminal charges. Nevertheless, in *Strathclyde Regional Council* v *Porcelli*,[82] Mrs Porcelli successfully argued that sexual harassment could come within the provisions of the Sex Discrimination Act and was awarded compensation. Using legislation intended for one purpose to cope with a novel situation is never entirely satisfactory. The question of who can or cannot benefit might be totally arbitrary. A far better solution is to have legislation which deals specifically with the issue.

Finally, legislation which is a product of the United Kingdom Parliament may have to take into account the United Kingdom's membership of the European Economic Community and the obligations under the Treaty of Rome. The European Community has been particularly active in promoting measures to outlaw sex discrimination. What might have begun as a policy designed to ensure that the workforce of one member country could not compete unfairly with workforces in other member countries by paying its female workers lower wages than men now presents itself as a genuine commitment to the cause of equality. Numerous Directives[83] have been prepared on the subject and member states have been forced to bring their domestic law into line with the contents of those Directives, once they have been approved. Indeed it is always possible for a member state to do more than the Directive requires, provided this is still in accordance with European law. There have been occasions when the European Court has declared that the terms of a United Kingdom Act of Parliament are not in line with our obligations as a member of the European Community.[84] In these circumstances changes must be made to the United Kingdom's domestic law. As will become clear, membership of the European Community restricts this country's domestic legislative competence. More positively, from the point of view of women workers, it has led to changes in United Kingdom law designed to advance the cause of equal opportunities.

Enforcement

Some theorists consider that one of the marks of a fully developed legal system is the presence of rules concerned with determining whether or not the law has been breached. Although the 'British system of justice' is regarded by many as having much to recommend it, no system of law enforcement is perfect. There are of course various means by which law may be enforced. Observance of the law may be monitored by the police and by numerous government bodies, such as the Health and Safety Inspectorate, which is responsible for ensuring that employers observe health and safety legislation and which may instigate criminal prosecutions for its breach.[85] A great deal of the legislation under discussion, however, depends on the individual for its enforcement rather than an agency. Therefore, if an individual believes that he or she has been unfairly dismissed, has been the object of sex discrimination or has a claim for equal pay, it is their choice whether or not they pursue a claim.

It is not unusual for the individual to have to bear the burden of law enforcement. If a person is sold defective goods or is caused injury by another's negligence then it is a matter for that individual whether or not to pursue a claim for damages. Obviously there are disadvantages to such an approach. An individual must be aware of his or her legal rights or alternatively must have access to advice on the matter. This is particularly important where the right to claim has to be exercised within a comparatively short space of time. In addition, the individual may not have the resources available to finance a claim especially if success is not guaranteed, and the present legal aid scheme is far from generous. Finally, even individuals with the knowledge and resources to pursue a claim may find, should they be successful, that the defendant either lacks the resources to meet any award of damages or wilfully refuses to pay. The process of enforcement can thus limit the effectiveness of the law, a theme analysed in greater detail in Chapter 8. However well-meaning the terms of legislation may be, they count for little if it proves well-nigh impossible to obtain some form of recompense. Indeed, lack of a realistic remedy may be regarded by some as an indication that society attaches little or no importance to the issue in question.

The White Paper, *Equality for Women* (1974), suggested that anti-discrimination legislation represented a statement of intent and was the first step on the road to equality. If equality represented the ideal it has plainly not yet come to fruition. Given the time, the circumstances and the respect that has traditionally been paid to the notion of equality before the law, it may be that the legislation represented the best that

27

could be expected. Whilst it is possible to suggest changes to the law, it may appear pointless to do so in the light of what has been said. Many of those ideas with the most to offer – especially those that demand unequal treatment by way of positive discrimination – are ideas whose time has not yet come and may never do so particularly against the background of the current shift towards deregulation.

Chapter three

Policy and prejudice
The tangled web

The twentieth century has witnessed what appears to be a dramatic change in emphasis in the law's treatment of women workers. The restrictions of the past have been progressively removed and in their place a policy of equality has been pursued in legislation such as the Sex Discrimination Act 1975 and the Equal Pay Act 1970. Although the benefits of this legislation are not restricted solely to women, it is women who are commonly regarded as gaining the greatest advantage from these Acts. Some might even argue that matters have reached the stage where women workers are at no substantial disadvantage as compared with their male counterparts.[1] It is this belief that the authors set out to challenge. Those positive steps which have been taken in pursuit of equality are rendered less effective because there appear to be several easily identifiable and not necessarily compatible themes in the law which relates to women. In the course of this chapter three such themes will be examined – paternalism, the promotion of equality and the granting of additional rights – on the basis that each represents a thread in the law's treatment of working women.

Legal paternalism arises where the law is used to restrict an individual's freedom in the interests of that individual. The promotion of equality, on the other hand, relies on laws which require that men and women are treated equally. When the law grants additional rights, however, it does so because the individuals who benefit are seen to require more favourable treatment than others. Paternalism and the granting of additional rights thus result in people being treated differently; the promotion of equality requires the same treatment. There is, therefore, a discrepancy and a potential conflict in these particular uses of the law. There are of course many other uses to which the law might be put, some of which may be regarded as essential, while others, such as laws permitting slavery, are ruled out because they do not further the cause of justice. The law may, for example, be enlisted to protect one person from another, to protect property or in order to oppress. There is a good deal of controversy regarding the values which legal rules should endeavour to uphold. Over the centuries legal theorists have suggested a number of ideals – such as the value of life– whose implementation will guarantee human well-being.[2] The theoretical debate which surrounds this issue has had certain practical effects, for example in the considerable emphasis that is now placed on human rights. It has also caused attention to be focused on other abstract notions, including equality.

A government chooses how it wishes to use the law on the basis of government policy. In Chapter 2 various forces were discussed – social, political, economic and moral – which can influence the content of legal rules. These forces shape the policies which are adopted by diverse groups including the political parties. If one takes as an example a period of severe economic recession with rising unemployment and escalating inflation, differing policies may be put forward in order to resolve such a crisis. One group may advocate government subsidies to shore up ailing industries and economic help to those areas with particularly high rates of unemployment. In contrast, others may argue that inefficient and outdated industries should be allowed to fail, whilst new technology takes their place. The diverging nature of these policies is influenced by the political, moral and economic stance of the body advocating them. The legal system is a device, and it is by no means the sole device, for putting policies into practice. The government with its parliamentary majority has almost exclusive control over the legislative machinery and is able to implement its policy in this fashion. Others can only hope to have an indirect influence on the content of legislation.

Even the government will not rely exclusively on legislation to give practical effect to its policy goals. Other devices such as government circulars[3] may prove a viable alternative to or supplement of legislation. Neither should it be imagined that the government's control of the machinery to introduce and repeal legislation makes it pointless for other political parties, organisations and pressure groups to have alternative policies. Provided such groups are not in breach of the law, they may be able to go some way to put their alternative policy into practice. Indeed, it is possible to challenge in a court the very legality of a government policy as represented in an Act of Parliament.[4] It should not be assumed that, once a policy has been decided upon by central government and is given the force of law, the issue is closed.

If government policy, as it exists from time to time, dictates the choice of how law is to be used (paternalism, equality or whatever else may be chosen), it is logical to ask exactly what the policy has been towards working women. The answer, judging from modern legislation, seems to be that recent governments, with more or less enthusiasm, have adopted the pursuit of equality as a policy goal. This raises the question of the nature of 'equality' and whether the elimination of discrimination (that is a requirement that men and women are treated equally) is the equivalent of equality of opportunity. Whatever the answer, it must also be recognised that the mere existence of legislation which purports to eliminate discrimination does not necessarily mean that such a goal is or will continue to be government policy. An Act of Parliament may remain on the statute books whilst amendments create so many exceptions that the original goal becomes meaningless. In any event, as was pointed out in Chapter 2, legislation represents only part of the story. Industrial tribunals and the courts are responsible for interpreting that legislation as well as developing and applying the common law. In performing that task the policy behind the legislation may be overlooked either out of ignorance or deliberately. Judicial decision making may not be the objective process that it is sometimes represented to be. An analysis of the content of current legislation may produce convincing proof that the overall trend is towards the elimination of discrimination, but an examination of the spirit in which the legislation is applied or the way it is reconciled with the principles of the common law may show that such a trend is being thwarted.

Finally, it is possible that current policy may be undermined where the law is used in ways which are incompatible. If the elimination of discrimination is supposedly the overriding goal, paternalistic laws contradict this, unless of course both men and women are treated in this fashion. There is abundant evidence however that, in the past, it was women who were the major focus of paternalistic treatment, so that they were, for example, excluded from working in certain industries[5] while the hours they could work in other occupations were limited.[6]

The object of this chapter is to determine what is current policy on the treatment of women, and what factors, if any, prevent that policy from being fully effective and to that end each of those three uses of law identified at the start of this chapter will be discussed.

Paternalism

The term 'paternalism' is one which is well known to lawyers since it is central to a debate which originated in the nineteenth century and still continues today: that is, when can the law legitimately be used to restrict the liberty of the individual? John Stuart Mill in his essay *On Liberty*[7] was categorical in his belief that paternalism was not a legitimate basis for legal intervention. Apart from some minor concessions – to protect the very young, for example – he was adamant that the desire to act in others' best interests might simply present an excuse for those in power to have society reflect their values and hence exercise a form of tyranny. Mill wrote:

the sole end for which mankind are warranted, individually or collectively, in interfering with the liberty of action of any of their number is self-protection. That the only purpose for which power can be rightfully exercised over any member of a civilized community, against his will, is to prevent harm to others. His own good, either physical or moral, is not a sufficient warrant. He cannot rightfully be compelled to do or forbear because it will be better for him to do so, because it will make him happier, because, in the opinions of others, to do so would be wise or even right.[8]

Over the years jurists have returned to this debate, particularly when faced with a practical dilemma which has moral overtones such as the law's treatment of homosexuality or prostitution.[9] Though the question is raised most frequently in relation to sexual morality, the issue of when the freedom of the individual can legitimately be curbed is central to law and legal systems. Even if one accepts John Stuart Mill's premise that the law should be used only to prevent behaviour likely to cause harm to others, one can argue endlessly over what exactly that might mean. Undoubtedly it would include physical harm, but does it extend to financial or emotional harm? For example, does an individual have the right to indulge in a habit such as smoking, drinking or drug taking when its consequences might be to cause physical harm to that individual and emotional upheaval to his or her family? Apart from seeking to clarify what exactly is included in the term 'harm', some commentators have disagreed with the fundamental premise put forward by Mill. Jurists such as Stephen[10] and Devlin[11] have argued that society is justified in using the law to underpin those values which are seen as essential to the well-being of that society. The question of whether the individual harms anyone but himself or herself by their conduct is immaterial if the integrity of society is threatened.[12] Others have suggested that, in certain circumstances, it is proper to protect the individual from self-inflicted harm.

In an essay entitled 'Paternalism',[13] Gerald Dworkin gives various instances in which paternalistic legislation appears justified. The first of these is where it is a 'kind of insurance policy which we take out against making decisions which are far-reaching, potentially dangerous and irreversible'.[14] In these circumstances the individual consents to the state acting on his or her behalf on the basis that at some future date the individual may disregard or not truly appreciate the long-term damage he or she might do to themselves. The second instance involves decisions that might be reached 'under extreme psychological and sociological pressures'.[15] Once more Dworkin emphasises that without those pressures the individual might make a reasoned choice. As it is, the individual is not able to do so, and without legal intervention might arrive at a decision which is not capable of being reversed. The third situation which might warrant legal intervention 'involves dangers which are either not sufficiently understood or appreciated correctly by the persons involved'.[16] On this basis an individual might be prepared to run a considerable risk, particularly if its immediate result is some kind of pleasure or benefit, at the same time disregarding or being ignorant of what might be a very real danger.

From the situations described by Dworkin it would appear that they all have one element in common, namely the potential inability of the individual to make an informed choice. As others have pointed out, John Stuart Mill's thesis of individual choice rests on the premise that, whatever the situation, the individual can and does make not only an autonomous, but also a rational choice regarding their own personal well-being. In reality this may be far from the truth:

> Mill endows the average individual with 'too much of the psychology of a middle-aged man whose desires are relatively fixed, not liable to be artificially stimulated by external influences; who knows what he wants and what gives him satisfaction or happiness; and who pursues these things when he can'.[17]

In theory, therefore, there appears to be a good deal of strength in the argument that some measure of paternalism is an essential quality of any modern legal system. The problem is of course where to draw the line beyond which the 'nanny' state will not interfere. As Dworkin himself admits, there are a great many everyday human activities which carry with them a considerable risk. They include cigarette smoking and driving. Since it is not practicable totally to forbid such activities an effort is made to warn individuals of and protect them from the dangers involved. The strength of these warnings is perhaps tempered by potential losses in revenue and appeals to the rights of the individual.

An analysis of paternalism is directly relevant to the laws affecting working women because it appears to be the guiding force which once inspired much of their treatment. The legislation which banned women and children from the mines and regulated their hours of work is commonly described as 'protective' legislation,[18] implying that there was a paternalistic motive behind the legislation. To suggest that legislation of this nature, which restricted the way women organised their working lives and the work they undertook, was motivated by the desire to protect women workers from dangers which they might not properly appreciate is to make a number of assumptions which require very careful scrutiny.

In the first place is there the slightest evidence that such legislation was inspired by paternalistic motives? As Dworkin himself admits:

almost any piece of legislation is justified by several different kinds of reasons and even if historically a piece of legislation can be shown to have been introduced for purely paternalistic motives, it may be that advocates of the legislation with an anti-paternalistic outlook can find sufficient reasons justifying the legislation without appealing to the reasons which were originally adduced to support it.[19]

Indeed, when legislation is first proposed, its supporters may be influenced by diverse motives. If one takes the legislation designed to exclude women from performing certain jobs which are inherently dangerous – working underground for example – there may have been those whose motives were altruistic in advocating this legislation in the sense that their interference with a working woman's freedom of action was for her 'welfare, good, happiness, needs, interests or values'. There may have been others who supported this legislation purely out of self-interest, since the employment of women and children may have been regarded as depressing wages to the disadvantage of male employees. Still others may have supported the proposed legislation because they regarded men and women working together in such proximity as immoral. As accounts of this legislation make clear, it may be well-nigh impossible to isolate the motives behind it.[20]

Whilst it is feasible that such legislative moves were inspired by paternalism, it is hard to accept that the same motive lies behind the legislation and judicial decisions which excluded women from the professions. These occupations were far from hazardous, although some of the judgments in a case such as *Jex-Blake* v *Senatus of Edinburgh University*,[21] where seven women sought the right to attend medical school and graduate from the university, might suggest otherwise. Lord Neaves stated:

> It is a belief, widely entertained, that there is a great difference in the mental constitution of the two sexes, just as there is in their physical conformation. The powers and susceptibilities of women are as noble as those of men; but they are thought to be different, and, in particular, it is considered that they have not the same power of intense labour as men are endowed with. If this be so, it must form a serious objection to uniting them under the same course of academical study. I confess that, to some extent, I share in this view, and should regret to see our young females subjected to the severe and incessant work which my own observation and experience have taught me to consider as indispensable to any high attainment in learning.[22]

Lord Neaves in this case, as have other judges in other cases, claimed to be acting to promote women's 'best interests'.

If it is accepted that, to a degree, the legislation and judicial decisions under discussion were inspired by a desire to act in the best interests of women, this still leaves unanswered the question – why women? It is true, of course, that some of the protective legislation applied also to children but male workers were never restricted to the same extent.[23] At a time when women are progressively being freed from these restrictions,[24] there is no suggestion that the same logic requires that children should cease to be protected and paternalism remains acceptable in their case. In relation to women, however, the reasons formerly used to justify such treatment have been discredited. Women were deemed to be inferior in intellect and strength to men and best suited to a domestic role or to occupations which duplicated that role, such as domestic service, where there was never any attempt at legislative regulation. This perception was then used as a justification for restricting in law a woman's role as a worker on the basis that she might not appreciate what was in her best interests.

Paternalism demonstrates that, once a particular class or group of individuals is defined as vulnerable, it legitimises the use of law to protect those individuals. The judgement that the group or class is vulnerable is open to challenge and may change as the years pass. What the paternalistic approach does *not* insist upon is that the group singled out for protection in law should, as a consequence, be accorded inferior treatment. If, for example, it is decided that a woman is vulnerable because of her potential to bear children, that may be a reason for protecting her from hazards at work. The decision might be taken to protect her by excluding her completely from the workplace. Alternatively, work practices could be modified to eliminate, in so far as it is possible, potential dangers. In principle, both approaches are paternalistic, but the former results in the woman being treated in an inferior fashion, the latter as deserving of special consideration. The logic of paternalism is to use the law to protect, and it is not inevitable that the desire to protect must put the individual at a disadvantage. It is essential to appreciate this fact and that, in the past, paternalism has often been used in a negative and not a positive fashion.

Conversely, it may be argued that the laws in question, far from being used in a paternalistic fashion, were being employed as a device to repress women and to guarantee that men retained the upper hand. This explanation is, however, flawed since, at the time that this so-called protective legislation was being passed, other laws were being enacted which, for the first time, allowed women to retain control over their property after marriage[25] and gave them rights in relation to any children of the marriage.[26] The law, whilst insisting that a women's place was in the home, was apparently prepared to allow her more rights there than had previously been the case. Another defect in the argument that protective legislation was a means of repression of women is that over the years its repeal had little immediate practical effect, which would suggest that women's behaviour was influenced by factors far more varied than simply the presence of legislation. For example, until 1919 the legal profession was closed to women.[27] The restriction was then removed but very few women chose to take advantage of this. It was not until the 1970s that women began to enter the legal profession in appreciable numbers until now they constitute, for example, almost half the new recruits each year to the solicitors' profession.[28] Perhaps, given the 'image' of the legal profession and the need, until comparatively recently, to pay a premium to be trained rather than receive a wage, it is hardly surprising that women failed to take advantage of the removal of legal barriers. Nevertheless, if women were being and believed themselves to be oppressed, one would expect that the disappearance of the source of oppression would mark a change in their behaviour.

Paternalistic legislation is arguably more insidious in its impact and its removal does not take account of the fact that it may have played a part in shaping attitudes in society at large or in confirming attitudes that were already present. If that is so, these attitudes must also be eradicated, in addition to the repeal of the offending legislation. The weight of the legislative evidence drawn from the nineteenth century constantly emphasises that women were to be treated differently from men and were to be shielded from taking responsibility for themselves. It is, therefore, hardly surprising that the piece by piece removal of this legislation did little seriously to dent those attitudes which underpinned it.

Given the gradual repeal of most of the protective legislation, paternalism may no longer appear as an objective of the law in its treatment of working women. Yet this view rests simply on the elimination of the most glaring examples and does not attempt to resolve whether legislation which applies equally to male and female employees is interpreted in a paternalistic fashion when applied to women. On that point the law as it relates to health and safety at work is worth considering.

Since the nineteenth century, legislation governing safety standards at work has sought to protect the individual worker from the hazards of the workplace. An employer is under a common law duty of care to provide for the safety at work of each individual employee.[29] The employer may also be liable in damages to an injured employee for breach of statutory duty should the employer fail to comply with the requirements of the numerous statutes and regulations governing health and safety at work.[30] Additionally, the employer will be liable to prosecution for failure to comply with health and safety legislation including the Health and Safety at Work Act 1974. Section 2 of the Act provides, amongst other things, that the employer may be fined for failing to provide, so far as is reasonably practicable, a system of work and a working environment which is safe and without risks to health.

Whilst it is proper that an employer should safeguard the health and safety of employees against known dangers, it remains unresolved how far this concern may be pursued. If a particular substance poses a threat to a woman's fertility, has an employer the right to prevent female employees from working with that substance, even though the working system can reduce the risk of contamination and women employees are prepared to accept the risk they run? Alternatively, if workers have to handle a substance which could pose a threat to a pregnant woman or to her unborn child, can an employer refuse to employ women of child-bearing age in that job on the basis that they might become pregnant at some future date? It also seems pertinent to enquire whether employers express the same level of concern over a man's reproductive capacity as over that of a woman. The purpose of the legislation is the protection of workers, yet it would seem harsh, where the danger is confined to workers of one sex, to go so far as to exclude workers of that sex, particularly if it is possible to reduce the danger. Again, if workers do not currently possess that characteristic which makes them particularly vulnerable, it seems wrong to remove them on the basis that they might at some future date possess it. The same logic would justify excluding men from stressful occupations since they are more susceptible to heart attacks than women and it would be in their own best interests not to employ them in any occupation which aggravates that risk.

What little guidance there is to the law's attitude towards such problems is to be found in *Page* v *Freight Hire (Tank Haulage) Ltd*.[31] Mrs Page, a divorcée aged twenty-three, was employed as a tanker driver transporting chemicals. She was informed that she could not drive tankers carrying dimethylformamide (DMF) because the makers had warned her employers that it was dangerous to women of childbearing age and that special precautions should be taken in such cases. DMF also had other unpleasant side effects which applied equally to men and women. Mrs Page indicated to her employers that she was aware of the risks, did not want children and was prepared to grant her employers an indemnity. The employers refused her offer and in somewhat confused circumstances she ceased to be employed. She subsequently complained that she had been discriminated against by her employer contrary to the terms of section 1 of the Sex Discrimination Act 1975. It was held that Mrs Page had been the object of discrimination, because a male employee would have been allowed to continue carrying DMF.[32] In this particular case, however, the employer had a defence based on section 51(1) of the Sex Discrimination Act 1975 (now amended) which permitted discrimination if this was necessary in order to comply with a legislative provision pre-dating the 1975 Act. Here it was successfully argued that the Health and Safety at Work Act 1974 justified the employer's actions in safeguarding the health of Mrs Page. The employer did not have to show that preventing Mrs Page from driving the tankers in question was the sole course of action possible, but merely that, in the circumstances, the employer had sought to achieve what the 1974 Act required.

This decision suggests that the general policy which underlies the health and safety legislation may be applied differently to female as opposed to male employees. As far as is practicable any threat to an employee's health and safety should be eliminated from the workplace, but in the case of hazards which might pose a specific threat to women, the law would appear in certain circumstances to sanction the removal of the female employee rather than the hazard. In other words, under the guise of paternalism a woman is accorded inferior treatment in that she is deprived of her job. This reasoning may be carried to such lengths that, even though a woman is not yet at risk, if, for example, the risk is confined to pregnant women, it may still be possible to treat a non-pregnant woman differently without being considered to have acted in an unlawfully discriminatory fashion. That this represents a very unsatisfactory state of affairs has been acknowledged by the European Court in *Johnston* v *The Chief Constable of the Royal Ulster Constabulary*.[33] This case examined the European Community Equal Treatment Directive[34] and the provision in that Directive which allows exceptions to the equal treatment principle where the intention is to protect women, particularly as regards pregnancy and maternity.[35] The European Court held that this 'exception' must be interpreted strictly and not simply in order to exclude women where men would not be excluded. The principle of equal treatment was said to require that 'derogations remain within the limits of what is appropriate and necessary for achieving the aim in view'.[36] Therefore, the standard to be applied in such circumstances may well be that of proportionality and the alternatives to excluding women must be considered. Consequently, if a hazard might have been eliminated with little in the way of cost and disruption, then it would appear out of all proportion simply to exclude women.

The length to which this reasoning could and should be carried is obviously a matter for speculation. Dworkin in his essay 'Paternalism' stated: 'If there is an alternative way of accomplishing the desired end without restricting liberty although it may involve great expense, inconvenience, etc. the society must adopt it.'[37] This same attitude is reflected in the United States Equal Employment Opportunity Commission policy statement on reproductive and foetal hazards.[38] In evaluating the position taken by an employer on such matters the Commission requires evidence regarding the nature of the hazard, scientific proof that it represents a reproductive/foetal hazard, the stage at which harm may be caused and whether alternative methods of protection may be utilised. On this last point, the Commission's view is that 'where a reasonable less discriminatory alternative exists, it must be used'.[39] Reasonableness will be assessed in terms of cost and efficiency. Even if there is a proven risk that cannot be eliminated, the Commission will enquire whether 'the employer's policy is under or over inclusive'.[40] For example, exclusion of all women of childbearing age could not be justified since many women will be able to establish infertility. In addition, if the evidence shows that the risk to the foetus does not occur until late in pregnancy, exclusion of all fertile women would not be justified; any exclusion should be limited to those women in the vulnerable stage of pregnancy.[41]

Because section 51 of the Sex Discrimination Act, as originally drafted, condoned discriminatory actions which were legitimate under the terms of legislation passed prior to 1975, it appeared not to be consistent with the Equal Treatment Directive.[42] Section 51 was therefore amended in the Employment Act 1989.[43] Even in its amended form, section 51 will allow discriminatory treatment of women provided this is sanctioned by earlier legislation, including the Health and Safety at Work Act, and is necessary for the protection of women as regards pregnancy or maternity or other circumstances giving rise to risks specifically affecting women. It remains to be seen whether this provision is interpreted in the light of the example set by the European Court and the United States. Regrettably, there appears to be a good chance that, if the circumstances of *Page* were to be repeated, the decision would be the same. In contrast, were men but not women to be excluded from the workplace because of a threat to their reproductive capacity, this would apparently amount to sex discrimination since the amended section 51 creates an exception only where a woman's capacity to reproduce is put in danger. Faced with a threat to a man's reproductive capacity, an employer might have to remove the risk rather than the employee or else chance being in breach of the Health and Safety at Work Act.

If it becomes harder to exclude a woman from the workplace on the basis of some hazard to her health and safety, employers may fear repercussions in relation to the civil law liability to their employees. The tort of negligence rests on the basis that in certain circumstances an individual owes a duty of care to another. Failure to observe that duty of care may result in a finding of negligence and liability to pay damages to the individual who has suffered harm. If, therefore, despite all the precautions taken by an employer, a woman worker has her fertility impaired or gives birth to a severely handicapped child, what will be the legal consequences for the employer? In acting in a non-discriminatory fashion, will the employer have been rendered liable in a civil action? If the employer is shown to have behaved reasonably in the precautions taken, then the answer is no. Nor would there be a case to answer under the Congenital Disabilities (Civil Liability) Act 1976. The Act provides that an individual may be liable to a child which is born disabled as a result of an occurrence which took place before its birth,[44] but it is a defence for the employer to show that the employee was fully aware of the risks that he or she was running and agreed to take them.[45]

The philosophy of paternalism represents a particular theory about the use to which law should be put. Whilst there appears to be general acceptance of the fact that the law should be used in order to prevent one individual from doing harm to another, there is less agreement on the extent to which an individual should be restrained by the law from doing harm to himself or herself. John Stuart Mill undoubtedly goes too far when he argues that such an approach can rarely be justified. Given the complexities of life it seems acceptable that in certain carefully limited circumstances the state will take it upon itself to act in our own best interests. In the case of women this may involve acknowledging their childbearing role and protecting them accordingly by, for example, awarding them special concessions. In the past, however, paternalism has been used as a way of focusing on these differences and then using them as a pretext for excluding women from certain activities. In short, whilst paternalism may be acceptable in itself, this ceases to be so when the consequence is not to compensate for differences, but to penalise for their existence. This can lead to the added problem that, even when the protective legislation which is based on exclusion is removed, as is happening at present, the attitudes underlying it may take a great deal longer to eradicate.

Reference has already been made to the process of deregulation and its repercussions. If the paternalistic legislation currently being repealed was intended to be in the best interests of women, what was it designed to shield them from? Was it threats to their physical, mental or moral well-being? From exploitation in the form of low wages? From dangers to their unborn children? Any or all of these factors may have played some role. Deregulation may do little to eradicate this persistent image of the 'weaker sex' but it may represent a fresh opportunity to exploit women workers by the payment of low wages. In theory none of this should be possible, since with the demise of paternalistic legislation, equality is in the ascendancy. It is, however, one thing to affirm a commitment to this principle; it is a separate matter to devise a policy and legislation which effectively put that principle into practice.

This raises a final thought as to whether, as paternalism is expunged from the workplace, it is simultaneously making itself felt in the family.

In particular, do the powers possessed by the state to intervene in matters of child care and the ability of the courts to determine the custody of children and divide family assets on the breakdown of a marriage represent the erosion of the individual's right to do what he or she perceives to be in their and their family's best interests? The controversy over the adoption of mixed race children by white families may be an expression of that tendency. The question may appear particularly pertinent in view of the fact that much of that intervention on behalf of state and court is justified as being in the best interests of any child of that family. It has been suggested that the division between public and private, regulated and unregulated, workplace and family might provide the key to women's subordination. Perhaps the key lies not here, but in the use of the law to promote paternalism, which then gives an excuse to treat women in an inferior fashion, rather than allowing them to make their own choices.

The promotion of equality

The underlying policy of the Sex Discrimination Act 1975 and the Equal Pay Act 1970, together with subsequent amendments, is the attainment of equality through the elimination of discrimination. The law is being used to ensure that women are treated equally with men, and married with single persons, in employment and that discrimination on the grounds of sex or because a person is married is avoided. Put in this way the whole issue appears remarkably simple – treat men and women alike and the problems of the past will be at an end. In reality, the equal opportunities legislation of the 1970s raises a number of issues:

(i)   What is meant by the term equality?
(ii) Once the theory of equality has been clarified, how best should that be embodied in practical legislative terms?
(iii) If the law is to be used to put the theory of equality into practice, will any exceptions to such a policy be justified?
(iv) How compatible is the policy of equality with that of paternalism and in order to achieve the former must the latter be eliminated?

The ideology of equality

The term equality is one much used in relation to the English legal system. In his book *An Introduction to the Study of the Law of the Constitution*, Dicey made it a principle of the rule of law that everyone was treated equally under the law.[46] At the time he meant no more than that everyone was subject to the law, rather than that they enjoyed equal rights under the law. Indeed in the nineteenth century and earlier, everyone most emphatically did not enjoy equal rights under the law. Rights, such as the right to vote, were restricted and only gradually was the franchise extended.[47] One of the grounds for restricting rights was based on sex, with women being denied certain rights which were available to men. In his essay, 'The subjection of women', John Stuart Mill put forward his explanation for the inferior position which women found themselves in at that time. In his view it rested on the power which men possessed over women:

> the adoption of this system of inequality never was the result of deliberation, or forethought, or any social ideas, or any notion whatever of what conduced to the benefit of humanity or the good order of society. It arose simply from the fact that from the very earliest twilight of human society, every woman (owing to the value attached to her by men, combined with her inferiority in muscular strength) was found in a state of bondage to some man.[48]

The law in its treatment of women simply recognised this reality. As Mill wrote, 'Those who had already been compelled to obedience became in this manner legally bound to it.'[49] This led Mill to assert that the way to achieve change was by eliminating the legal disabilities suffered by women. Hence, in his opinion, law had a key role to play and could be used to secure for women those rights which previously they had not enjoyed, such as the right to vote. Once men and women enjoyed equal rights under the law then, in Mill's eyes, women would no longer experience the subjection in public and private life that had previously been their lot. In interpreting equality to mean equal rights under the law, Mill was following in the best liberal traditions, and the history of the women's movement at that time and on into the twentieth century shows such a course being pursued. Rights were demanded and obtained in both public and private life. Important though these gains were, the equality achieved by the securing of equal political and legal rights for women did nothing to outlaw the discriminatory treatment of women. Legislation such as the Married Women's Property Act 1882 which allowed women to retain control of their property after marriage did little for those women who were economically dependent upon their husbands and had no resources of their own. Nor was there in the legislation giving women the vote and access to public office anything to prevent discrimination. It was at that time perfectly lawful to treat women less favourably than men.[50] On her marriage a woman might be forced to give up her job or she might be refused employment on the basis that women were not suited to perform certain tasks.[51]

The policy of equality which aimed simply at securing equal political and legal rights for women did little to benefit the 'average' woman. This is not in any way to denigrate the efforts of the women and men who campaigned for equal rights under the law. The fact that women were unable to vote or that married women were deprived of the control of their property were glaring examples of discrimination on which a political campaign might focus. Arguably, without first obtaining these rights, the efforts by women to improve their position might have proved even more problematic.

It became apparent that the kind of equality achieved by insisting on equal political and legal rights was insufficient. In the 1960s and 1970s a new and more radical form of equality was pursued, namely equality of opportunity. Genuine equality of opportunity demands more than the mere elimination of discrimination, because men and women do not start with equal advantages, but the legislation at that time concentrated on the elimination of discrimination, as a route to equality of opportunity. The battle against discrimination was spearheaded by the Equal Pay Act 1970 and the Sex Discrimination Act 1975. The Equal Pay Act aims to eliminate discrimination by providing amongst other things that a woman must receive the same pay as a man if she performs the same job, a job rated as equivalent or a job of equal value. The Sex Discrimination Act also aims to outlaw discrimination which it defines as having two forms, direct and indirect. Section 1(1) of the Act provides:

A person discriminates against a woman in any circumstances relevant for the purposes of any provision of this Act if –

(a) on the ground of her sex he treats her less favourably than he treats or would treat a man, or

(b) he applies to her a requirement or condition which he applies or would apply equally to a man but –

    (i) which is such that the proportion of women who can comply with it is considerably smaller than the proportion of men who can comply with it, and

    (ii) which he cannot show to be justifiable irrespective of the sex of the person to whom it is applied, and

    (iii) which is to her detriment because she cannot comply with it.

The same definition of discrimination extends not only to men (section 2) but also to the married (section 3) although the latter applies only in the context of employment. Taken together with section 6 which deals with such discrimination in employment, the 1975 Act thus ensures that an individual who refuses a woman a job simply because she is a woman or because she is married is guilty of direct discrimination. To its credit, however, the Act recognises that discrimination can be more subtle than this. The imposition of conditions such as height limits or age limits with which fewer women can comply can have a discriminatory effect even though they apply equally to men and women and, therefore, unless such conditions can be justified the Act renders their use unlawful on the basis that they amount to indirect discrimination.

Though these Acts displayed a new and welcome approach to improving the position of women in society, they can be criticised. In seeking to eliminate discrimination, both Acts stress the importance of treating men and women equally. Exactly what this means is open to interpretation. On the one hand it might simply carry the implication that men and women are to be given an equal chance to obtain those goods/benefits which society has on offer. In their book, *Equality and Sex Discrimination Law*,[52] O'Donovan and Szyszczak argue that this approach is flawed:

> For instance, in discussions of anti-discrimination legislation it is often assumed that once barriers to competition are removed women, who have been historically discriminated against, will show their prowess and compete equally. But this conception of equality is limited, for it abstracts persons from their unequal situations and puts them in a competition in which their prior inequality and its effects are ignored.[53]

A more radical notion of equal treatment would acknowledge and attempt to eliminate some of the 'background inequalities' that women face when they compete with men.[54]

On the face of it, the radical notion seems to have much to recommend it. It is difficult, however, to isolate those 'background inequalities' and to determine how to compensate for them. They could include poverty, poor education and lack of expectation as a product of historical legacy. But the current anti-discrimination legislation does not appear capable of taking account of such factors. For example, girls may be less likely to remain at school, to obtain qualifications such as GCSEs or to continue to study the subjects which qualify them to enter certain occupations. An employer who requires potential employees to possess certain educational qualifications might well be imposing a condition that considerably fewer women than men can satisfy. That employer will, however, not be guilty of discrimination if the conduct in question can be justified by the needs of the business. Concepts such as indirect discrimination seem incapable of dealing with the underlying causes of inequality, as opposed to its more obvious manifestations.

Faced with calls for a more radical notion of equal treatment, there are those who, far from accepting the justice of this argument, dispute it. In his book *Positive Discrimination* John Edwards doubts the wisdom of such an approach.

> The objective to be achieved by equality of opportunity is to rule out morally arbitrary characteristics from the determination of chances,

and hence to rule out such factors as sex, ethnicity, and social background. However, as we have seen, there are many other characteristics that affect life chances and ability to compete, that are also arbitrary from a moral point of view and ought also therefore to be corrected for. Where the radical interpretation of equal opportunity proves to be unrealistic is in its assumption that a truly fair meritocratic system requires the elimination of all morally irrelevant characteristics from the determination of chances. In reality, in a meritocratic system, we do accept some morally arbitrary characteristics (such as drive and intelligence) as being at least functionally relevant to winning the prizes and achieving desired offices.[55]

Certain important points may be deduced from a discussion of what constitutes equal treatment. In the first place everyone seems agreed that men and women should be allowed to compete on equal terms for the benefits that society has on offer. An individual should not be ruled out because of the colour of their skin or their sex, but of course because of that single factor an individual may have suffered other disadvantages, such as poor education, which may prevent competition on equal terms. Nor is there any guarantee that those disadvantages are experienced by every woman or by every individual who is black. The very complexity of the issue seems to provide the perfect excuse for doing nothing. But, as Lord Scarman has cautioned (in the context of race relations), there may be greater dangers in ignoring the problem than in taking steps to correct it: 'I ask myself: can we hope to unite the peoples inhabiting the United Kingdom into one civilized society without policies designed to advance minorities who we can see by and large are disadvantaged?'[56] As well as those 'disadvantages' which prevent women from competing on equal terms with men, there is another factor that needs to be taken into account. Even when women have succeeded in securing a particular benefit for themselves, they may lose it or, alternatively, fail to extract the maximum advantage from it because of domestic responsibilities. In this fashion, advances in the public sphere of the workplace may fall victim to lack of progress towards equality in the private sphere of the home. Some way has to be devised to cope with this, otherwise the gains made by women may be insignificant. It appears doubtful whether in this context the anti-discrimination legislation has any substantial contribution to make. The granting of additional rights may therefore have more to offer.

The concept of equality which the anti-discrimination legislation seeks to promote is fundamental to the interpretation of this legislation. As will be seen in subsequent chapters, both the Sex Discrimination Act and the Equal Pay Act are extremely complex legislative provisions and have been the subject of considerable judicial scrutiny. Any conclusions on how the courts interpret the policy embodied in these Acts will be left to those chapters, but there is still the question of whether the underlying policy of the anti-discrimination legislation is compatible with those other uses to which law is put, such as paternalism. Nor is the anti-discrimination legislation itself a coherent, unified code. The Equal Pay Act is concerned with contractual terms and conditions, making it relevant as regards earned income but not state benefits. The Sex Discrimination Act applies to employment, training and related fields, education, housing and the provision to the public of goods, facilities and services, but has no effect on the status of women in relation to such matters as social security or taxation. This is crucial since these issues are very relevant for working women. Nor did the anti-discrimination legislation have any effect on relations within the family. This has been regarded by some commentators as of especial importance:

> The reforms addressed the issue of the economic dependence of women on men but ignored, and therefore left untouched, the division of labour within the family whereby women as wives, mothers and daughters, irrespective of their labour market activities, do most of the work of caring – for children, for men, for the sick and the old. The state has never taken anything but a tiny share of the responsibility for this work; women still do most of it and most of it unpaid.[57]

Though written some time ago, this statement still holds good, as government urges that care for the old and the sick should be undertaken in the community. It is unquestionably the case that, when and if that burden of care is apportioned, in the majority of cases it falls on the woman, thus jeopardising her prospects of engaging in paid employment.

Not only are there many areas of human activity where no effect has been given to the principle of equality, but also, even in those areas where the principle does operate, there are exceptions. The White Paper *Equality for Women* indicated that 'all exceptions weaken the principle of non-discrimination'.[58] The guiding principle for such exceptions as there were was said to be the following:

> The aim must be, therefore, to limit exceptions to the necessary minimum. These must include provisions to ensure that the legislation does not apply to personal and intimate relationships and that the application of the principle of non-discrimination does not produce manifest anomalies or absurdities.[59]

The Sex Discrimination Act 1975 did incorporate a number of exceptions,[60] many of which, including the genuine occupational qualification exception, have been the subject of sustained criticism.[61]

Evelyn Ellis in her book *Sex Discrimination Law* views many of these exceptions as resting on past practices rather than genuine reasons for discrimination:

the legislation also recognises a band of situations in which the sex of the employee can be relevant....[T]he only completely unobjectionable such situation is where the biology of a woman genuinely renders her unable to do the job in question or necessitates that she be treated in some way different from her male colleagues. The Sex Discrimination Act, however, also includes many more controversial cases in which social or cultural values are called into play. In many of these instances, it will be seen that the Act appears to create a wider defence than is really necessary and thus to undermine the principle of equality.[62]

It is undoubtedly the case that the more exceptions there are to basic principle the more this detracts from the status of that principle. If women are to be treated equally, it appears contradictory to have a Sex Discrimination Act which indicates when and where discrimination will be legitimate. Nor is there an attempt to make such exclusions as narrow as possible. Instead, the Act adopts a broad approach which may give those seeking to avoid the full force of the Act ample opportunity to do so. Thus, if less favourable treatment for women is sanctioned 'where the biology of a woman genuinely renders her unable to do the job in question or necessitates that she be treated in some way different from her male colleagues',[63] this could lend itself to exploitation by employers some of whom might argue that a woman is excluded from undertaking certain work simply because she has the potential to bear children.[64]

If the end result of a policy designed to eliminate discrimination is to be the promotion of equality of opportunity, considerable thought has to be given to what exactly is meant by this. The intention might be simply to give men and women an equal starting point, at the same time ignoring those inherent inequalities from which women suffer, such as those caused by child care responsibilities. Alternatively, the notion of equality of opportunity might be interpreted more broadly and some attempt be made to take account of those disadvantages a woman suffers by virtue of being female. Whilst biology does not predetermine a woman's destiny, it is certainly a factor which prevents her from achieving her potential. Arguably, even if the judiciary were to adopt the most enlightened stance possible, there would be no guarantee that women would be treated as favourably as men. This is because the law still makes use of the notion of paternalism, not in order to benefit women, but to treat them in an inferior fashion. Paternalism could be used as the basis for granting women additional rights, and therefore make the objective of equal opportunities more attainable. In reality it appears that the exact opposite happens. Further, there are important areas of law, such as that body of law regulating the family, where the concept of equality of opportunity for women has little application or, indeed, relevance. Even if, therefore, the concept of equality of opportunity is employed as constructively as possible, many women will extract little benefit, and it has yet to be seen what the approach of the courts will be.

Additional rights

Granting additional rights to women is justified by the disadvantages they experience, which may derive from their education or from their role as mothers and for which they ought to be compensated. This proposition raises a number of issues which require closer examination before any conclusions can be reached on whether this is a desirable course of action. Undeniably women do suffer disadvantages as compared with men, but this is not true of all women nor does every woman endure the same level of detriment. Objections might therefore be raised to granting all women the same rights. Consequently, it might be either necessary or desirable to grant rights only to those women who are in need, that is, only those who have suffered or are currently experiencing some disadvantage. The alternative to granting additional rights on a selective basis would be to argue that, since in the past women have been discriminated against as a group, awarding them additional rights as a group is defensible.

Apart from the criteria used to grant additional rights, the form those rights would take requires clarification. Should 'rights' mean exactly that, such as the right to return to one's job after the birth of a child? In that context, the creation of a right seems a sensible solution. In a different context this may not be the case. If the aim is to compensate women for a perceived shortcoming in the education which some of them have received, then all women might be granted access to higher education. Apart from the practical difficulties this would involve, there would be other deeper-seated objections. Besides ignoring the good education that some women will have received, the idea of awarding rights to a group seems ideologically at odds with the current emphasis on individual rights. A more acceptable approach might be to grant to every individual the right to the best education possible, though this seems unworkably vague. Alternatively, use could be made of positive discrimination, an experiment that has been tried in the United States.

Positive discrimination is a much discussed and often much misunderstood concept. John Edwards, in his book *Positive Discrimination*,[65] defines it as a process where *the criteria used to identify beneficiaries and potential beneficiaries are different from those for which the benefit is being given.* If the reasons for giving a benefit or social good are need or merit or restitution or rights, and the recipients are identified solely according to their needs, merits, deserts, or rights, that is *not* positive discrimination. If, in fulfilment of the same objectives, recipients are chosen according to other criteria, such as ethnicity, sex, race, and – more arguably – age and residential location, that *is* positive discrimination.[66] [Italics in original.]

It would amount to positive discrimination should every university in England agree to admit a specified quota of women, regardless of the fact that some possessed qualifications inferior to those of men refused places. Using Edwards's definition of positive discrimination, preferential treatment could be justified on the basis either of need or of women's right to be compensated for past discriminatory treatment. The difficulty yet again is that not all women have suffered in this fashion and need to be compensated. Edwards bases his rejection of the concept of positive discrimination on theoretical as well as practical grounds. He regards sex as an arbitrary basis on which to distribute goods or benefits. The practical consequences of ignoring this, he argues, may be a loss of esteem by the group that is preferred and a reaction on the part of others. It is worth recording that Edwards does concede that racial minorities or women may have some substance to their complaints of inferior treatment. His solution is to improve the procedure for individual claims. 'It seems platitudinous to say so, but it may well be that there is no really effective alternative to improved and more effective machinery for individual compensation for discrimination through the courts.'[67]

The desire to grant women additional rights in order to make reparations for past treatment, to compensate for current practices and to take account of the burden of domestic responsibilities seems doomed to meet with failure. Clearly the theoretical objections which have been raised are not an insuperable barrier and any government determined enough to pursue a policy of positive discrimination could do so. To a government not so inclined, those same objections may serve as a convenient excuse for not taking action. On a more practical level, as the law currently stands, any organisation, such as a local authority or university, minded to embark on its own programme of positive discrimination might well be in breach of the law. Their favourable treatment of women is likely to be judged unlawful discrimination against men.

To all intents and purposes, therefore, it would not appear possible to award women different rights. In reality, however, there are circumstances where a woman can lawfully be treated more favourably than a man. For example, details are given elsewhere[68] of special training programmes that can be established for women. Women are also entitled to take maternity leave and return to their job after the birth of a child.[69] The existence of these additional rights may be justified on grounds which are perfectly acceptable and appear far removed from any notion of positive discrimination. Where the law gives a woman the right to maternity leave before and after the birth of a child, as well as the right to return to her job, the basis for granting those additional rights appears to be biological. They can be enjoyed only by women because only women can be pregnant. The special training programmes are described as positive action rather than positive discrimination. Employers are not forced to establish such programmes, instead the matter is left to their discretion, though it has to be said that the legislation is quite specific on when and how that discretion can be exercised.[70] As Edwards points out, positive action may be acceptable to some where positive discrimination may not, since the two are seen as 'different and easily distinguishable animals'. He begs to differ though he does concede that some examples of positive action are acceptable.[71]

In the light of what has been said, it may appear well-nigh impossible to grant additional rights to women, with the exception perhaps of rights related to pregnancy. One solution would be to build up a network of additional rights which are available to those of both sexes who need them, such as the right to have time off when children are sick or more flexible working hours. In this fashion, accusations of sex discrimination could be avoided and the law could go some way towards making it easier for men and women to combine paid employment with domestic responsibilities. The fundamental problem with this solution are the lengths to which this reasoning can, and should, be carried. Clearly the award of additional rights would prove costly, if, for example, it were to involve the provision of comprehensive child care facilities by the state. Other individuals and other projects might have equally strong cases for state help. The essential merits of awarding additional rights then becomes secondary to the issue of how state help should be apportioned.

Of the many ways which can be devised to improve the position of women in society, awarding additional rights appears the most problematic. Those difficulties reach a peak when a method is sought of compensating for past injustices, such as childhood poverty. The approaches discussed to date will do little to achieve this with the exception of positive discrimination in its most 'positive' sense. Clearly there are other groups, such as ethnic minorities or the disabled, who might benefit from similar treatment and might argue that they have a stronger case than women. Faced with such an intractable situation, the temptation is to do nothing and that perhaps is the greatest problem of all.

Three approaches to the treatment of women have been analysed. In their time all three have influenced the content of laws affecting women. Undoubtedly the preferred approach at present is the elimination of discrimination and the other two are peripheral. Yet they are not so peripheral that they cannot have an effect upon the success of the campaign to achieve equality. In the case of paternalism, this is a deleterious effect in so far as it serves as an excuse to treat women in an inferior fashion. The award of additional rights offers more positive prospects if it were not for the fact that the philosophy it epitomises runs directly counter to the notion of eliminating discrimination. At the same time, it may well further the struggle towards equality of opportunity. In short, the law's treatment of women reveals a tangled web of policies rather than a single consistent approach.

Chapter four

Patterns of employment

In recent years the position of women in the labour market has become the subject of scholarly research as well as straightforward statistical record. This is entirely appropriate in the light of women's increasing participation in paid employment and also very welcome in this context since it makes it easier to describe that section of the population with which this book is concerned. It is not sufficient merely to point to the growing figures of economically active women since, whilst this indicates the absolute number, it gives no idea of what might be termed the 'patterns' of their working lives. The identification of such patterns can, however, be problematic, not least because there are no universally agreed definitions of the commonly used descriptive categories of part-time, full-time, homeworkers and the self-employed.

It is generally accepted that part-timers are a disadvantaged section of the workforce as compared with full-timers,[1] but this leaves open the question of what constitutes part-time work. The Department of Employment considers those who work fewer than thirty hours a week to be part-timers. The definition adopted by employer or employee may, however, produce quite different results.[2] A part-timer may be loosely categorised as anyone who does not work what is considered to be a standard week in that particular occupation or industry. One employer's full-timer may be another's part-timer and the absence of a consistent definition makes accurate comparisons difficult. It should be borne in mind, therefore, that for these purposes, 'part-time' is not a term of art but simply denotes someone who does not work the hours considered to be standard in that job. Indeed, in the particular context of this book, the fact that someone works part-time becomes crucial only when their legal rights are affected as a consequence, for example where they do not work sufficient hours to qualify for employment protection rights. More generally the law may have a role to play, not in excluding part-timers from the protection of the law, but in alleviating some of the disadvantages they suffer and outlawing the discrimination practised against such workers. The law must take account, however, of the fact that part-timers are not a homogeneous group of workers, and that they may be working part-time for a whole variety of reasons, including a genuine preference for shorter hours.

Homeworking is, perhaps, a less well documented and less frequently encountered phenomenon than part-time work. Statistics compiled to show the extent of the working population may not even take account of this section of the workforce. One reason for this is the difficulty of defining and locating such workers who may pay no income tax or national insurance, and may not even classify themselves as workers. For example, the woman who earns commission as an agent for a mail order catalogue firm may not consider this to be 'work'. A distinction has sometimes been drawn between those working at home and those working from home. The former tend to be women, perhaps working part-time, the latter tend to be full-time, male workers including for example, tradesmen, sales representatives and insurance agents. Despite the many forms of homeworking, it raises certain common legal problems. These centre on the number of hours individuals work and whether or not they are employees, both factors being crucial in determining whether employment protection legislation applies. In practice, many homeworkers appear confused over their status as employees or self-employed and whether and to what extent legislation, such as the Health and Safety at Work Act 1974, affects them. In addition to this confusion over legal rights, some homeworkers may find themselves in a disadvantageous position in relation to such matters as pay and occupational benefits. The 'low profile' of some homeworkers must make them at the very least a potential target for exploitation.

The self-employed are another group who feature in some of the employment statistics mentioned in this chapter. The term self-employed simply means that someone is not an employee.[3] The immediate consequence of this is to put that individual outside the scope of the employment protection legislation and to put the onus on them to make provision for eventualities such as sickness and retirement. Where the status is freely accepted in the full knowledge of what it entails, this is legitimate. Many workers may not, however, be aware of all the practical consequences and some firms who wish to avoid legal responsibilities for their 'employees' may impose the label of self-employed regardless of worker preference. Research has shown that homeworkers are particularly susceptible to finding themselves described, correctly or not, as self-employed. It is, of course, a legal issue for the courts to decide whether an individual is self-employed, but this is of little use or comfort to those workers who are unhappy with their description, but who do not have the financial resources or the collective strength of a trade union to challenge it.

The final group of workers who may not be included in official statistics are those who work on a temporary or casual basis. A manufacturer faced with a sudden rush of orders may engage individuals on a temporary basis for a few weeks or months. The workforce taken on may work full-time, part-time, on the premises or at home. They may be regarded as employees or as self-employed. Temporary or casual work can raise any one of a combination of the problems previously referred to. In a time of economic uncertainty it may appear an attractive proposition to have workers whose services can apparently be dispensed with at very short notice.

These diverse patterns of work have particular significance for women whose paid employment outside the home has been traditionally affected and interrupted by domestic and especially child care responsibilities. Such constraints on women's abilities to participate fully in the labour market adversely affect not only their general career prospects but also the *legal* protection available to them, since much of the current employment legislation (as opposed to that dealing more directly with discrimination) is predicated on the notion of permanent, full-time employment.[4] This is exemplified by the requirement that the 'employee' must have worked for at least sixteen hours a week for two years in order to be protected from unfair dismissal or to claim redundancy pay or maternity rights.[5] It is laudable that the law should seek to grant rights, for example, to pregnant employees, but less commendable that it should do so in a manner which excludes many potential beneficiaries.[6]

If laws which relate to working women are to be relevant and effective, it is essential to have a clear picture not only of how many women there are in the labour market (in employment or actively seeking it) but also of what proportion of these work full-time and what proportion are part-timers. Similarly, it is also necessary to discover how many of these women are married, whether they have dependent children and the ages of those children. The status of a woman as a wife and/or a mother has an impact on her working life quite disproportionate to the effect that family circumstances have on her male counterpart. The final element in the pattern is supplied by the kind of jobs done by women, since those women working in segregated jobs doing so-called 'women's work' tend to have lower wages and worse terms and conditions of employment.

Trends in employment

In June 1987, of the estimated 21.3 million employees in work in Great Britain, 11.6 million were men and 9.7 million were women (see Table 4.1). Women, therefore, constituted 45 per cent of workers in employment.[7] It is significant that the statistics indicate that, while male employment has been falling, the participation rate of women has shown a steady increase. In 1971, for example, of the 21.6 million in employment, women numbered 8.2 million or only 38 per cent of the workforce.

Table 4.1 Employment trends 1971–87[8]

Great Britain June	1971	*Millions* 1976	1981	1986	1987
Employees in employment	21.6	22.0	21.4	21.1	21.3
All male	13.4	13.1	12.3	11.6	11.6
All female	8.2	8.9	9.1	9.5	9.7
Full-time female	5.5	5.4	5.3	5.3	5.4
Part-time female	2.8	3.6	3.8	4.1	4.3
Self-employed	2.0	1.9	2.1	2.6	2.8
H.M. Forces	0.4	0.3	0.3	0.3	0.3
Total employed	24.0	24.3	23.8	24.0	24.4
Total unemployed	0.7	1.3	2.4	3.1	2.8
Working population	24.7	25.5	26.1	27.1	27.2

Source: Women and Men in Britain, EOC, 1988

When the Department of Employment published its Labour Force Estimates and Projections for 1980 to 2000 these showed an expected overall increase in the numbers in the labour force to 28.6 million,[9] with the vast majority of this growth occurring in the female labour force which is expected to rise to 12.7 million or 44 per cent in 2000. This is to be contrasted with the figures for male participation which is projected to show a slower increase to a peak in 1990 and then a small decrease.

The picture which emerges from these figures is one which clearly demonstrates a greater participation in the labour market by women than has been seen in recent years. One reason for this increase in the activity rate of women is the decline in the numbers of young people of both sexes in the labour force because of the fall in the number of births after the 1960s 'baby boom'. As the number of school leavers seeking work decreases employers are aiming recruitment policies at women and particularly at those women who may have left paid employment because of domestic commitments and responsibilities, though, as one report has pointed out, women who have been out of the labour market 'are unlikely to be attracted back to the sort of unattractive, low-paid and unskilled jobs traditionally filled by minimum age school leavers, especially since many such women are highly qualified'.[10]

Employers may find it more effective to seek to retain the female employees they already have by, for example, introducing 'career breaks' which are designed to allow employees to take breaks from employment for several years while still maintaining contact with their employer and, in some cases, having a guaranteed right to return to employment. In this respect, the practical consequences of a shortage particularly of skilled workers may well ultimately have a greater impact on the incidence and the conditions of employment of female workers than much of the legislation designed to assist them, although once the demographic crisis is over, employers may be reluctant to continue with such practices. In that, at least, legislation has more to recommend it than market forces.

Occupational profiles

For many years women were assumed to be primarily concerned with their domestic roles and therefore to have no desire to work outside the home unless it was for 'pin money' or when it could be fitted in with their other, more important duties. The very phrase 'career woman' implies a deviation from the norm: a woman, perhaps single and childless, choosing employment rather than domesticity. The statistics cited in Table 4.1 showing the number of women in the labour market indicate quite clearly that it is wrong to assume that women are not part of the 'real' working population.[11] Women, like men, work for a variety of reasons. Research has shown that, even amongst married women working part-time, a substantial proportion are not working for pin money but for essentials and, moreover, in one survey, 52 per cent of all working women gave as a reason for working that they enjoyed it.[12]

In order to challenge traditional views and to establish a more accurate picture of the working woman, studies have been undertaken to investigate the patterns of women's working lives. In 1982 a *Research Report on Women's Working Lives* was produced by Elias and Main, based on the National Training Survey 1975-76 and showing the work histories of women and the role of part-time employment.[13] In 1980 the Women and Employment Survey (WES) was carried out by the Department of Employment and Office of Population Censuses and Surveys and the findings were published in 1984.[14] From the wealth of information in these and other studies[15] conclusions may be drawn about the way women view employment, the segregation of labour, the effectiveness of anti-discrimination legislation and, of course, the way that women's employment is affected by their responsibilities within and their attitudes to their families. In particular, it is possible to construct occupational profiles of women which show the extent to which women take breaks from employment and whether women tend to change jobs more often than men. Both of these charges are frequently made against working women by those who maintain that women lack commitment to paid employment and put domestic responsibilities first, thus making them a different proposition from men as employees.

The Women in Employment Survey 1980 showed that, on average, women work for four to five employers throughout their working lives with the highest rate of change amongst women in their first five years of work, when, incidentally, it is also high for young men. It was also found, however, that women are more likely to leave an employer for a job-related rather than for a domestic reason. In other words, women, like men, leave one employer for another employer rather than, in all cases, fading from the labour market. They did, of course, sometimes leave work for domestic reasons. This happened about 40 per cent of the time and was more likely to happen in the first ten years after the birth of a first child. Although even in those years domestic reasons are not the main reason for changing jobs, it was found that occupational change is closely linked to the presence of dependent children. Women with children tend to have had more jobs than childless women and to experience greater 'vertical mobility', a term used to describe movement between different levels of jobs. Significantly, this is frequently downward mobility so that women returning after childbirth may do so to a lower level job. This is especially true if they return part-time.[16]

The 1980 Survey also established, as shown in Table 4.2 that not only is it now normal for a woman to work full-time until her first child is born but also that, although almost all mothers have a break from employment, a very high proportion return to work, are doing so more quickly and, increasingly, are returning between births and not waiting until the youngest child is at school. At its very simplest this means that women are spending more of their working lives in the labour market.

The 1980 Survey also examined women's attitudes to work. Views were collected from working and non-working women on women's roles at home and work and, from working women, their views on their jobs and employment. Most women (71 per cent) felt that married women have the right to work if they wish[18] but it was also found that for most women, paid employment, though seen as important and beneficial, was still secondary to family commitments, though the response depended on age, status and qualifications, with older, non-working women holding the traditional views, while young working women especially those with higher educational qualifications were, not surprisingly, likely to hold less traditional views.

Table 4.2 Proportion of women who have made a return to work within varying intervals of first birth: women with first births in five year periods from 1950 to 1979[17]

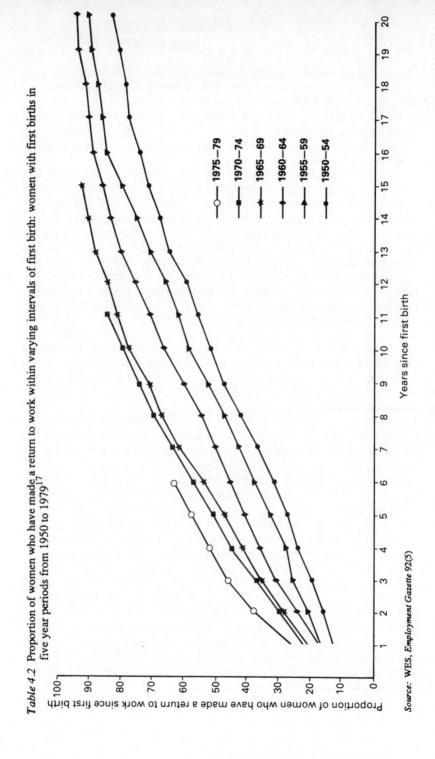

Source: WES, *Employment Gazette* 92(5)

Table 4.3 Usual weekly hours worked in main job, employees and self-employed[20]

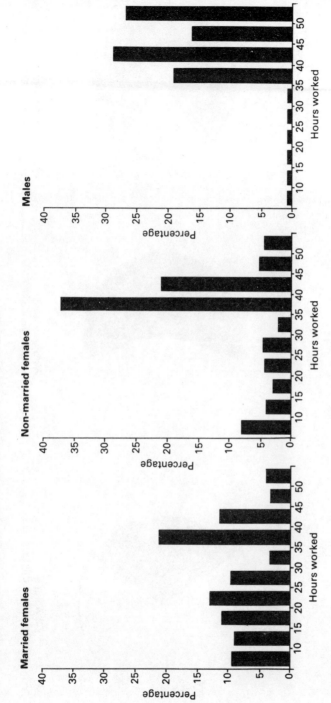

Source: Department of Employment Gazette, reproduced from *Women and Men in Britain*, EOC, 1989

Table 4.4 Working women by family status and full- or part-time employment, 1985[22]

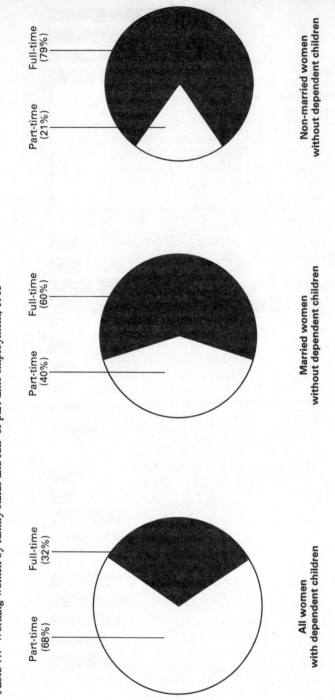

Full-time
(79%)

Part-time
(21%)

**Non-married women
without dependent children**

Full-time
(60%)

Part-time
(40%)

**Married women
without dependent children**

Full-time
(32%)

Part-time
(68%)

**All women
with dependent children**

Source: Women and Men in Britain, EOC, 1988

Part-time working and homeworking

There is little doubt that, in general terms, both part-time employees and homeworkers are disadvantaged groups as compared to full-time employees. There are signs that pressure from the European Community has assisted part-timers, for example in relation to non-discriminatory access to occupational benefits (discussed at greater length in Chapter 7). Currently, however, both part-timers and homeworkers appear worse off in terms of pay, benefits such as sick pay and paid holidays, and legal protection. It is significant, therefore, that the vast majority of part-timers are women. In particular, as Table 4.3 shows, the majority of married women who work are part-timers.[19]

The obvious question as to why women choose to work part-time if their conditions of employment are demonstrably worse than those of full-timers invites the equally obvious answer that many of these women have little choice. It is clear that the hours worked by women are influenced if not dictated by the presence or absence of dependent[21] children and by the age of those children.

Table 4.4 shows that of all women with dependent children a staggering 68 per cent were working part-time. Marriage by itself is also a very important factor since married women without dependent children evidence a 40 per cent part-time rate.[23]

The personal or family circumstances of a woman therefore exert an enormous impact on her working life (and see pp. 64–66 on working mothers). The effects of this full-time/part-time distribution must not be underestimated. At a very basic level, it has already been noted that the legal protection available to employees is generally dependent on them having worked sixteen hours per week for two years.[24] There is some consolation for part-timers in the fact that the 1980 Survey found that 60 per cent of part-timers (as defined by the women themselves)[25] *were* covered by the employment legislation and among those not covered insufficient length of service rather than insufficient hours was the main reason. Any legal protection which is subject to qualifying conditions makes women susceptible to loss of rights if government policy changes. A White Paper was produced in 1986, *Building Businesses Not Barriers*, in which it was proposed to raise the current thresholds for qualifying weekly hours of work. The sixteen-hour qualification was to be raised to twenty hours and the exception which allows employees to qualify after working for five years for between eight and sixteen hours was to be raised to between twelve and twenty hours. Statistics available at that time indicated that a significant proportion of married women workers would have been prejudiced by such a change.[26]

Apart from the straightforward question of qualifying for employment protection rights, part-time working has more complex conse-

61

quences. The 1980 Survey found that women in part-time employment tend to work in different kinds of jobs from full-time employees and, further, that part-timers are likely to be in 'lower-level' work involving sales, semi-skilled or unskilled work. In that survey more than half of part-timers had manual jobs as opposed to less than one-third of full-timers. This picture is supported by statistics from the New Earnings Survey 1987, which shows that 75 per cent of those employed in the occupational grouping 'catering, cleaning, hairdressing and other personal services' were women and of those 54 per cent worked part-time. In 'selling', 58 per cent were women and 32 per cent of those were part-time. By contrast, of those employed in 'professional and related supporting management and administration' although 69 per cent were women only 24 per cent were part-time.[27]

Some people might be surprised at the sheer number of part-time jobs that exist. Until recently any growth in employment has been principally in female part-time jobs. But a Training Commission Report noted a sharp rise in new *full-time* jobs for women in the twelve months to March 1988. Indeed, 141,100 new full-time jobs were filled by women, more than treble the previous year and significantly more than the 129,000 new part-time jobs filled by women. This might reflect the way in which employers are responding to the fall in the number of school leavers by altering recruitment strategies.

Table 4.5 below, however, shows the general trends in part-time working over the years 1971 to 1987, based on the Department of Employment definition of part-time.

Bearing in mind that working women who have children are constrained in the hours they can – or wish – to work, it is significant to note that when they return to employment after childbirth, they are far more likely to experience *downward* occupational mobility if they return part-time. Indeed, 45 per cent of women going back part-time experience this,[29] though it does vary as between occupations. Teachers are likely to maintain status, nurses for example are not.[30]

Part-time workers are not the only disadvantaged section of the workforce. Homeworkers may also experience similar problems, but these workers are often overlooked. In part this is due to scarcity of information concerning the incidence of homeworking and the composition of the workforce. Those studies which have been made suggest that the range of occupations undertaken either in the home, or using the home as base, are very varied. They include manufacturing, teaching, clerical work, computing, childminding, selling and service occupations such as hairdressing. Reference has already been made to the distinction between working at home and working from home. Research has suggested that the majority (73 per cent) of those working at home are women, and the majority (71 per cent) of people working

Table 4.5 Employment trends 1971 to 1987 (1971 = 100)[28]

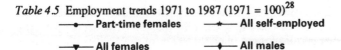

———•——— Part-time females   ———*——— All self-employed

———▼——— All females   ———◆——— All males

———■——— Full-time females

Percentage

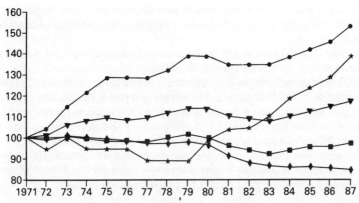

Source: *Women and Men in Britain,* EOC, 1988

from home as a base are men.[31] There also appears to be a variation in the hours worked by men and women, with women in general working part-time and men working full-time. The explanation for this is presumably women's domestic commitments which may have persuaded them to undertake homework in the first place. The reasons for homeworking are, however, exceedingly diverse and the traditional image of a homeworker as a woman with young children, forced to adopt this work pattern, is less than accurate. Some female and the majority of male homeworkers seem positively to favour this option, referring to the flexibility it offers them. It has also been suggested that for those women with traditional views on 'a woman's place', homework may represent an acceptable compromise. Levels of pay also tend to vary, with some homeworkers being extremely well paid. Once again there appears to be a disparity between men and women, leading one writer to conclude 'The great majority of people with very low hourly earnings are women, while the majority of high-earners are men.'[32]

Pay apart, many homeworkers will not have access to occupational benefits such as paid holidays or sick pay. Neither may they have access to state benefits since their level of earnings may well be below the threshold for the payment of national insurance contributions. Their employers may class them as self-employed, thereby evading certain legal obligations owed to employees. Another feature of homework may be its unpredictability, resulting from fluctuations in the amount of work available. Sometimes there may be plenty of work, sometimes none, reducing the homeworker's status to that of a temporary or casual worker. The invisibility of homeworkers has made them of peripheral interest to those who frame protective legislation. Even where the law may be interpreted to cover these workers it has to be borne in mind that an individual working in isolation at home, or from home, and who is unlikely to belong to a trade union, may be unaware of any legal rights or, even if aware, may be reluctant to pursue them because of fears of losing her job.

One final point is worth noting before turning to working mothers. Amidst the downward mobility, less favourable employment conditions and lower status enjoyed by part-timers, the General Household Survey published in 1982[33] indicated that women and part-time workers express greater job satisfaction than men and full-timers, the exception to this being women homeworkers.[34] Such levels of satisfaction may be attributable in part to women's lower aspirations. If the choice is between part-time work or no work, the choice is illusory. Essentially, many women accept a low rate of pay and adverse conditions of employment in order to combine paid work and domestic responsibilities.

Working mothers

It is apparent that motherhood is no longer seen as the occasion for a permanent or even a lengthy absence from paid employment. Conversely, the presence of young children has a great impact on the likelihood of women working and the hours worked. There are distinctions to be drawn, however, not only between mothers and childless women but also between lone mothers (single, widowed, divorced, separated) and those with partners.

In 1985 the General Household Survey produced figures which support what most would suspect, namely that the younger her child, the less likely it is that a mother will be working. Nevertheless, amongst married couples with a child under four years old, 30 per cent of mothers were working, 7 per cent full-time and 23 per cent of them part-time. These percentages increased with the age of the youngest child, so that by the time the youngest was ten years old or more, 66 per cent of mothers were working, 40 per cent part-time.[35]

A survey of mothers' employment for the years 1977–85 gave a graphic illustration of the effect of dependent children on a woman's working life. Before the youngest child reached the age of five, the percentage of married women working full-time was only 5 per cent. Once the youngest child reached five, that percentage increased to 20 per cent.

Table 4.6 Mothers' employment 1977–85

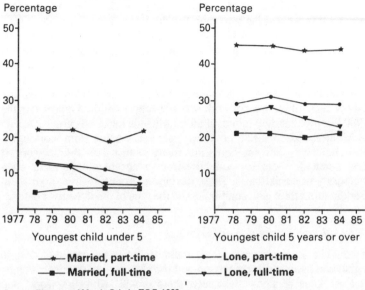

Percentage   Percentage

Youngest child under 5   Youngest child 5 years or over

——⋆—— **Married, part-time**   ———•——— **Lone, part-time**
——■—— **Married, full-time**   ———▼——— **Lone, full-time**

Source: Women and Men in Britain, EOC, 1988

The corresponding rise amongst married women working part-time was from just over 20 to over 40 per cent[36] (see Table 4.6).

It is notable from Table 4.6 that between 1978 and 1984 employment amongst lone mothers fell dramatically where the youngest child was under five years old. Even where children are of school age, levels of employment of lone mothers have fallen (though note the higher proportion of lone mothers who work full-time).[37] The reasons for the differences lie partly in the difficulties faced by lone mothers in finding adequate child care arrangements and partly in the intricacies of the social security system which ensure that it is not worthwhile to take paid employment unless the wages are either so low that they are below the threshold of earnings allowed before state benefits are reduced or else are considerably above the threshold.[38]

Child care facilities in this country are generally recognised as lamentable.[39] There is an enormous gap between supply and demand, not only in local authority nurseries but also in affordable private care. Many women are thus unable to seek full-time employment and elect for jobs where the hours allow them to combine work and caring for children. Even part-timers, if they are not working at home, have to make arrangements for child care. Where children are not in school, 83 per cent of part-timers and 93 per cent of full-timers had to make special arrangements.[40] Once children are at school, the variation increases – 70 per cent of full-time and 47 per cent of part-time working women with children aged five to ten years made child care arrangements. Of those making provision for child care, very few women used institutional or non-family care. The two commonest arrangements were first the husband and secondly a grandmother.[41] It is the importance of husbands in these arrangements which illustrates yet another drawback for the lone mother who is faced with the same paucity of non-family care, but also lacks the kind of support provided by a partner – 47 per cent of mothers in work with pre-school children reported in the 1980 Survey that they relied on their husbands for child care.

Motherhood does not, obviously, prevent women from working. It does, however, limit the hours that many women feel able to work. It may persuade them to work at home or accept employment on a temporary or casual basis. These deviations from full-time, permanent work in turn affect pay, conditions and the type of job done by women.[42]

Occupational distribution and earnings

It would be depressing in the late twentieth century to admit that, despite legislation against discrimination and the changes in attitudes amongst at least some sections of society, there is still 'women's work' and 'women's wages'. Unfortunately, depressing though this is, it is patently still the case. Part of the problem stems from the fact that women are clustered in relatively few occupations, a phenomenon which may be explained partly by the prevalence of part-time work in those jobs (though it is debatable whether this is cause or effect) and partly by the complex issues of women's education, aspirations and expectations.

As regards the industrial distribution of employment, in 1987[43] women formed the majority of workers in medical and other health services (80 per cent); footwear and clothing (73.5 per cent); personal services, for example hairdressing and cleaning (71 per cent); education (68.5 per cent); hotels and catering (67 per cent); retail distribution (63 per cent); sanitary services (60 per cent); and banking and finance (55 per cent). Retail distribution, education and medical services are the largest employers of women and, together with hotels and catering, the largest employers of part-timers.[44] There is, moreover, evidence not only that women are concentrated into relatively few occupational areas but also that within the workplace itself segregation occurs as between jobs. The 1980 Women in Employment Survey found that 63 per cent of women were in jobs done only by women at their workplace. Such segregation was more likely in relation to part-timers.

This kind of separation of women's work and men's work is, of course, not universal, and women can always be found across the range of employment. Nevertheless, the segregation that does occur has important consequences – or more accurately it is one of several inter-related factors which contribute to the general pattern of women's working lives. One of the most obvious effects of segregation relates to conditions of employment enjoyed by workers and, in particular, their rates of pay.

Rates of pay

The Equal Pay Act was passed in 1970 and implemented in 1975, a transitional period being allowed, in theory to give employers the opportunity to adjust women's rates of pay to those of men doing like work or work rated as equivalent. The Act appears to have had a fairly dismal success rate in closing the gap between women's and men's earnings. This was not entirely surprising if, as seems clear, women and men often do not do 'like work' or work that has been given the same rating under a job evaluation scheme. In theory, more women should benefit from the right to claim equal pay with men where the women are doing work of 'equal value'. The equal value amendment, in force from January 1984 as a result of a decision of the European Court of Justice that United Kingdom law did not comply with European Community requirements, should assist women but, as yet, despite some notable individual successes, does not appear to have affected the earnings gap.[45] Whether one considers hourly or weekly earnings it is clear that women's wages are very noticeably lower than those of male workers.

The 1988 New Earnings Survey shows that women's average gross hourly earnings (excluding the effects of overtime) are 75.1 per cent of men's. The gap is even greater in relation to average weekly earnings because, even allowing for overtime, men work longer hours. Over half of working women earn less than £152 a week, while only 19 per cent of men do so.[46] It is noticeable that women's hourly earnings improved, relative to men's in the mid-1970s, a period during which the existence of an incomes policy assisted the lower paid in general. Those years also coincided with the coming into force of the Equal Pay Act 1970. Latterly, however, wages have increased more at the higher end of the income scale and have improved more for non-manual than manual workers. Women, it is true, feature largely in the non-manual occupations but, since they tend to be in the lower-grade jobs, they have not benefited as much.

The various factors which may explain the earnings gap between women and men, which include job segregation, part-time employment, the predominance of women in traditionally low-grade, low-paid jobs are, of course, closely interlinked and, in any event, tell only part of the story. The New Earnings Survey 1987[47] showed that within particular occupations there is a gap between what women and men earn and this has been unaffected by the equal pay legislation. In nursing and midwifery, for example, where women make up 89 per cent of the work-force, their earnings are 90 per cent of the men's. Amongst sales staff, shop assistants and shelf fillers, 65 per cent are women and they earn 75 per cent of what men earn.

There is no one factor which will account for women's comparatively low pay. Though part-timers have lower earnings than full-timers (54 per cent of part-timers earned less than £1.50 per hour in 1980 as compared to 30 per cent of full-timers),[48] that difference is explicable largely by the type of job done by part-time workers. Indeed, the Women in Employment Survey discovered that even more significant than working part-time was the fact that it was a 'women only' job. Segregation had an effect, moreover, not only on pay but also on other conditions of employment and on chances of promotion and training.

It is said that statistics may be used to prove anything, and it is undoubtedly the case that where statistics abound the results may appear confused or inconclusive. However, despite the abundance of figures available on working women (only a sample of which are referred to here), it is possible to see the emergence of a remarkably clear pattern. Women follow different paths from men during their working lives and for many women these are dead ends. It would be wrong, however, to assume that because of this working women form a homogeneous group. Working women, far more than working men, have work histories which form a complex picture of movement between full-time and part-time work, between skilled and unskilled work, between permanent and casual jobs. There is no 'typical working woman', a fact which legislators would do well to note. For the purposes of this book we need not delve into the motives which might impel women to make the decisions they do about work. We must note simply that even today women are operating within limits placed on them by domestic responsibilities which, by and large, leave male colleagues untouched. Women are, numerically, not far behind men in the labour force but, taken as a group, are nowhere near attaining the same kind of employment opportunities and conditions or career structures. It is with these important differences in mind that the rest of the book must be read.

Chapter five

Women's rights at work

For a woman to extract the maximum benefit from her participation in the labour market she must be free to exploit to the full the talents she possesses and must be shielded from discrimination based on her sex or childbearing potential. In addition, the rewards she receives as a consequence of her efforts should be the same as those received by a comparable man. The aim of this chapter and Chapter 6 is to examine whether that body of law primarily enacted for the benefit of women, namely the anti-discrimination legislation, has allowed women successfully to achieve these objectives. There are various factors which militate against success. In the first place, the law is limited in its ability to bring about social change. Secondly, although from the 1970s onwards there has been a commitment to an equal opportunities policy, the manner in which that policy has been pursued has not been single-minded, nor has sufficient attention been paid to the distinctive patterns of women's employment in determining policy goals. Thirdly, an analysis of the terms of the anti-discrimination legislation, and its interpretation in the courts, exposes additional weaknesses. In particular, a 'credibility gap' emerges between the policy which the legislation purports to implement and the manner in which the law is applied in practice.

There are three major pieces of legislation designed to improve the situation of working women. These are, first, the Sex Discrimination Act 1975 together with its associated legislation, second, the Employment Protection (Consolidation) Act 1978, and, finally, the Equal Pay Act 1970. The first two Acts are dealt with in this chapter and the Equal Pay Act is the focus of Chapter 6. Each of these Acts deals with a particular issue. The Sex Discrimination Act and the Equal Pay Act share the same aim, namely the elimination of discrimination and the promotion of equal opportunities but the two Acts are mutually exclusive. The Equal Pay Act is concerned with the terms and conditions in a woman's contract of employment which should include the rate of remuneration she receives. The Sex Discrimination Act covers issues not dealt with in the contract of employment as well as a much wider range of activities. The Employment Protection (Consolidation) Act sets out the protection which is accorded a pregnant employee and is more accurately described as part of the employment legislation as opposed to the anti-discrimination legislation.

When several pieces of legislation are intent on dealing with a problem, difficulties are almost inevitable and discriminatory activities can and do fall through the legislative net. This happened in *Meeks* v *National Union of Agricultural and Allied Workers*,[1] where a part-time secretary was paid less per hour than a full-timer. The Industrial Tribunal considered that a requirement making it necessary for an employee to work for thirty-five hours per week in order to qualify for the higher hourly rate was indirectly discriminatory. It constituted a condition with which proportionately fewer women than men could comply and which the employer could not justify. The Tribunal went on to hold, however, that the discrimination in question was not unlawful since it concerned the payment of money and this was specifically excluded from the scope of the Sex Discrimination Act. Unfortunately, the Equal Pay Act, which was intended to cover such circumstances, was at that time of no use since all the secretaries were women and no male comparator was available.[2] The combining of the anti-discrimination laws into a single Act would simplify matters to some extent and the Equal Opportunities Commission has recommended that there should be an Equal Treatment Act.[3]

An evaluation of the effectiveness of the current law should begin by describing the attitudes and behaviour adopted by employers which, whilst they prejudice a woman's chance of employment, are so deeply rooted in the system that it is easy not to think of them as sexually discriminatory. It is not uncommon, for example, for job vacancies to be informally advertised by word of mouth. Women who are out of the job market may be prejudiced by never hearing of these opportunities. The success of the law in facilitating women's free access to the labour market must therefore be measured against the prevalence and persistence of the kinds of practices and assumptions which constitute obstacles to obtaining employment.

Obstacles to employment: the practice of discrimination

Research studies have revealed a number of stages in the process of gaining and retaining employment which may be handled in a discriminatory fashion, knowingly or not, by employers. These stages may be identified as follows:

(i) Job description.
(ii) Recruitment.

   (iii) Characteristics perceived to be necessary in a potential
        employee.
   (iv) Promotion and training.
   (v) Availability for work.

Though attention is directed at practices which adversely affect women, there is evidence that men, as well as married persons, can suffer
the effects of ill-conceived assumptions. Some employers, for example,
have the preconceived idea that women are more dextrous than men or
that married persons are less reliable than those who are single.

Job description

The way in which a job vacancy is described or advertised can be
crucial. Obviously, a potential applicant may be required to have certain
qualifications. Thus applicants for the post of driving instructor must
have a driving licence and an acceptable driving record. There is
evidence, however, that requiring candidates to possess certain formal
qualifications, such as GCSEs or A levels, can work unfairly against
women if the subjects specified are those which women are unlikely to
have studied.[4] It may seem that the solution to this lies not with
employers but with the education system – both teachers and students –
so that peer pressure, individual expectation and the inflexibility of
some schools ceases to discourage girls from studying relevant
subjects.[5] That ideal ignores, however, the rigidity of what some
employers specify as essential qualifications, even where there may well
be some alternative which is just as satisfactory.[6] This puts the onus on
employers to consider very closely the reason for insisting on certain
qualifications, particularly when they are qualifications which,
traditionally, women do not possess.

Apart from formal qualifications, a job description may specify other
characteristics which applicants should have. Two of the commonest
requirements are that job applicants should be in a definite or preferred
age range and be geographically mobile. Research undertaken into
recruitment in the retail and clerical sectors demonstrated that over two-
thirds of employers expressed some preference regarding the age of
candidates applying for vacancies.[7] The researcher's conclusion was
revealing: '[the] preferred age range is thus precisely the age at which a
considerable number of women are prevented from working because
they are bearing and raising children'.[8] The motives behind the
imposition of age requirements raise quite separate and difficult issues.
Their use reflects expectations concerning the kind of behaviour and
abilities that are commonly assumed to manifest themselves at certain
ages. Alternatively, an employer may believe that the younger a person

is the less he or she needs to be paid. Whilst age discrimination does affect both sexes, it is undoubtedly a factor which can be conclusive in a woman's failure to find a job which suits her experience and abilities or, indeed, any job at all. One study of job advertisements indicated that of the 11,500 advertisements monitored, almost one-fifth required applicants to be aged thirty-five or under.[9] This must have an adverse effect on many women who, at around that age, are taking time off to have or to care for children. On their return to the labour market a considerable number of those women are over the age of thirty-five. Employers who wish to recruit graduates and also impose an age limit of thirty or thirty-five may prejudice the chances of women since a greater number of women than men return to higher education *after* caring for their families and the use of age limits can again effectively prevent women from obtaining employment.[10]

Geographical mobility may be required of job applicants, notably in professions such as banking or selling. This too can actively deter women, particularly married women, from applying for such posts. This is unfortunate since there is evidence that the requirement may not be rigidly adhered to once an individual is in post.[11] Those selecting or screening potential applicants may themselves assume that women are less mobile than men, though logic would suggest that much depends on the particular individual. A married man might, in reality, be less geographically mobile than a single woman. Indeed the condition is one which, if applied rigorously, could excessively affect all married persons, if employers are disposed to regard marriage as a bar to mobility.

Recruitment

The way in which vacancies are publicised can adversely affect women. Section 38 of the 1975 Act does outlaw, directly or indirectly, discriminatory advertisements, including those which use terms that are not sexually neutral, such as 'waiter' or 'salesman', unless it is made clear that both sexes may apply. Employers can, however, evade the spirit of this section by placing advertisements in journals that are unlikely to be read by women or using recruitment techniques that do not involve advertising. Neither does the legislation attempt to eradicate sexist language with its implication that certain jobs are performed by women, others by men.

If a job is extensively advertised in newspapers and job centres, this should alert the widest range of individuals. Alternative methods of filling vacancies are used, however, such as internal appointments, selecting potential employees from a waiting-list of interested persons or choosing someone to fill a vacancy on the basis of personal recommendation. All these alternatives effectively restrict the field of applicants for a post. For example, if only internal candidates are considered and they are all male, a male monopoly is created and perpetuated.

As well as making efforts to publicise a vacancy, employers should give some thought to how a vacancy is filled. Arguably, the more closed and informal the appointment process is, the more opportunity it allows for discrimination, deliberate or otherwise. If employers are forced to articulate their criteria for appointment and justify their choice, this may encourage fairer selection.[12] It has to be said that even when the appointment process is apparently made fairer the opportunity remains to discriminate, as case studies have shown.[13] Nevertheless, since methods of recruitment do play a role in restricting women's access to employment, they should not be neglected in any 'equal opportunities' policy.

Personal attributes

Individuals selecting potential employees may well have preconceived ideas about the attributes required by the successful applicant. This can adversely affect women, particularly if the attribute sought is one which women are, rightly or wrongly, thought unlikely to possess. There will be no mention of these qualities in any job description and this makes it all the more difficult for a woman to disabuse any potential employer. For some jobs a degree of physical strength may be assumed to be necessary. A study into equal opportunities at British Rail provided one such illustration. 'Almost all the men interviewed felt that some jobs were too *heavy* for women, and that their more limited physical strength ruled them out in some occupations.'[14] Objectively this presumption was incorrect, but it meant that women were not given the chance to show that they could cope, and thus they were excluded from certain jobs.

Other research has demonstrated the adoption of a 'protective' attitude towards women which is then used to justify a refusal to give them certain jobs. One researcher quotes an insurance recruiter as making the following remark:

> If it's a girl who's selling and she says to the client, 'I'll take you to lunch', he'll obviously read more into it than that. If the broker's wife knew about it, she'd be a bit worried. And again, selling insurance often involves night calls. Now how does a lady cope with that if she calls on a man's house at night?[15]

On this occasion a woman's sexuality is being used as an excuse to deny her employment under the guise of acting in her own best interests. For some employers, a woman's physical attractiveness is one of the factors

73

in determining whether or not she obtains employment. Clearly there are jobs where the way a woman (or a man) looks could be important, but denying a woman employment simply because she is middle-aged or overweight is a particularly offensive form of discrimination, which is not, however, necessarily unlawful.[16] The anti-discrimination legislation relies on comparisons between men and women, not between young and old, pretty and plain. Legislation has been proposed which would outlaw discrimination on the grounds of age.[17] The problem of being considered too old is one which can equally well affect men, though in their case age may more frequently be associated with a loss of stamina and drive rather than image and looks. There is no indication, however, that, in an effort to outlaw these practices, English law will go as far as some American states which outlaw discrimination on the grounds of physical appearance.[18]

Once a woman has obtained employment her physical appearance may well be the source of additional difficulties. She may find herself the recipient not only of comments on the way she looks and dresses but also of unwelcome sexual advances. Such behaviour falls under the general description of sexual harassment. This phenomenon, the existence of which has only recently been acknowledged by the English courts, can have serious consequences in the recipient's working life. This is made clear in the TUC's guidelines on sexual harassment at work which define behaviour of this nature as:

> repeated and unwanted verbal or sexual advances, sexually explicit derogatory statements made by someone in the workplace which are offensive to the worker involved, which cause the worker to feel threatened, humiliated, patronised or harassed, or which interfere with the worker's job performance, undermine job security or create a threatening or intimidating work environment.[19]

Women appear to be the major targets of this behaviour and there is some suggestion that the problem can be particularly acute when women find themselves working in what was previously an all-male environment. This may discourage other women from contemplating such employment if they feel that they are likely to be the object of such behaviour. Sexual harassment can take many forms, from assaults, threats and sexual propositions to bad language and the display of 'page three' pin-ups by male workers, and it remains to be seen where, legally, the line will be drawn between 'acceptable' and 'unacceptable' behaviour.

Sexual harassment reflects one view that men have of women. Another assumption often made is that working women do not want a career, since at some stage they will marry and start a family. Apart from preventing a woman getting a job in the first place, this assumption may be used as justification for employing her in a post with little in the way of prospects or denying her promotion. This statement is typical:

> The average trainee has lived in seven different places by the time they become a manager. Women won't put up with this. They'll fall by the wayside. Women are going to leave and get married and have children, whatever the extreme feminists say.[20]

Not all recruiters would regard women in this fashion, but the presence of such attitudes represents another obstacle to women's access to employment. On occasions, of course, women are regarded as particularly suited to undertake certain work. It is perhaps unfortunate that when this does occur, the work in question is often repetitive and low paid. 'The job is boring, tedious and monotonous. Men wouldn't do it. Women will. It's their temperament. They won't complain, they just get on and do it. It's not a career, it's just a job.'[21]

Promotion and training

Once a woman is in employment she must have access to whatever training opportunities are available in order to advance her career. Without this she may find it impossible to progress, and lack of training may account in part for statistics which show that in large organisations women often occupy low-grade positions.[22] Women also need access to those jobs that are looked upon as providing the necessary breadth of experience for promotion. A study undertaken in the banking industry suggests there is a strong link between training and promotion. 'Some posts provide good training and are the first step in the line of promotion. Others are cul-de-sacs and it is extremely difficult to back out – especially if one is not a man.'[23]

Training also has an important part to play in securing women access to employment which in the past has been regarded as a male preserve. If women lack the skills to do a particular job they can legitimately be denied employment. The Sex Discrimination Act allows a limited form of 'positive action' in relation to training, and the existence of these provisions is an acknowledgement of the fact that 'Even where the employer eliminates the source of discrimination, long-standing job segregation may discourage women from applying for a job where it is perceived as traditionally done by men'.[24] Under the terms of section 48 of the Sex Discrimination Act an employer may give women employees access to training facilities in order to allow them to take up a particular kind of work. The employer must, however, show that women were under-represented in that area in the previous twelve months, and this requires him to produce figures as evidence that no women or comparatively few women were doing that work in the relevant period.

An employer can also provide training for female employees and non-employees alike if, nationally or regionally, women are under-represented in certain work. Finally, an employer is allowed to discriminate in permitting access to training where individuals 'are in special need of training by reason of the period for which they have been discharging domestic or family responsibilities to the exclusion of regular full-time employment'.[25] Since, in the main, it is women who undertake such responsibilities, they stand to reap the major benefit from this provision.

Training, and in particular training that is specifically targeted at women, can have a useful role to play in ensuring that women do gain access to employment where traditionally they have not been represented. Union pressure apart, the onus lies on employers to initiate schemes of this nature and for a variety of reasons they may be reluctant to do so. In the first place, there is the legislation's insistence that various conditions are satisfied and employers may be unsure whether their schemes qualify. The possible reactions of the established workforce could also act as a disincentive, as could the costs of the training programmes. In these circumstances employers may prefer to do nothing, though the predicted labour shortage of the 1990s might cause some to rethink their position.

Armed with the necessary skills, women should be free to seek and obtain promotion on the same terms as men. The conditions attached to a vacancy, or the way in which it is advertised can, however, discourage women from seeking promotion. Women may also feel, rightly or wrongly, that men receive more favourable treatment when it comes to promotion:[26]

> Women are given equal opportunity to reach about grade eight, but beyond that promotion opportunities are so rare that managers tend to favour men in the belief that they are more likely to be the 'breadwinner' in their families and so need the opportunity to further their careers more.[27]

Availability for work

Women are not always available for full-time work. On the one hand, a woman may be temporarily absent from work immediately before and after the birth of a child. To prevent employers from sacking their pregnant employees or refusing to let them take time off, the law gives a woman the right to take maternity leave and return to her job.[28] In order to qualify for that right, however, various conditions have to be satisfied. For example, a woman must be an employee and must have worked for her employer for sixteen hours per week for two years.[29] Consequently, many pregnant women will be unable to benefit from this right and may face the loss of their jobs. In such cases a pregnant employee would have to look to the Sex Discrimination Act in order to gain some protection from dismissal.

Apart from temporary absences, a woman may be forced or may choose because of her family responsibilities to take part-time work.[30] Although in the past part-time work has tended to be associated, not entirely accurately, with unskilled work, it is now frequently encountered in the skilled professions, as employers seek to retain the services of well-trained employees. In general, part-time workers receive inferior treatment as compared to full-time employees and this is manifested in a variety of ways. Depending on the number of hours worked part-timers may receive less in the way of legal protection. Their employers may well exclude them from occupational benefits, such as sick pay and pension schemes, as well as special entitlements such as low interest mortgages, although recent legislative changes may reverse this trend.[31] If redundancies are necessary, part-timers are often the first to lose their jobs. Nor do part-timers fare any better when it comes to state benefits. If their earnings are below £46 per week they do not have to make national insurance contributions, and consequently receive no national insurance benefits, such as a retirement pension, in their own right. Part-timers, the majority of whom are women, are clearly discriminated against, but the question is whether this is always unlawful and can form the basis of a claim under the Sex Discrimination Act.[32]

Whilst there is no denying the poor treatment that some part-timers receive, their position may be better than that of homeworkers. Homework can involve either the carrying out of paid work at home or using the home as a base for work. Reference has already been made to the diversity of homework and the fact that paid work in the home is likely to appeal to women with family responsibilities.[33] In one sense it is difficult to generalise about homeworkers. For example, research has shown a wide variation in pay from the well to the low paid. A common problem, however, is the legal status of homeworkers as employees. In order to benefit from the employment legislation, one has to be an employee.[34] In contrast, the Equal Pay Act and the Sex Discrimination Act are not so limited but the comparisons which these Acts require between the treatment of men and women may pose problems for female homeworkers.

The law's response: breaking down the barriers?

The behaviour and attitudes described in the previous section constitute some of the problems faced by working women. What must now be considered is how effective the law is in dealing with these problems.

The relevant law is found principally in three pieces of legislation: the Sex Discrimination Act, the Equal Pay Act and the Employment Protection (Consolidation) Act. The Equal Pay Act is considered in Chapter 6. This chapter will concentrate on the Sex Discrimination Act, which aims generally to eliminate discrimination, and the Employment Protection (Consolidation) Act, which grants specific rights in respect of pregnancy and childbirth.

Sex Discrimination Act 1975

Direct discrimination

The efficacy of the law depends, at least partly, on the way in which discrimination is defined and interpreted. The Sex Discrimination Act 1975 begins by drawing a distinction between direct and indirect discrimination. Direct discrimination occurs where a woman is treated less favourably than a man simply because of her sex.[35] If a suitably qualified women is refused a job, for example in a car showroom, where there are no female sales representatives, she can argue that she would have been offered the job if she had been a man and that this is unlawful direct discrimination as defined in sections 1 and 6 of the Act. If this has any claim to be an effective test,[36] then the motive of the person accused of discriminating would not appear relevant but, rather, their actions must be viewed objectively in order to determine whether discrimination has occurred. To allow motive to justify directly discriminatory behaviour detracts from any attempt to achieve equality of opportunity since it legitimises and perpetuates gender-based prejudice. If direct discrimination were acceptable on the basis that, for example, an employer genuinely believed that one woman working in an all-male workshop would find life very difficult, this would frustrate attempts to eliminate discrimination. Indeed, the deep-rooted assumptions that can lead to a woman receiving less favourable treatment may not be regarded by the person who holds them as discriminatory, and, arguably, the practical effect of allowing a consideration of motive would be to reduce dramatically the number of instances of direct discrimination.

The 1975 Act does not mention motive as a factor in determining direct discrimination and there are several decisions where the court has affirmed motive is irrelevant. In *Strathclyde Regional Council* v *Porcelli*,[37] it was pointed out that the relevant provision of the 1975 Act, section 1(1)(a), 'is concerned with "treatment" and not with the motive or objective of the person responsible for it'.[38] The House of Lords in *R* v *Birmingham City Council*[39] took the same approach, Lord Goff commenting that:

The intention or motive of the defendant to discriminate...is not a necessary condition to liability; it is perfectly possible to envisage cases where the defendant had no such motive, and yet did in fact discriminate on the ground of sex. Indeed...if the council's submission were correct it would be a good defence for an employer to show that he discriminated against women not because he intended to do so but, for example, because of customer preference, or to save money, or even to avoid controversy.[40]

In view of this decision it was surprising to find the Court of Appeal taking what appeared on its face to be a totally different approach in *James* v *Eastleigh Borough Council*.[41] The local authority allowed those who had reached state pension age free entry to a swimming pool. Since the state pension age is sixty-five for men but sixty for women, the policy resulted in a retired man of sixty-one being charged for entry whereas his sixty-one-year-old wife was allowed free use of the pool. The defendant in this case argued that since free access was available to all of state pensionable age, there was no discrimination on the ground of sex. The effect might be to prejudice men, but that was not why the rule was imposed; it was simply a consequential effect of a gender-neutral policy. In the opinion of Sir Nicholas Browne-Wilkinson and the other members of the Court of Appeal, there was no direct discrimination against Mr James.

This decision was impossible to reconcile with the objectives of the Sex Discrimination Act. The Council had chosen a sexually discriminatory way of providing a benefit, presumably for administrative convenience. Nevertheless, it did discriminate, whereas the criterion of free entry to all those who had retired from paid employment would not have done so, but would have been more difficult to implement. Perhaps such considerations were present in the minds of the Court of Appeal who foresaw the problems that an alternative finding might cause.

Whatever may have been behind the decision of the Court of Appeal it is clear that James *was* treated less favourably on grounds of his sex: his wife did not have to pay whereas he did, because he was a man. That may have resulted from the anomaly of differential state pension ages, but that itself is based on sex. The Court of Appeal justified its decision by choosing to distinguish between the intention behind and the reason for the behaviour. The Council in *James* intended to discriminate between men and women, but did so in order to benefit those in reduced circumstances, that is, all those eligible to receive the state pension. This was not unlawful discrimination because the motive was not discriminatory.

The Court of Appeal in *James* could not, of course, ignore the House of Lords' decision in the *Birmingham* case. An attempt was made to distinguish it on its facts, on the basis that Birmingham City Council was guilty of unlawful sex discrimination because it had deliberately allocated more places in selective secondary education to boys than girls and this was using 'overtly sex based criteria'. Eastleigh Borough Council differed because it had not used such criteria and had no covert motive of sex discrimination.

The reliance by the Court of Appeal on the discriminator's reasons and motives was an extremely worrying development. It did not, however, withstand the scrutiny of the House of Lords,[42] although it is worth noting that even in that court the judges were not unanimous; the decision in favour of Mr James was by three judges to two. The majority in the House of Lords pointed out that 'pensionable age' is derived from the Social Security Act 1975 section 27(1) where it means sixty-five for a man and sixty for a woman. That age governs not only when a person qualifies for a state pension, but is also used as the basis on which men and women qualify for a variety of concessions such as free travel and National Health Service prescriptions. Referring to the Court of Appeal's view that there was no direct discrimination because both men and women were required to be of pensionable age (thus making it a gender neutral requirement), the House of Lords noted that such reasoning is based on and vitiated by a fallacy. By distinguishing between men and women the state pensionable age is itself directly discriminatory since it treats women more favourably than men 'on grounds of their sex'. Any other differential treatment of men and women which adopts the same criterion must equally amount to direct discrimination. To state that a concession is available to all of pensionable age is shorthand for saying women of sixty and men of sixty-five.

The House of Lords, having thus clarified what might have already been thought of as clear, went on to reiterate the view expressed in the *Birmingham* case. To construe the phrase 'on ground of her sex' in section 1(1)(a) as referring to the discriminator's reason for doing the act was wrong. Moreover, the *Birmingham* case is indistinguishable from *James*. Motive – however pure – is irrelevant: 'the purity of the discriminator's subjective motive, intention or reason for discriminating cannot save the criterion applied from the objective taint of discrimination on the ground of sex...'.[43]

Although the House of Lords has once more given a clear indication that direct discrimination does not depend on motive, the progress of *James* v *Eastleigh Borough Council* through the courts illustrates some important points about law and the nature of the legal system. At the very least, it provides evidence of how an accepted interpretation of a section or sub-section can be disrupted, even if temporarily.

Complainants and their legal advisers are neither assisted nor inspired by these disruptions and this has consequences for the numbers of individuals willing to undertake litigation unassisted. It is notable that in both the *Birmingham* case and in *James* the Equal Opportunities Commission was involved, as it regarded them as important test cases. From what has been said about the judicial process, this change of judicial direction should not come as a surprise. Departures from assumed orthodoxy do not always work to the detriment of the policy goal of equality of opportunities. Unfortunately, such departures are unpredictable both in their occurrence and their results.

Motive apart, a woman seeking to prove that she has been the subject of direct discrimination has other obstacles to surmount. A woman who unsuccessfully applies for employment and believes that she was refused a job because of her sex has to be able to demonstrate this. Since employers are under no general legal duty to give unsuccessful candidates reasons for their failure to gain employment,[44] the Sex Discrimination Act allows a potential complainant to request information from the 'employer' with a view to substantiating suspicions of discrimination.[45] General information on the qualifications of the candidates can be obtained but not their names and addresses so that it is not possible to link specific qualifications to a particular candidate.[46] Access to relevant information is clearly vital since the onus is on the woman to initiate a claim and make out a prima facie case. An alternative procedure, known as discovery, does exist, and this can be used to force an employer to produce relevant documents, but discovery is available only once an action has commenced and not as a preliminary measure.[47] The court exercises its discretion when determining whether or not to order discovery and past practice has shown a reluctance to do so if the documents in question contain sensitive personal material.[48]

On the basis of the information supplied by the employer, a woman may discover that the other candidates for the job were better qualified or more experienced or had qualifications equivalent to hers. If this is so, and given that she may not know precisely what qualifications the successful candidate had, it may be hard for her to allege direct discrimination since there is no evidence from which adverse inferences may be drawn. Alternatively, if it emerges that she was the best qualified candidate, then she may have the basis for a claim, since it is now possible for her to argue that a man in her circumstances would have been offered a job and that therefore she has been treated less favourably on the grounds of her sex. Inference does have an important part to play in cases of direct discrimination and the courts have acknowledged this fact. In *Wallace* v *South Eastern Education and Library Board*[49] it was stated that:

Only rarely...will direct evidence be available of discrimination on the grounds of sex; one is more often left to infer discrimination from the circumstances. If this could not be done, the object of the legislation would be largely defeated, so long as the authority alleged to be guilty of discrimination made no expressly discriminatory statements and did not attempt to justify its actions by evidence.[50]

An employer can of course attempt to explain away these apparently discriminatory inferences and ultimately the tribunal hearing the case must determine whether that explanation is convincing. In *Khanna* v *Ministry of Defence*[51] it was said:

If the primary facts indicate that there has been discrimination of some kind, the employer is called on to give an explanation and, failing clear and specific explanation being given by the employer to the satisfaction of the industrial tribunal, an inference of unlawful discrimination from the primary facts will mean the complaint succeeds.[52]

Presumably any explanation must be aimed at removing the discriminatory inference. It must be distinguished from the situation where a difference in treatment is admitted. Whatever the motive behind such action, it will, following the decision in *James*, amount to discrimination on the grounds of sex.

Indirect discrimination

In order to prove that she has been the victim of indirect discrimination, a woman must, according to the terms of the 1975 Act,[53] show the existence of a requirement or condition which applies equally to both men and women. If a considerably smaller proportion of women as compared with men can comply with that condition and, irrespective of sex, there is no justification for imposing it, then, providing the complainant cannot, to her detriment, comply with it, there is indirect discrimination. Despite the complexity of its definition, the purpose of including indirect discrimination is plain. In theory, it appears to be the ideal instrument with which to tackle some of those practices, such as the imposition of age limits, mentioned in the earlier part of this chapter. In practice, the interpretation given to the various aspects of the concept has not always been helpful, although the Employment Appeal Tribunal has stressed that:

The purpose of the legislature in introducing the concept of indirect discrimination into the 1975 Act...was to seek to eliminate those practices which had a disproportionate impact on women...and were not justifiable for other reasons....If the elimination of such practices is the policy lying behind the Act, although such policy cannot be used to give the words any wider meaning than they naturally bear it is in our view a powerful argument against giving the words a narrower meaning thereby excluding cases which fall within the mischief which the Act was meant to deal with.[54]

There might appear to be nothing intrinsically difficult in demonstrating the existence of a condition or requirement, but, at the very least, this ignores the fact that on some occasions the reasons why a woman has been unsuccessful in obtaining employment will not have been articulated and hence cannot amount to a condition or requirement. Vague suspicions that a particular condition is in operation are not sufficient for the purposes of the Act. Some of the decided cases stress that the words 'condition' and 'requirement' are not to be given a narrow construction since this would not be in accordance with the policy of the Act.[55] Instead, the terms have been described as 'plain, clear words of wide import fully capable of including any obligation of service'.[56] However, it does also appear that any condition or requirement must represent an essential prerequisite the lack of which will be decisive. Thus, in *Perera* v *Civil Service Commission*[57] potential recruits had only to satisfy one essential requirement, namely possession of a professional qualification. Their suitability on the basis of other criteria was also assessed, but failure to satisfy any of these criteria was not an automatic bar to employment. The claim of indirect discrimination was therefore unsuccessful in so far as these criteria did not constitute either a condition or a requirement. The consequence of this decision is that employers can evade charges of indirect discrimination by arguing that although they take into account certain criteria which may have a disproportionate impact on women, there are circumstances when, at their discretion, they might be prepared to waive them. As has been pointed out, 'This is unfortunate. To focus solely on absolute barriers to the employment of women is to ignore the impact in practice of non-absolute criteria which may have a considerable adverse impact and be totally unjustifiable.'[58] It is even more unfortunate in view of the fact that the terms of the Act do not justify adopting this approach. If particular criteria are used to select or retain employees then it is accurate to describe them as conditions or requirements whatever the likelihood, remote or otherwise, that they will not be insisted upon.

An instructive illustration of some of the problems created by the terms 'condition' and 'requirement' can be found by comparing two cases. In *Home Office* v *Holmes*[59] a full-time civil servant requested permission to work part-time because she was a single parent with two small children. The refusal of her request and the requirement that she work full-time were held to amount to indirect discrimination. The insistence on full-time work was treated as a requirement or condition with which proportionately fewer women than men could comply, essentially because of their domestic responsibilities,[60] and the employers were unable to produce any justification for its imposition. More recently, however, in *Clymo v Wandsworth London Borough Council*[61] a branch librarian on return from maternity leave asked for permission to job-share. Her employers refused her request since they felt that this was not compatible with the managerial responsibilities of her job. She was, however, offered the alternative of sharing her husband's job as senior assistant librarian at no loss in income. She refused this offer and complained that she had been discriminated against. The Employment Appeal Tribunal had various grounds for rejecting her claim including the fact that the need to work full-time was not a requirement or condition within the meaning of section 1(1)(b) of the 1975 Act, but was part of the nature of the job. Apart from the fact that this conflicts with the decision in *Holmes*, it is difficult to see why on this occasion the insistence on full-time work was not categorised as a requirement or condition. The reliance placed on the 'nature' of the job seems to invite uncertainty, particularly in view of the fact that in *Clymo* no attempt is made to explain this expression. Instead, the court appeared content to take the employer's word on this issue:

> it seems clear that in many working structures whether in industry or public bodies, local government or elsewhere, there will be a grade or position where the job or appointment by its very nature requires full-time attendance. At one end of the scale if a cleaner was required to work full time it would clearly be a requirement or condition. Whereas in the case of a managing director it would be part of the nature of the appointment....it will be for an employer, acting reasonably, to decide – a managerial decision – what is required for the purposes of running his business or his establishment.[62]

This decision, along with *Holmes*, may prove to turn very much on its own facts but, for now, it represents a retrograde and unsympathetic interpretation of the law. It may even be argued that it is quite simply wrong on this point, even if it is accepted (as was suggested in *Holmes*) that in some circumstances full-time working cannot be said to be a requirement or condition.[63] One commentator has pointed out that what the tribunal had to say about the nature of the job was more relevant to an attempt to justify the need to work full-time than to establishing a requirement or condition in the first place.[64] It has also been intimated that the complainant's refusal to compromise might have convinced the tribunal that she was an undeserving case.[65] However, for the time being at least, the employer's discretion can effectively transform what appears to be a condition or requirement into something that is part of the nature of the job.

The next step in establishing indirect discrimination is to show that, although the condition or requirement is applied equally to men and women, the proportion of women who 'can comply' with it is considerably smaller than the proportion of men. In making this calculation, account is taken of women who 'can comply' in practice, rather than in theory.[66] If this were not so, the task of proving indirect discrimination could be extremely difficult. For example, if geographical mobility is a requirement for a particular job, the fact that, in principle, women may be no less mobile than men ignores such considerations as the responsibility that women take for caring, either for the elderly or for children. In attempting to substantiate the disproportionate impact of a particular condition on women, the complainant can produce statistical evidence, though judicial attitudes to this vary.[67] Much may depend on the circumstances of the case. The whole question of disproportionate impact raises the difficult issue of identifying the appropriate pool for comparison. If the requirement is for geographical mobility, should the comparison be with the working population as a whole, or with workers in that particular profession or workers in that particular firm? There is no hard and fast answer to this, nor to what amounts to a 'considerably smaller proportion'. It is left to the industrial tribunal hearing the matter to decide what is appropriate in the circumstances. As a result some very idiosyncratic decisions have emerged. One of the best known of these is *Kidd* v *DRG (UK) Ltd*[68] where it was claimed on behalf of Ms Kidd that the selection of part-timers for redundancy ahead of full-timers was indirectly discriminatory on the basis that women as compared with men and married women as compared with single women were less able to comply with a requirement to work full-time because of their domestic responsibilities. Ms Kidd, who was a married woman with two children, failed in her claim because the Industrial Tribunal considered that there was no evidence of what she had alleged:

> they were not prepared to accept without evidence that within this section of society a requirement to be in full-time employment (as a condition of ranking for redundancy selection on a seniority basis) was one with which a considerably smaller proportion of married than of unmarried women could comply. It was implicit in their decision...that they were similarly unprepared to accept without evidence that within the same section the same requirement was one with which a considerably smaller proportion of women than of men could comply.[69]

At first sight this seems an outrageous finding and one totally at odds with common sense. Yet in criticising this conclusion it must be understood that the Industrial Tribunal were not looking at the population as a whole. The reference to 'this section of society' was to the pool the Tribunal had chosen for the purposes of comparison, namely 'the section of the population for whom the need to provide care for children at home represents a potential obstacle to a parent's acceptance of full-time employment'.[70] Using this as a yardstick, which the Employment Appeal Tribunal held was permissible, the Industrial Tribunal refused without evidence to reach any conclusions on the condition's possible adverse affect on women, totally ignoring the fact that the pool selected was itself inherently biased since those who were more likely to be able to comply were omitted.

The decision in *Kidd* can be contrasted with that in *Clarke* v *Eley (IMI) Kynoch Ltd*.[71] Yet again a company's policy of selecting part-timers ahead of full-timers for redundancy was alleged to be indirectly discriminatory. Here the claim was successful since the Employment Appeal Tribunal affirmed the Industrial Tribunal's finding that the number of women who could comply with a requirement to work full-time in order to avoid selection for redundancy was considerably smaller than the number of men. The reasoning in *Clarke* thus appears totally at odds with that of *Kidd*. The incompatibility between the two decisions was rationalised in *Kidd* which is the more recent decision. 'Any difference follows only from the application by the Tribunals...of flexible criteria to the varied circumstances confronting them.'[72]

The pool for comparison is presumably one of those flexible criteria and exactly how it is defined may go a long way to explaining any discrepancy. Yet to dismiss conflicting decisions in this fashion is to tolerate conclusions such as the one arrived at in *Kidd* which are based neither on statistical data nor on common sense. Clearly, a tribunal can resolve a case only on the basis of the evidence which is presented to it. If no statistics are available to prove a particular point it cannot assume it to be true. More problematic is how far a tribunal can use common sense in determining whether fewer women than men can comply with a particular condition. Arguably, common sense indicates that more men than women will be able to work full-time. Some tribunals will be prepared to accept this and will resolve a case on this basis. Others may insist that evidence is produced of this. In other words, what appears common sense to one tribunal may not be viewed in the same way by another tribunal. Common sense can be used as a double-edged weapon and on some occasions may be employed in a manner which is totally unsympathetic to any equal opportunities policy.

Attempting to show that considerably fewer women than men can comply with a condition or requirement is no straightforward task. Its vagueness may leave a complainant unsure what she has to prove and how she should go about proving it. It is perfectly legitimate for the parties to an action to agree beforehand what the appropriate pool should be, though this may not be feasible if a party believes that a particular pool will give them an advantage. Lawyers sometimes argue in favour of ill-defined tests on the basis that they allow a degree of flexibility. In this context, however, the use of any comparison apart from that between men and women in the population as a whole runs the risk of itself being chosen in a discriminatory fashion. The same is true of the tribunal's determination as to whether fewer women than men can comply with a requirement. If a tribunal relies on 'common sense' in reaching a conclusion, it may run the risk of perpetuating traditional views of a woman's role in society. Alternatively, if a tribunal is to rely exclusively on statistics, there is the difficulty and perhaps cost involved in obtaining them, not to mention any problem in interpreting them. The greater objectivity of this approach seems preferable, though it assumes that statistics do not have a discriminatory bias to them. There is also a chance that a deserving case could be lost simply because there are no statistics to support a common-sense belief that discrimination has occurred. Perhaps the real difficulty is the rigid way in which indirect discrimination is defined. It seems legitimate to suggest that the elements which make up the concept of indirect discrimination could be more sympathetically interpreted, since, even if a prima facie case is made out, employers can attempt to justify their actions.

It is worth asking why an employer who has indirectly discriminated against a woman is given the chance to justify the conduct on grounds other than sex. One possible explanation would seem to be that the concession recognises that certain working practices exist that an employer may not be able to eliminate. It might be argued that the end result of the legislation should not be to force employers to adopt practices that are totally at odds with the efficiency and profitability of their businesses. In certain circumstances, it may be essential that employees work full-time or that part-timers are made redundant before full-timers, however harsh the consequences are for women. The difficulty in accepting this outwardly attractive explanation rests on the fact that in different contexts the courts have interpreted legislation giving rights to women in a fashion that is inimical to the best interests of the employer.[73] When this has been pointed out, the court's response has been that difficulties for employers may well be one of the consequences of improving the position of working women. It should not, therefore, be automatically assumed that, by giving employers a chance to justify their conduct, any explanation they care to offer should suffice. Unfortunately, the legislation does not use a term such as 'essential' or 'necessary' which might emphasise this fact. Instead it uses a less well-defined expression – 'justifiable'. Over the years the interpretation of this term has fluctuated. Early in its history, an employer was required to show that a condition was necessary as opposed to convenient.[74] This stringency was gradually relaxed, however, in favour of an interpretation which took greater account of the employer's needs until, in *Ojutiku* v *Manpower Services Commission*,[75] the term 'justifiable' was said to mean no more than that 'if a person produces reasons for doing something, which would be acceptable to right-thinking people as sound and tolerable reasons for so doing, then he has justified his conduct'.[76] A comparison was drawn between 'justifiable' and 'necessary', with the former representing a different as well as a lower standard. Plainly, greater emphasis was being placed on the employer's needs, though it was not clear how those needs should be assessed.

Following the judgment in *Ojutiku*, the law appeared to be in a confused state, with statements in the European Court of Justice and the House of Lords raising doubts over the correctness of the decision. In *Bilka-Kaufhaus GmbH* v *Weber von Hartz*[77] and *Rainey* v *Greater Glasgow Health Board*,[78] both equal pay cases, the need to show objectively that a condition was necessary was reasserted. This led one commentator to conclude 'it appears that, in order to establish justifiability today, it must be shown to the satisfaction of the tribunal that the requirement is "necessary" to achieve a legitimate demand of the employer'.[79] This statement must now be seen in the light of the Court of Appeal's decision in *Hampson* v *Department of Education and Science*[80] (a race relations case). The decision in *Ojutiku* is held still to be binding, but the Court in *Hampson* is of the view that, far from offering clear guidance on the interpretation of the expression 'justifiable', the majority in *Ojutiku* gave no definite indication of the correct test to apply. The exception was Stephenson LJ and his test is adopted in *Hampson* and restated in the following fashion: ' "justifiable" requires an objective balance between the discriminatory effect of the condition and the reasonable needs of the party who applies the condition.'[81] This test and the decision in *Ojutiku* which is its source are said to be reconcilable with the House of Lords' judgment in *Rainey*. Moreover, the court in *Hampson* stresses the desirability of a uniform test for determining whether actions are justifiable. Although none of these decisions relates to sex discrimination, it must be assumed that the term 'justifiable' in the 1975 Act will be interpreted in the light of the test in *Hampson*.

It may appear that the uncertainty over the term 'justifiable' has, at long last, been resolved. Arguably this is not the case since the test in *Hampson* allows a good deal of scope for judicial discretion. Indeed Balcombe LJ emphasised that, in determining whether a particular action was justifiable, a tribunal would have to make a value judgement.[82] The difficulty is that in balancing the employer's needs against those of a woman who has suffered discriminatory treatment, corporate needs may automatically assume greater weight. Therefore, the position of working women in relation to this particular aspect of indirect discrimination seems as unpredictable as ever.

The final element in the definition of indirect discrimination emphasises the complainant's need to show she has suffered a detriment because she cannot comply with the condition in question. Few cases seem to have turned on this point which was included to prevent hypothetical cases being argued before the courts. Whether the complainant has suffered a detriment at the time when the condition or requirement becomes applicable is a matter for the tribunal hearing the case to decide.[83]

Proof of either direct or indirect discrimination is far from easy. Whilst it is possible to extract some general guidance from the cases, each decision turns on its own particular facts and contradictory decisions make it hard to take the circumstances in one case and state that in future all similar or indeed identical behaviour will be discriminatory. This makes it difficult to comment upon the legitimacy of the employment practices considered elsewhere in this chapter, such as the way jobs are advertised, age limits and geographical mobility.

There are several decisions which demonstrate that the use of age ranges has the potential to amount to unlawful indirect discrimination. In *Price* v *Civil Service Commission*,[84] candidates for the post of Executive Officer had to be at least 17 and under 28 years of age. Figures show that between these ages women may withdraw from the labour market in order to raise their families.[85] Price successfully claimed in this case that proportionately fewer women than men can comply with the condition and that it amounts to indirect discrimination. It is, of course, highly probable that employers will try to justify their behaviour, perhaps on the ground that they need a well-balanced workforce, as was unsuccessfully argued in *Price*. Employers could use other less blatant devices to ensure that they attract applicants in a particular age range. The most obvious would be to offer a level of pay that would be attractive only to those embarking on a career and not to a woman with experience who is seeking to return to the job market. On various counts it might be difficult to prove that this amounted to indirect discrimination, for example in relation to showing the existence of a 'condition' or 'requirement'.

Although there are no reported decisions[86] on geographical mobility, it has the potential to be considered indirect discrimination since women with family responsibilities, and married persons in general, might have difficulty in complying. Undoubtedly there are professions where this requirement could be regarded as justifiable. The paradox is that, where it is not, a successful claim of indirect discrimination might confirm the commonly held belief that women are less mobile. Of course, in assessing the suitability of a particular applicant for a specific post, resort should not be had to stereotypical assumptions. A woman who is refused employment on the basis that 'women are not geographically mobile' might therefore be able to claim *direct* discrimination since she has been treated less favourably than a man.

The way in which job vacancies are filled may in certain circumstances prove to be unlawfully discriminatory. In *Lock* v *Lancashire County Council* [87] it was the practice to fill vacant positions for fire control operators from a waiting list. The names on the list were, in the main, those of firemen's wives and the facilities for fire control operators were designed for women. In those circumstances the rejection of a male candidate for the post of fire control operator amounted to direct discrimination. Other informal recruitment practices may fall into the same category if it can be shown that the end result is to exclude applicants of a particular sex. [88]

Even if a woman secures a place on a short-list and is interviewed for a post, this does not prevent those interviewing her from harbouring certain prejudices. If these become apparent from the line of questioning adopted this can amount to discrimination. In *Gates* v *Wirral Borough Council*, [89] for example, the complainant was the sole female candidate interviewed for the post of headteacher. She was asked questions regarding her marital status which were not asked of the male candidates. This was held to constitute discriminatory treatment. Questioning of this nature may be indicative of the belief that women do not want careers but jobs which they can abandon in favour of their families. If, however, an employer asks these questions of all applicants it appears that the practice is perfectly valid. Moreover, employers may still assume, whatever answers they receive, that women do not put their careers first. This raises a more fundamental point as to whether or not, if women are now prepared to do that, they should be applauded. It could be argued that, in part, the effect of the anti-discrimination legislation is to persuade women to adopt so-called male attitudes towards employment.

Although sexual harassment in the workplace is perceived by women to be commonplace, there is no mention of the term 'sexual harassment' in the anti-discrimination legislation. Nevertheless, in *Strathclyde Regional Council* v *Porcelli* [90] conduct amounting to sexual harassment was held to constitute direct discrimination. Here the complainant was the subject of sexual remarks and other offensive conduct indulged in by two male colleagues in an effort to make her leave her post. The argument that the individuals in question would have been equally unpleasant to a male colleague whom they disliked, and that therefore Mrs Porcelli's treatment was not on the grounds of her sex as the Act demands, was rejected. Instead, the point was made that some of the treatment inflicted on Mrs Porcelli took the form it did because she was a woman and that a man would not have been treated in the same way. 'It follows that, if a form of unfavourable treatment is meted out to a woman to which a man would not be vulnerable, she has been discriminated against.'[91]

In *Porcelli* the conduct in question was designed to drive the complainant out of her job. In some instances this will happen simply because the woman cannot any longer tolerate the behaviour. In *Bracebridge Engineering Ltd v Darby*[92] Mrs Darby resigned after a single very unpleasant incident of sexual harassment. The Employment Appeal Tribunal confirmed that a single action, provided that it was sufficiently serious, could constitute sexual harassment and give rise to an action for sex discrimination. Apart from a successful claim for sex discrimination, Mrs Darby could recover damages for unfair dismissal. Her employers' failure properly to investigate her claim of sexual harassment was a breach of their implied duty of trust towards an employee.

Apart from resigning, requesting a transfer or being dismissed, there may be occasions when the person who has endured sexual harassment remains in post. Since section 6 of the 1975 Act requires the victim of sexual discrimination to suffer a detriment, there may be doubts over whether this particular requirement has been fulfilled. The decision in *De Souza v The Automobile Association*[93] removes those doubts by indicating that this condition will have been satisfied if 'the putative reasonable employee could justifiably complain about his or her working conditions or environment'.[94]

The concept of sex discrimination has been used to render unlawful many instances of sexual harassment. The less satisfactory aspect of the law on this topic concerns the woman who complains of sexual harassment but who may herself use sexually explicit language or behave in what is classed as a provocative fashion. In *Snowball v Gardner Merchant*[95] the complainant alleged that she had been sexually harassed. It was held permissible in these circumstances to question her about her own sexual attitudes in order to show that she had suffered little if anything by way of detriment to her feelings. In other words a woman who behaves in a familiar or flirtatious fashion with some of her colleagues or dresses 'provocatively' may have to tolerate unwanted advances from a colleague on the basis that she can expect little else because of her own behaviour. The fallacy here is to fail to distinguish between how a woman may choose to behave outside work with a partner of her own choice and the right she must have at work (or elsewhere) to reject unlooked for advances. The question of how she dresses or behaves is in any event irrelevant where she has made it plain that the conduct complained of is unwelcome.

On many occasions when sexual harassment occurs, the guilty individual will be an employee. Employers are constantly urged to ensure that no sexual harassment occurs in the workplace. Indeed, the 1975 Act makes employers liable for acts of sex discrimination performed by their employees, unless an employer can show that all such steps as are reasonably practicable have been taken to prevent the conduct in question.[96] The decision in *Balgobin* v *London Borough of Tower Hamlets*[97] suggests that the standard required of an employer in these circumstances is very low indeed. As long as there is some attempt at supervision this may be deemed adequate and the Employment Appeal Tribunal seemed to indicate in Balgobin's case that sexual harassment might be well-nigh impossible for an employer to control.

Promotion procedures, it was argued earlier, may also work against a female employee if there is no well-defined procedure. In *Watches of Switzerland* v *Savell*[98] it was alleged that just such an informal process amounted to indirect discrimination. Here there was a pool of candidates for promotion to manager. These candidates were appraised by various members of the higher management team and decisions made on who would or would not be promoted. This procedure was criticised on several grounds, including the fact that persons under consideration were not interviewed and that criteria for promotion were not made known. The end result, it was argued, was a procedure that was indirectly discriminatory since, in order to be promoted, a woman had to satisfy:

the criteria of a vague, subjective, unadvertised promotion procedure which does not provide any or any adequate mechanisms to prevent subconscious bias unrelated to the merits of candidates or prospective candidates for the post of manager.[99]

On this occasion the complainant failed to establish indirect discrimination, since no evidence was produced by her to show that she had suffered a detriment. On the contrary, she had most definitely been considered for promotion. This serves as yet another illustration of how difficult it may be to show that a woman's failure to be promoted amounts to unlawful discrimination.

The final factor that may have an untoward effect on a woman's career is her inability to work full-time because of family responsibilities. From the decisions in cases such as *Holmes* and *Clymo* it seems uncertain whether a refusal to allow a woman to work other than full-time amounts to indirect discrimination. Much would now seem to depend on the job itself and whether it is part of the nature of that job – whatever that might mean – that full-time work is necessary. It is also unclear, after decisions such as *Clarke* and *Kidd*, whether practices such as making part-timers redundant ahead of full-timers amounts to indirect discrimination. In these circumstances, the justification put forward by the employer may be crucial, as may be the interpretation placed on the definition of indirect discrimination.

A women who is pregnant or who has children may be able to gain protection from the Sex Discrimination Act in a number of ways. For example, an employer who decides to dismiss a pregnant employee may be in breach of the Act. In *Hayes* v *Malleable Working Men's Club*[100] the Employment Appeal Tribunal distinguished an earlier decision which had refused to accept the proposition that dismissal on the grounds of pregnancy could amount to discrimination.[101] That earlier decision is a good example of how an inflexible and literal approach to the words of a statute can frustrate the policy which the 1975 Act is designed to implement. Since the Sex Discrimination Act relies on comparisons between men and women, it was concluded that the impossibility of comparing a pregnant woman with a pregnant man pointed inexorably to the impossibility of employing the anti-discrimination legislation in this context. In *Hayes* this sweeping proposition was rejected and the Employment Appeal Tribunal accepted that of the many situations where a woman's pregnancy could lead to her dismissal, in principle, some at least might amount to discrimination. Although the decision in *Hayes* seems to adopt a more flexible approach, the difficulties inherent in that decision should not be underestimated. All that it establishes is that a *claim* may be brought, and the outcome in individual cases will depend very much on their facts.[102] It is not sufficient for a pregnant employee complaining of discrimination simply to show she was dismissed for some reason connected with her pregnancy. In order to comply with the *Hayes* modified approach to the definition of discrimination, a pregnant employee must show that her treatment is less favourable than that which would be accorded a man in an analogous situation. Hence if an employer would dispense with the services of a man who would be absent through illness for a number of months, a decision to do the same when a woman is forced to take time off because of her pregnancy is prima facie not discriminatory.

Not only pregnant employees but also working mothers may gain some limited protection from the Sex Discrimination Act. In *Hurley* v *Mustoe*,[103] Mrs Hurley was employed part-time as a waitress by the manager of a restaurant. When the owner discovered this fact Mrs Hurley was told to leave since he had a policy of not employing women with young children and she fell into this category. The Employment Appeal Tribunal held in this case that Mrs Hurley had been the victim of discrimination. Since there was no evidence to support a claim that the identical condition was applied to men, it was concluded that Mrs Hurley had been treated less favourably than a man and thus directly discriminated against. Alternatively, the condition in question (no children) could be complied with by fewer married than single persons. It was to those persons' detriment since they would not be employed and, therefore, this would amount to indirect discrimination unless some justification existed for imposing that condition. Despite claims that employees with children were unreliable and a threat to the viability of small businesses, there was no evidence produced to support this. In addition, there was felt to be no necessity for such an all-embracing condition. Even if some women with young children were unreliable, it was not necessary to exclude all women with young children. Instead ways should be devised, such as the taking up of references, to allow employers to be more selective in this matter.

The decision in *Hurley* v *Mustoe*, welcome though it undoubtedly was, is limited in what it achieves, since it merely outlaws an employer's outright refusal to employ working mothers. What the anti-discrimination legislation may fail to cope with effectively is the lack of flexibility a woman may experience once she becomes a mother. The need to care for her child may force her to work part-time instead of full-time or to switch from a skilled or semi-skilled job to unskilled work and accept a loss of income. Whilst the anti-discrimination legislation as currently drafted is better than nothing, the manner in which the legislation is framed means that it offers a limited means of redress.

Some of the practices which are detrimental to women employees amount in law to unlawful discrimination and each finding of discrimination must have a positive effect since it makes clear not only that discrimination exists, but also that it is not acceptable to society. The number of claims alleging sex discrimination in any year must, however, represent the mere tip of the discriminatory iceberg.[104] In addition, not every claim will be successful. The complex definition of discrimination, and the restrictive way in which some terms have been interpreted may work against women and prevent the policy underlying the Act being successfully implemented. Indeed, a comparison might be made between the approach of the English courts and that of the European Court of Justice which appears to have been more constructive in its use of the concept of discrimination.[105] From an objective perspective, one may be forced to conclude that the 1975 Act has had little practical impact. Whilst ways could be found of stating a clearer equal opportunities policy in less equivocal terms, breaches would still occur that went unpunished because of defects in the legislation or in its application. Perhaps the real value of law as currently drafted is the attention it focuses on particular issues, but even judged on that basis the law does not effectively outlaw discrimination.

Employment Protection (Consolidation) Act 1978

In the past it was common for a woman to leave employment once she decided to have a family. Many factors contributed to this situation, not least the feeling, which is still encountered, that a mother should remain at home with her children. On the other hand, even if a woman wished to return to employment after the birth of her child, there was no legal requirement for her employer to keep her job open and she might therefore be forced to seek a new job. Her prospects of obtaining employment would not be enhanced by the fact that, as a mother, employers might consider her an unreliable employee and, consequently, discriminate against her. Undeniably the position in law of a working mother has improved considerably over the last twenty-five years. She can, for example, benefit from the anti-discrimination legislation in a number of ways. Furthermore, a working mother is accorded a number of additional rights, such as the right to return to employment once her child is born. It is a matter for debate whether these additional rights are more effective in benefiting women than the rules which seek merely to eliminate discrimination, and whether, in practice, the law plays any more than a peripheral role in the protection of working women from employer prejudice (whether based on managerial convenience or innate sexual bias).

There are a whole range of additional rights that could be granted to working mothers or, more accurately, to those employees who take responsibility for child care. These include the right to work flexible hours, the right to take time off to care for a sick child and help from central government to cover the costs of child care. At present the additional rights which have been conferred are confined to pregnancy and maternity leave.[106] The Employment Protection (Consolidation) Act 1978 and the Social Security Act 1986 together give four rights to a pregnant employee. They are:

 (i) the right not to be unfairly dismissed because of pregnancy;
 (ii) the right to return to the same job after confinement;
 (iii) the right to paid time off for ante-natal care;
 (iv) the right to Statutory Maternity Pay.

The granting of individual rights appears directly to contradict the desire on the part of the law to eliminate discrimination. This much is acknowledged since additional rights in relation to pregnancy are considered an exception in the anti-discrimination legislation.[107] Indeed, it might seem that the award of additional rights is simply another manifestation of that desire to protect women by reference to their childbearing role, which has been described as paternalism. To a degree this must be true since the health of the mother-to-be and her child is the basis of the right to have access to ante-natal care. Arguably the manifestation of paternalism here is distinct from that discussed earlier. In the past paternalism has been used as an excuse for treating women in an inferior fashion. Here a woman is acknowledged as being in need of special treatment, but in order to allow her to compete on equal terms with men. If that is the aim of these additional rights then one might expect to see them made as freely available as possible and not subject to conditions or arbitrary qualifying periods.

Right not to be unfairly dismissed

Section 60 of the 1978 Act provides that if an employee is dismissed because she is pregnant or for some reason connected with her pregnancy then that will amount to unfair dismissal. In order to qualify for this protection an employee must have two years' continuous employment.[108] This qualifying condition applies generally to complaints of unfair dismissal, though some exceptions do exist. The method by which continuity of employment is calculated is the same as is used elsewhere in the 1978 Act. In order, therefore, for a week to count towards the two-year period an employee must be employed for sixteen hours a week. If an employee is employed for between eight and sixteen hours a week, it will take five years to qualify. The existence of these conditions undeniably reduces the number of women who may benefit from this particular right. A great many women work part-time[109] and some at least will never work sufficient hours each week to qualify. In addition, women working part-time or in unskilled jobs may change employers frequently, never stopping long enough to work the requisite number of years. As for women homeworkers, since their status as employees may be in doubt, subject only to its determination in a court of law, and their hours of work fluctuate, they too may have a difficulty in benefiting. In these circumstances, is there any justification for the existence of these conditions?

The most obvious explanation is that they protect an employer from the disruption caused to his undertaking by female employees whose work is interrupted by pregnancy. If all female workers were to qualify immediately for this protection, this might cause an employer considerable inconvenience. There is no reason to believe, however, that a woman's absence because of pregnancy would not prove equally disruptive after two years as before it. Far from being justified, the condition appears to be more a way of forcing a woman to earn any additional rights rather than being automatically granted them. Although the general right not to be unfairly dismissed is dependent on a similar qualifying period, the question is whether the policy which protects all individuals from unfair dismissal is the self-same policy which requires the protection of a pregnant woman. The answer might well be no, since the overall aim of unfair dismissal is to protect the employee from losing that valuable right which a job may represent, whilst the purpose of protecting pregnant employees is to secure them equality of opportunity.

Leaving aside the qualifying conditions, there are two exceptions to the protection which the law accords a pregnant employee.[110] The basis for these exceptions is the inability of the employee to carry out her job. On the one hand, this may be because her pregnancy makes her incapable of doing the work. Alternatively, it may be because, by continuing to employ her in that job, the employer would be in breach of his legal obligations. The 1978 Act does, however, provide that, even in these circumstances, before an employer may dispense with his pregnant employee's services he or she must offer her any suitable vacancy which is available.[111] Failure to do so may render what is in principle a justified dismissal, covered by one of the exceptions, unfair. The key issue is whether these exceptions are given a broad or narrow construction. The typical case is a pregnant employee who is forced to take time off because of illness associated with her pregnancy. Can she be sacked on the basis that she is no longer capable of adequately performing her job?

Until comparatively recently a distinction was drawn between pregnancy and illnesses associated with pregnancy. If an illness prevented an employee from performing her job, then the exception was considered inapplicable. The legislation refers to a woman being incapable of performing her job because of her pregnancy and, in the past, tribunals accepted that a woman suffering from an illness associated with her pregnancy is incapable of work because of that illness.[112] Lately this generous construction was rejected in *Grimsby Carpet Company* v *Bedford*[113] and 'incapable because of her pregnancy' has been interpreted as including illnesses associated with pregnancy. The reason given for this change of heart was in order to make industrial sense out of the legislation, the implication being that the previous construction placed too great a burden on employers. When, however, it is recalled that the purpose of the legislation is to award rights to pregnant women, the courts' concern for employers seems misplaced. In future it would appear that an employer may fairly dismiss a pregnant employee who is suffering from an illness related to her pregnancy, such as hypertension, although this is subject to the employer acting reasonably in all the circumstances and reasonably believing that the employee is incapable of performing her job. Hence, a few days lost because of morning sickness would not be grounds for dismissal.

When one of the exceptions to section 60 is applicable, a dismissal on the grounds of pregnancy is not automatically unfair, but it may become so unless due regard has been paid to the rules of reasonableness governing dismissals in general[114] and to the need to offer an employee any suitable available vacancy. Failure to do so will render the dismissal unfair. Undoubtedly some pregnant employees benefit from this provision although the employer is under no obligation to create a special post, merely to consider whether an existing vacancy is suitable. If, therefore, a pregnant employee is no longer capable of lifting heavy loads, then a post involving lighter duties may prove satisfactory provided the employee has the skill to perform it.[115] Clearly, however, this duty imposed on the employer is of little use to those who are suffering from an illness associated with pregnancy which renders them incapable of work.

Qualifying conditions and exceptions apart, the courts have asserted the need to adopt a robust interpretation of what will amount to a pregnancy-related dismissal. Where the employer is faced with the need to make redundancies, one possibility which might be contemplated is to select a pregnant employee for dismissal, as opposed to applying normal rules of selection, such as 'last in, first out'. In *Brown* v *Stockton on Tees Borough Council*[116] the House of Lords held that to select a woman for redundancy because she is pregnant and will require maternity leave is an unfair dismissal within the terms of section 60. This decision was particularly welcome for the assertion in it that the disruption that an employer may suffer when a woman takes maternity leave is a price which has to be paid for the promotion of equal opportunities.

This willingness to implement the spirit of the law was repeated in *Clayton* v *Vigers*.[117] Mrs Vigers, a dental assistant, took maternity leave with the intention of returning to work after the birth of her child. During that leave she was dismissed since her employer claimed that he was unable to engage a temporary replacement. The Employment Appeal Tribunal refused to disturb the Industrial Tribunal's finding that Mrs Vigers had been dismissed because of her pregnancy. It was stressed that the relevant words in section 60 ought to be read widely so as to tackle the mischief at which the statute was aimed.

Right to return to work

Section 45 of the 1978 Act gives a woman the right to return to the job she had before the birth of her child, provided she returns within twenty-nine weeks from the week in which the date of confinement falls. Besides being subject to the two years' continuous employment requirement, this right has various notification provisions associated with it, such as the need for an employee to give notice of her intention to return to work.[118] Failure to observe these provisions can lead to a loss of rights.[119]

The whole issue of maternity leave and the right to return has been further complicated by the fact that some employers allow their employees more generous benefits than those provided for in the 1978 Act.[120] These benefits may be set out in the contract of employment and, clearly, the willingness of employers to offer more than the statutory minimum is a step to be welcomed. The 1978 Act acknowledges that this may well be the case by indicating that where an employee has rights under the statute and under her contract of employment she may combine the two and take advantage of whichever is the more favourable in any respect.[121] The extent to which an employee can 'pick and choose' in these circumstances was considered in *Bovey* v *The Board of Governers of the Hospital for Sick Children.*[122] Mrs Bovey was employed as a full-time physiotherapist, Grade 1. She was entitled to maternity leave and could have returned to her full-time post. Instead, she agreed with her employers to return as a part-time physiotherapist, Basic Grade. It was contended that by combining her statutory and contractual rights Mrs Bovey could return as a part-time physiotherapist, Grade 1. This argument was rejected, primarily on the basis that the right to return part-time was not a term in the employee's contract of employment but simply a concession from her employer. Even if it had been a contractual right, the tribunal was of the opinion that there was a limit to the degree to which rights might be subdivided. In their view the part-time element was not capable of being split from the basic grade element. To have determined otherwise would, it was suggested, have been a recipe for industrial disruption. To justify a judicial decision simply on the basis of avoiding industrial disruption is a very unsatisfactory practice. As the House of Lords stressed in *Brown* v *Stockton on Tees Borough Council*, a legislative provision may exist in order to promote equal opportunities and as a consequence industrial disruption may be unavoidable.

There are various grounds on which an employer may legitimately prevent an employee from exercising her right to return. The basis for creating exceptions to the right to return rests partly on the need to relieve an employer from the burden, whether it is financial or administrative, which an employee's absence may cause. Employers may claim that it is not reasonably practicable to allow an employee to return, but where there are more than five employees, the employer must offer the employee any suitable available vacancy.[123] Redundancy is another permissible reason for preventing an individual exercising her right to return, though this too is subject to the employer being obliged to offer any suitable available vacancy.[124] In *Community Task Force* v *Rimmer*[125] Mrs Rimmer became redundant while on maternity leave. Her employers failed to offer her an alternative position which became available, not because she was unsuitable, but because her employers had been threatened with loss of funding by the Manpower Services Commission if they offered the post to someone who was not long-term unemployed. Although her employers argued that consequently the vacancy in question was not 'available', the Tribunal rejected this approach. The fact that the Community Task Force might suffer unpleasant consequences by giving the post to Mrs Rimmer was irrelevant, since the post was theirs to give.

The right to return is subject to considerable qualification. Many women find it impossible to benefit from its existence and even those who can take advantage of it may find it an empty right without additional rights such as access to child care facilities. There are a variety of practical problems facing a woman who wishes to return to work[126] and it is important to recognise that the mere fact that a right is in place does not guarantee it will be observed.

Time off for ante-natal care and Statutory Maternity Pay

It is commendable to encourage a pregnant employee to take care of herself and to award her some kind of benefit whilst she is on maternity leave. Some employers offer considerably more generous terms than those of the state scheme. The right to take time off for ante-natal care seems uncontentious in the sense that it has rarely been the subject of litigation[127] and, in the absence of evidence to the contrary, one must assume that employers respect the right. Statutory Maternity Pay, however, is far from straightforward, particularly on the issue of who qualifies. The whole matter will be examined in greater detail, together with other state benefits, in Chapter 7.[128]

In the course of this chapter the provisions of two important pieces of legislation have been examined in some detail. As a result it is possible to draw some general conclusions on the effectiveness of those specific pieces of legislation. The Sex Discrimination Act represents a laudable but in many ways unsatisfactory attempt to outlaw discrimination. The definition of discrimination, and in particular of indirect discrimination, is relatively complex and the situation has not been improved by certain judicial decisions which place a good deal of emphasis on the needs or wishes of the employer and neglect the essential purpose of the legislation, namely the promotion of equal opportunities. The extent to which a measure designed to eliminate discrimination can promote equal opportunities must as ever be in doubt.

A disturbing feature of the legislation is the discretion it gives tribunals, for example in their ability to select an appropriate pool in determining whether or not there has been indirect discrimination and to resort to common sense. Earlier in this book it was argued that the 'feel' judges have for the law ensures that their decisions are not outrageous but in line with previous authority. When contemplating the decisions from industrial tribunals upwards one is left with a sense of confusion as the law moves first in one direction and then in another. Whether this can be attributed in part to the composition of the tribunals or is symptomatic of the rather open-ended way in which the legislation is drafted is a matter for debate. Finally, the effort devoted to analysing the Sex Discrimination Act may seem almost futile since, comparatively, so few women actually take advantage of it and pursue a case through the courts. That may be indicative of procedural defects or it could be that the 1975 Act has little relevance to certain categories of workers. There is no legal reason preventing a homeworker, for example, from bringing a claim under the Act, but such workers, lacking union or peer group support, may be unaware of their rights or be reluctant to challenge their employer.

Elsewhere in this chapter, it was suggested that, even if the drafting of the 1975 Act was impeccable and its interpretation the most advantageous for the promotion of equal opportunities, it would achieve little more than it does at present. If this proposition is correct, does it demonstrate that the desire for equality is a misplaced urge and one that can never be effectively achieved? The view has been expressed that, even if equality could be achieved, all it ensures is that women behave like men. The entry of women into paid employment might have been expected to bring about changes in the workplace – what is sometimes referred to as the feminisation of the workplace. This is based on the notion that women possess particular qualities, being, for example, more co-operative and less confrontational in the way in which they work. Moreover, it is argued that women see their families as being as important as their work. By accepting equality, it is arguable that women are accepting entry into the workplace on men's terms and not on their own. Women should perhaps devote more attention to promoting their values than to accepting those of men.

The Employment Protection (Consolidation) Act is very specific in that in this context its sole purpose is to guarantee pregnant employees certain rights. In a sense what it seeks to achieve is the very antithesis of equality since it acknowledges that in these circumstances working women require special treatment. The granting of additional rights was a policy examined in Chapter 3 and the comment was made that this is one way in which women can be compensated for the caring role which society still expects them to fulfil. Of course, some associate the granting of additional rights with positive discrimination, a process which is unlawful under English law. In reality it would be possible to build up a network of such rights – for example the right to take parental leave – and not be 'guilty' of positive discrimination by allowing both men and women to take advantage of them. This might also go some way to removing stereotypical attitudes towards caring. As matters stand at present this appears to be a policy which the United Kingdom is very reluctant to pursue, as illustrated by its unwillingness to accept a European Draft Directive on parental leave.[129]

Where additional rights have been conceded they have been made less effective because working women have to qualify in order to take advantage of them. Employers may also in certain circumstances be able to avoid conceding such rights. Moreover, the way in which the legislation has been interpreted and applied by the industrial tribunals is indicative on occasions of the origin of these rights in the employment rather than the anti-discrimination legislation. In other words too much attention is paid to the employer's needs as opposed to those of the pregnant employee.

Finally, the existence of this statutory framework giving pregnant employees additional rights is no guarantee that full advantage will be taken of them. The reasons for this appear complex. Some women may feel that any prolonged absence will lead to difficulties when they return. Others may be aware of the resentment among colleagues and possible disruption in the workplace. The end result of this process, to quote one commentator, is that 'even such an important women's reform as this is not necessarily utilized by those who were meant to benefit'.[130]

Chapter six

Women's wages

The relationship between a worker and an employer is based, in law, on contract. That contract represents in most cases a 'wage–work' bargain in which the worker undertakes to provide her own labour and skill in return for the employer's promise to pay wages. This bargain is so fundamental to the way in which society is currently structured that levels and forms of reward are inevitably an area of conflict, not only as between the opposing interests of capital and labour, but also between different groups of workers. The setting of wage levels is a function of the continuing interplay of supply and demand and the relative bargaining strengths which result from the wider economic context, including the impact of demographic trends on the availability of labour. Indeed, it is this latter factor which may eventually have the greatest effect on women's wages and their other terms and conditions of employment. The distribution of wages amongst a workforce depends not only on general economic influences but also on more specific matters which may include productivity, endeavour, ability, qualifications, experience and status. Levels of pay may also, however, depend on one's sex or on the colour of one's skin.

As a matter of policy, the law aims to outlaw overt bias. Covert discrimination is theoretically dealt with by the notion of indirect discrimination based on the disproportionate impact that specific requirements have on a particular group, though the efficacy of indirect discrimination in eliminating institutionalised bias is especially susceptible to the vagaries of judicial interpretation.[1] The Sex Discrimination Act 1975 attempts to achieve equality of opportunity for women by the elimination of discrimination, that is by treating like cases in the same way regardless of sex. In adopting that route to equality the 1975 Act was simply following the lead given in the Equal Pay Act 1970. The use of a uniform approach in the two Acts was deliberate. From the outset those who advocated equal pay were adamant that it must be part of the wider movement towards equal opportunities on the basis that if women are relegated to 'female' jobs the right to equal pay is considerably, if not totally, devalued. If, therefore, the legislation designed to eliminate discrimination is not adequate for the task, it may be argued that this has inevitable consequences for the success of the Equal Pay Act in its objective of equality of reward.

There is a fundamental flaw in both the 1975 and 1970 Acts because of their failure to deal with the root causes of women's inequality at work. It is particularly relevant in relation to these causes that women still seem to do different jobs as compared with men. While the figures in Chapter 4 show that women are playing an increasingly equal role in the labour market in numerical terms, they also show that the patterns of female participation are quite different. Statistical analyses of female employment demonstrate an intricate pattern of gender-based segregation operating both vertically, to create primarily female occupations, and horizontally, so that even in mixed jobs, women are concentrated in the lower grades.

Explanations for the gender-based segregation of the labour market make depressing reading for those hoping to achieve equality through legislation, since some writers assert that segregation occurs for reasons which begin to act on women years before they enter the labour market. Women are not appropriately educated or trained in subjects or areas which would open up 'male' jobs, nor indeed are they brought up to believe that such jobs are open to them.[2]

Added to these problems of education and expectation, women often have family or domestic responsibilities which largely preclude 'male' employment patterns, and thus the pursuit of promotion and training becomes futile. Lack of ambition is claimed to lead to lack of motivation and this in turn is said to lead to absenteeism and frequent job changes. On top of all of this there is the view still held by some employers that women are simply not capable of or suitable for certain tasks because of physical or emotional deficiencies or differences.[3] Put all of this together and the result is, first, employers who consider it pointless to invest money in training women, to promote them or to run the risk of challenging entrenched prejudices in a male workforce, and, secondly, women who by education, aspiration and lack of practical support filter into jobs already earmarked for women.

Another explanation for gender-based segregation centres on the theoretical division of the labour market into primary and secondary sectors.[4] The primary sector is principally the skilled, non-manual and higher paid sector, whereas the secondary sector is mainly manual and low paid. Women tend to concentrate in the secondary sector, for reasons which are circular. Employers who perceive women, as a class, to be unreliable and lacking in commitment will not consider them for primary sector jobs. Women who are then confined to monotonous, low-paid jobs fall prey to absenteeism and lack of motivation, thus reinforcing employers' prejudices against them. Whereas it is true that absenteeism seems associated with low-paid and monotonous jobs, in so far as men do those jobs, their absence rates are similar to the women's. Furthermore, absenteeism amongst women may be due to many causes other than a lack of commitment. Since many women are now the family wage earners, it is unlikely that a job would be lightly jeopardised. If a child is sick or otherwise needs care, the lack of alternative provision means that the woman may be absent though will rarely give the true reason for it.[5]

Only when the factors which account for gender-based segregation are identified can an attempt be made to eradicate that segregation. It is, however, easier to disprove some of the beliefs which inform the attitudes of employers than it is to influence the assumptions and expectations of women in their education and training. At this very basic level, the Sex Discrimination Act and the Equal Pay Act are of little relevance. A girl who leaves school with limited expectations about her working life has little to gain from the present legislation.

The consequences of gender-based segregation are reflected in the levels of women's pay since jobs done only or mainly by women attract lower wages. Variations in pay are, admittedly, not solely a function of sex discrimination but also reflections of worth and status. The bargain between employer and employee may be expressed in a variety of ways: a salary, an hourly rate or a piece rate, and the form that the bargain takes may itself signal social differentiation. 'Pay' is a term which may mean quite different things to different workers. A manual worker may be used to the idea of basic pay plus overtime rates or productivity bonuses. An office worker might expect pay to include paid holidays and sick pay. A professional in management would probably expect an employer to provide a salary package which could include a car, health insurance and pension scheme. These are matters left to the agreement between parties and their relative bargaining power, seen against the background of what is usual for that class of worker.

The influence of worth and status on pay means that women's wages pose a particularly complex problem. The reward a woman receives may be less than a man's because a woman's work is seen as being, by definition, worth less. Such a perception must have a considerable bearing on the successful operation of those laws which seek to eliminate discrimination unless these laws are so drafted and interpreted as to take account of such subtle prejudice.

Lawyers rarely find it necessary in applying the law (as opposed to understanding it) to grapple with socio-economic factors which underlie the legal model. It is possible to approach any law in a purely technical sense, divorced from the context in which it must operate and be made sense of. In the case of labour law that context is the labour market, the forum in which patterns of employment take shape and conditions of employment, including pay, emerge. In any market supply and demand provide the framework for more sophisticated structures which may to a greater or lesser extent seek to regulate the effects of an absolute principle of *laisser faire*. The labour market has, traditionally, been regulated by both voluntary and legislative means.

Voluntarism is reflected in the system of collective bargaining under which trade unions have taken over the task of negotiating terms and conditions of employment on behalf of groups of employees, rather than leaving it to the individual – who by and large has no economic power when compared to the employer. Traditionally, the role of the law was largely non-interventionist, leaving trade unions and employers to order their own affairs. Nevertheless, legislation has been used either to support collective bargaining, or as a substitute for it, or as a way of imposing certain minimum conditions on the parties, thus providing a floor of rights for individuals which may not be bargained away.

Laws requiring equal pay for men and women are neither a support nor a substitute for bargaining but rather represent a restraint on totally free bargaining since they curtail the full force of the market. It is those same market forces which appear to put a lower value on the work which women perform and work which is perceived as 'women's work' tends to attract lower rates of pay. This may result from a discriminatory, conventional valuation which simply asserts that women are worth less, or it may be based on pragmatism, for example an employer's fear of resistance from male employees or undercutting from competing employers.[6] Some jobs on the other hand are, objectively, worth less than others to an employer for gender-neutral reasons and, indeed, this is recognised in the legislation which allows the employer to justify pay differentials on grounds other than sex.

Apart from market forces, rates of pay are susceptible to more general social or political influences. Although the Sex Discrimination Act facilitates the entry of women into male-dominated occupations and the Equal Pay Act should ensure equal financial reward, inequality is more complex and not solely gender based. If there are two sales assistants, one male, one female, and he is paid £10 per week more than she is, this may be because he is more senior or has greater responsibility. It may, however, be due simply to the difference in sex: a clear case of sex discrimination where the law may assist. But if she works in Leeds and he works in London, or if they both work in the same city, but for different employers, it is more difficult to assess the part played by their sex in the different rates of pay. Alternatively, compare the wages of a miner or a steel worker with the lower rates of pay of a nurse. Each job is skilled and demanding, each is now, theoretically, open to both sexes. What then causes differences in pay: effort, strength, danger – or the assumption that a 'man's job' is worth more than 'women's work'? Even if the latter assumption can be proved, there is no current legal mechanism by which to challenge this. Finally, the male managing director of a multi-national company may have, amongst other benefits, a company car, subsidised mortgage, health insurance and a salary in excess of £50,000 a year. Compare him with the woman who cleans his office for fifteen hours a week for £35. It is at this point that the limits of the law are finally reached.

In the case of the sales assistants the law will eradicate differences solely due to sex and provided there is only one employer involved. In the second example, it will make it possible for women to enter previously all-male jobs, though it will not address the value which society places on the caring professions as opposed to the value the market decrees for industrial labour. In the third comparison it becomes even more apparent that a society rewards its members according to the principles which underlie its economic and political system. The distribution of wealth is, ultimately, not a legal but a political decision, which the law is used to support and enforce according to the wishes of those with power. The law thus reflects the values of the rulers of a particular society at a given time. To state that the cleaner is 'worth' as much as the managing director is a judgement about the just distribution of wealth. It would be possible to construct laws to allow for such equality but the debate is fundamentally political. The law is not necessarily always reactive. Laws may be proactive and help to shape popular beliefs or at least to alter climates of opinion but, even so, such laws are not passed in isolation from political power and political will. It is important, therefore, to bear in mind not only the current objectives of existing legislation but also the limits of what any law may achieve.

This chapter is concerned with pay and the impact of the Equal Pay Act.[7] Because, however, many working women are low paid, the picture would be incomplete without reference to the way in which the law purports to protect such workers, either by guaranteeing minimum rates or by supplementing income and so a section on low wages and social security is included.

Equal pay: the law

Inequalities of pay between men and women led to the passing of the Equal Pay Act in 1970: an attempt to eradicate discrimination by the simple expedient of raising women's pay to the level of their male colleagues employed by the same employer. It may now be asked to what extent, if at all, the law has proved successful. Even leaving aside the theoretical issues of the choice of elimination of discrimination as a basis for equality and of how far any law may successfully challenge the hidden, inbuilt bias which prevails in many sectors, it is clear that on a practical level the Equal Pay Act is deficient in its coverage, complex in its drafting and daunting in its procedures. The complexities of the law are exacerbated by the influence of European law, though it is precisely this latter body of rules which has occasionally provided a remedy in cases where the national legislation has been held not to meet European standards.

There can be little doubt that membership of the European Economic Community has brought with it changes that are to the lasting benefit of working women in this country. Indeed, the advent of the anti-discrimination legislation can be seen, at least partly, as a response to obligations which were to be incurred under the Treaty of Rome. The relationship between English and European law is not always a smooth, harmonious one. The problems raised range from questions of constitutional supremacy to issues of judicial interpretation, not only in the English courts but also in the European Court of Justice. Further, although the advantages that have already accrued are valuable, many other potential benefits are denied to women by the way in which Community measures are enacted, so that the use of the veto by the British government can effectively halt progress on many issues.

European law already forms a crucial part of the armoury of those fighting to eliminate sex discrimination, whether in pay or more generally. It is, however, with pay that the Treaty is itself specifically concerned and, thus, European law figures frequently not only in the decisions at a European level but also in many English cases. It is helpful, therefore, to preface an examination of the English legislation with an outline of the European provisions and to clarify how the two sets of rules interact and in what circumstances a woman in an English tribunal can call upon European law to aid her claim.

European Law

The substance of the law is contained in Article 119 of the Treaty of Rome and in a number of Directives which relate more or less directly to the issues of equal pay.

The Treaty of Rome

Article 119 provides that:

> Each member state shall...maintain the application of the principle that men and women should receive equal pay for equal work.
>
> For the purpose of this Article, 'pay' means the ordinary basic or

minimum wage or salary and any other consideration, whether in cash or kind, which the worker receives, directly or indirectly, in respect of his employment from his employer.

As a general rule of international law, treaty obligations are enforceable only by parties to the treaty, that is, by states or international organisations, and they cannot be relied upon directly by an individual citizen within the state.[8] Only if and when the treaty becomes part of national law by whatever is the appropriate constitutional machinery (in the United Kingdom by passing an Act of Parliament) may the individual citizen take advantage in the courts of rights and benefits contained within the treaty. At that stage, however, any available remedy is derived from the national legislation and not from the international obligations of the treaty.

In exceptional cases, however, a treaty may be of such a nature or drafted in such a way that its provisions are directly enforceable by an individual within a national court. The European Court of Justice (ECJ) has held that Article 119 of the Treaty of Rome gives such a right to an individual worker.[9] This means that, deprived of a remedy under English law, that is the Equal Pay Act, a woman may base her claim on European law, as contained in the Treaty.

Such an argument would not often, in practice, be of real benefit to an applicant, since Article 119 is itself of fairly restricted scope and, if there is a remedy to be had at all, it is likely that the 1970 Act will provide it. Nevertheless, certain cases which are *not* covered by the Act are caught by the more general wording of the Treaty and the point is, therefore, of more than academic importance. The scope of Article 119 is an inherently complex legal question as is amply illustrated by *Pickstone* v *Freemans plc*[10] (see pp. 123–124) where English law appeared at first not to comply with the requirements of European law so that, in the lower courts, it seemed that if Pickstone was to have any remedy it would have to be found in the Treaty. It was duly held in the Court of Appeal that Article 119 creates a separate right under which an individual may apply to an English court for relief. *Pickstone*, however, was a claim based on equal pay for work of equal value and, although the House of Lords confirmed the decision of the Court of Appeal that the applicant was entitled to equal pay, it did so on a different ground, and the question of the direct enforceability of the Treaty was considered by only one of the judges. In the opinion of Lord Oliver there are doubts as to whether Article 119 would be directly applicable in cases involving equal value as opposed to like work claims. This doubt stems from the way in which the Article is expressed. It states in bald terms that men and women should receive 'equal pay for equal work' and in *Defrenne*,[11] the case which established the direct enforceability of

Article 119, the female applicant (a Belgian air hostess) did the *same* work as the cabin steward with whom she compared herself.

Thus, although Article 119 may give a direct route to relief under the Treaty, it does so only in a limited number of cases which may well not include those where the work is not the same but is allegedly of equal value.[12] There are, however, Directives which supplement the Treaty and which may in certain circumstances widen the scope of European law.

The Directives

Directives are issued to member states, instructing them how to achieve the goals set by the European Community. They are, according to Article 189 of the Treaty of Rome, 'binding as to the result to be achieved' but they leave to the individual member state a 'choice of form and methods'. This raises quite separate issues of the direct enforceability of Directives. The ECJ decision in *Marshall* v *Southampton and South-West Hampshire Area Health Authority (Teaching)*[13] appears to have settled the matter by establishing that Directives may in certain circumstances have *vertical* but not *horizontal* effect. Translated, this means that whereas an individual may, subject to certain conditions,[14] enforce a Directive against the state or a public authority which represents the state,[15] the Directive cannot be used directly as between two private individuals. Miss Marshall succeeded because she was using a Directive (the Equal Treatment Directive) against her employer who, fortunately for her, was a public authority sufficiently identifiable with the state.

An employee in the private sector would appear, therefore, to be seriously prejudiced by the inapplicability of relevant Directives in a dispute with her employer. The harshness of these consequences has, however, recently been tempered by decisions of the House of Lords on the correct interpretation of English laws which are supposedly passed to give effect to obligations imposed by Directives. In *Pickstone* v *Freemans plc*[16] (see pp. 123–124) the House of Lords was able to find a remedy under the Equal Pay Act by interpreting the relevant English provision 'purposively', that is by reading words into the legislation in order to achieve what Parliament must have intended, namely compliance with the Equal Pay Directive. In a later case concerned with a Directive which governs employee rights on the takeover of a business, the House of Lords relied on its decision in *Pickstone* and again held that English law must be interpreted in a way which gives effect to Directives, even to the extent of the judges reading words into the legislation.[17] The importance of such decisions cannot be over-emphasised. The Directives, while they remain in theory directly unenforceable, are nevertheless given 'indirect direct' effect by the device of flexible or even creative construction of the English legislation.

The first Directive relating specifically to Article 119 was Directive 75/117, otherwise known as the Equal Pay Directive. The Treaty had been aimed principally at preventing unfair competition resulting from some states allowing employers to pay low(er) rates of pay to women workers and, also, at the general improvement of living and working conditions.[18] Progress under the Treaty was, however, uneven and in 1975 the Council of the European Community adopted a Directive to encourage the approximation of national provisions. The Equal Pay Directive provides in Article 1 that:

> The principle of equal pay for men and women outlined in Article 119 of the Treaty, hereinafter called 'principle of equal pay' means, for the same work or for work to which equal value is attributed, the elimination of all discrimination on grounds of sex with regard to all aspects and conditions of remuneration.
>
> In particular, where a job classification system is used for determining pay, it must be based on the same criteria for both men and women and so drawn up as to exclude any discrimination on grounds of sex.

This Directive is the one most obviously concerned with equal pay and it introduces the concept of work of equal value which was at issue in *Pickstone*. It is not, however, the only Directive relevant to equality of pay and working conditions.

Directive 76/207, the Equal Treatment Directive, makes frequent appearances in the area of equal pay. In this context, the crucial provisions are in Article 1 which provides:

1. The purpose of this Directive is to put into effect in the Member States the principle of equal treatment for men and women as regards access to employment, including promotion, and to vocational training and as regards working conditions and, on the conditions referred to in paragraph 2, social security....

2. With a view to ensuring the progressive implementation of the principle of equal treatment in matters of social security, the Council, acting on a proposal from the Commission, will adopt provisions defining its substance, its scope and the arrangements for its application.

The Equal Treatment Directive, as its title suggests, is wider in scope than the Equal Pay Directive and, unlike the latter, it is not expressly tied to a particular provision of the Treaty, a fact which, ironically, may make it more difficult for individuals to use. The references to a future

Directive on social security matters finally bore fruit in 1979. Directive 79/7 calls for equality of treatment in matters of social security covering, amongst other things, statutory schemes which protect against sickness, invalidity, old age, accidents at work, occupational diseases and unemployment. It does not, however, apply to survivors' benefits, nor does it require states to provide for equal treatment in relation to old age pensions and ancillary matters. It does, however, make reference to a further measure which is to deal with occupational social security schemes, and this appeared in 1986.

Directive 86/378 provides that men and women should be treated equally in schemes not governed by the 1979 Directive, that is contractual rather than statutory schemes. At the same time, however, the Directive expressly allows member states to defer the compulsory application of the principle of equal treatment in certain circumstances. In particular, states are allowed to defer equality in relation to the determination of pensionable ages for the purpose of granting old age or retirement pensions and also in relation to survivors' benefits. Equal pension ages and survivors' benefits have now been proposed in a Draft Directive, but since its implementation may be delayed by member states for up to three years, even if it is eventually adopted by the Council, the provisions are most unlikely to be binding until well into the 1990s.[19]

The four existing Directives may each be said to supplement to a greater or lesser extent the principle enshrined in Article 119. The constitutional aspects of the relationship between European and United Kingdom law remain complex, but the issue to be examined here is the extent to which the body of European law outlined above augments the rights granted under the Equal Pay Act 1970.

The scope of European law

Article 119 is directly enforceable by an individual in national courts[20] but is couched in the narrow formula of equal pay for equal work and as such is not necessarily of any greater scope, or therefore of greater value to an applicant, than the Equal Pay Act. In particular, the Treaty applies directly only to those forms of discrimination which are overt in the sense that they 'may be identified solely with the aid of criteria of equal work and equal pay referred to in [Article 119] without national and community measures being required to define them with greater precision'.[21] It is in this context that Lord Oliver in *Pickstone* expressed his doubts as to whether Article 119 can have direct application to a claim based on equal pay for work of equal value, rather than the same work, since equal value claims need additional machinery to fix criteria for assessing what is of equal value.[22]

Significantly, the Equal Pay Directive does refer to work of equal value but this takes the matter no further since the Directive has no effect independently of Article 119. In *Jenkins* and in other cases[23] it was argued that the Equal Pay and Equal Treatment Directives should have direct effect. Remaining silent about the latter Directive, the ECJ in *Jenkins* held in relation to the former that 'article 1 of Council Directive 75/117 which is principally designed to facilitate the practical application of the principle of equal pay outlined in Article 119 of the Treaty, in no way alters the content or scope of that principle as defined by the Treaty'. This would indicate that if a claimant finds no help from Article 119, it is futile to turn to the Directive on equal pay as an alternative, separate source of aid.[24]

On the other hand, if the Equal Pay Directive merely defines Article 119, the Treaty must require equal pay for work of equal value and it was on this point that the United Kingdom legislation was found in its original form not to comply with European law.[25] The Article alone, however, is simply not sufficiently detailed to determine such a claim and must be supplemented by further national measures which allow for calculations of what is of equal value.

The restriction of Article 119 to discrimination which is overt in the sense that it is definable without more detailed measures does not, apparently, mean that it cannot apply to what is commonly known as indirect discrimination.[26] Whilst the Treaty does not specifically refer to the different forms of discrimination, the ECJ had little hesitation in clarifying the point by deciding that Article 119 could apply to indirect discrimination, thus including discrimination against part-timers, the majority of whom are women.[27]

The Equal Treatment Directive is of far wider ambit than that on Equal Pay and by no stretch of the imagination can it be said merely to explain Article 119. It is of particular relevance to equal pay where the discrimination concerns retirement and consequent benefits.[28] Regrettably, therefore, the Equal Treatment Directive has also been held not to be directly enforceable, at least by individuals employed in the private sector.[29] Since Directives are aimed at the state, those employed by the state or bodies which can be identified with the state have been successful.[30] In so far as these cases related to differential retiring ages, the point has now been resolved by legislation which applies to all employees.[31] It is clearly unsatisfactory, however, that the usefulness of the Directive and the availability of rights depend on the identity of the employer, which from the employee's perspective is purely co-incidental.[32]

The intricacies of the relationship between European and United Kingdom law and problems in determining the precise scope of the former mean that there is nothing to be gained by seeking a European remedy unless the English law is deficient. Although neither the ECJ nor the English courts have yet been persuaded to accept the direct applicability of the Directives, the move both in the ECJ and in the English courts towards a purposive interpretation of the Directives and the laws enacted to comply with them does provide some cause for optimism. On the basis, however, that the Equal Pay Directive does not extend Article 119, one is primarily concerned, in practice, with the relationship between the Equal Pay Act and Article 119.

English law

Enacted in 1970, the Equal Pay Act came into force in 1975 at the same time as the Sex Discrimination Act. The five-year delay was intended to allow a period of voluntary compliance by employers – a hope which, in retrospect, was overly optimistic. Despite its title, the Equal Pay Act is wider in scope than simply pay, covering all terms and conditions that are included in the contract of employment. The legislation operates, however, only within the limits of the contract.[33] Conversely, Article 119 is restricted to pay, but not to rights arising only under the contract. It refers to cash or kind which the worker receives, directly or indirectly, in respect of employment from the employer.

The broader concept of pay in European law has proved valuable to applicants, and provided a remedy, for example, in *Worringham and Humphreys* v *Lloyds Bank Ltd.*[34] All the male employees of the Bank were required to contribute to the employer's pension scheme, a requirement which did not apply to female employees until they were twenty-five years old. Since men under twenty-five were paying pension contributions and their female contemporaries were not, Lloyds paid those men 5 per cent more than the women. This had no effect on net pay, as the extra 5 per cent was deducted towards the pension, but it meant higher gross pay for the men. Such discrimination was not unlawful under the Equal Pay Act,[35] but it was argued to be contrary to Article 119. When the question was referred to the ECJ it was decided that the pension contributions paid by the employer constituted pay under the Article, even though there was no contractual or other obligation to pay them.[36] This was overt discrimination and contrary to Article 119.

Worringham was a pensions case which involved a straightforward difference in gross pay. It should be compared with *Newstead* v *Department of Transport and HM Treasury*[37] in which an unmarried male civil servant complained that he was obliged to pay a percentage of his gross salary to a widows' pension fund whereas female employees were not. This was held by the ECJ not to breach Article 119. First, the gross pay of men and women was the same. Secondly, the arrangement did not contravene the Equal Treatment Directive, since that allows for

discrimination in relation to social security matters and the later Directives also permit discrimination in relation to retirement benefits. Both
the Equal Pay Act and Article 119 failed Mr Newstead whose complaint
was not that he was paid less than his female colleagues, but that he was
paying for benefits which were of no value to him, whereas the women
were excused from doing so.

Newstead's case must now be contrasted with *Barber* v *Guardian
Royal Exchange Assurance Group*,[38] where Mr Barber, made redundant
at the age of fifty-two, was denied the immediate pension available to
female colleagues. In an historic decision the ECJ held that this contravened Article 119. Barber was in an occupational pension scheme and
the benefits constituted pay, even though it was partly a substitute for
the state scheme (that is, a contracted-out scheme). This decision not
only upsets many assumptions about sex discrimination in pensions and
fuels the debate about the continuing discrepancies in the state scheme,
but also renders unnecessary much of the Social Security Directives.

The broader definition of pay under Article 119 has allowed the ECJ
to outlaw the total or partial exclusion of women from pension schemes
run by employers. In a case referred to it from the German Federal
Republic, the ECJ declared that to exclude part-time employees from an
occupational pension scheme was contrary to Article 119.[39] This
decision is important in two respects. By applying Article 119 to part-
timers, the ECJ established that it covers indirect discrimination: the
majority of the part-timers being female, the apparently neutral requirement that workers should be full-time to belong to the pension scheme
meant that women were disproportionately affected. The ECJ also held
that the benefits provided under the scheme did constitute pay within
Article 119, though in doing so it stressed the contractual, rather than
statutory, nature of the scheme in question.

Apart from pensions, Article 119 has been held in *Garland* v *British
Rail Engineering Ltd* to apply to concessionary travel facilities granted
to retired railway employees[40] on the basis that pay includes benefits
which are simply an extension of the benefits in respect of employment
which were available to employees during their working lives. The more
flexible definition of pay in Article 119 has also been used in relation to
redundancy pay. The Employment Protection (Consolidation) Act 1978
gives employees dismissed for redundancy a right to redundancy pay
calculated according to their age and length of employment with that
employer.[41] Originally, a man aged over sixty-four, or a woman over
fifty-nine lost one-twelfth of their redundancy payment for every month
over that age. In *Hammersmith and Queen Charlotte's Special Health
Authority* v *Cato*,[42] the Employment Appeal Tribunal decided that such
a provision in a contractual, as opposed to statutory, redundancy scheme
contravened Article 119, since *Garland* had established that pay did not

depend on the continued existence of a contract.[43] In *Secretary of State for Employment* v *Levy*[44] the Employment Appeal Tribunal held that statutory redundancy pay does not fall within Article 119. The issue in this case was complicated by the fact that the employer was insolvent and the claim by Mrs Levy, made redundant at the age of sixty, was against the Secretary of State in order that she might be awarded a redundancy payment from the Redundancy Fund.[45] Regardless of that, however, the Employment Appeal Tribunal was of the opinion that statutory redundancy pay is not pay within Article 119. The matter is, in any event, resolved in the Employment Act 1989, which requires men and women to be treated equally in both contractual and statutory redundancy schemes.

On the wider question, however, of what constitutes pay under Article 119, it is notable that Wood J remarked in *Levy* that there is no support from the ECJ for holding that statutory redundancy pay should qualify as pay. The accuracy of this must be measured against a decision of the ECJ not cited in *Levy*. In *Rinner-Kühn* v *FWW Spezial-Gebaudereinigung GmbH & Co*,[46] the ECJ held that where employees who worked fewer than ten hours a week were excluded from the statutory right to claim sick pay from the employer, this contravened Article 119, unless the adverse impact that the hours requirement had on women (because fewer women than men can work full-time) could be objectively justified.

If eligibility for sick pay is governed by Article 119, it is difficult to see why the same should not be true for redundancy pay, or indeed any other statutory payments. The *Rinner-Kühn* case, which was referred to the ECJ from the Federal Republic of Germany, has a far wider potential, however, than merely extending the scope of pay within Article 119. The exclusion of part-timers from the right to sick pay rested not on contract but on German legislation, just as workers in this country have to work for sixteen hours a week to claim various employment rights.[47] The ECJ not only decided that a statutory right to sick pay qualifies as pay, but that statutory exclusions or pre-conditions which discriminate indirectly against women must be justified not by the particular employer, but by the government of the member state on the basis of objective gender-neutral factors, rather than generalised statements. This opens the way to a challenge in an English court that similar statutory exclusions in the Employment Protection (Consolidation) Act 1978 are in contravention of European law, though it is always possible that an English court would find them justifiable.

On one level these cases simply highlight a divergence between English and European law. On another, they point to what may be inevitable differences of approach to the somewhat elastic concept of pay. The rather more generous attitude of the ECJ has, undoubtedly, assisted in what might otherwise have been lost causes.[48]

The operation of the Act

The structure of the Equal Pay Act is, on the face of it, relatively straightforward. It operates by automatically incorporating an equality clause into the contract of every person employed at an establishment in Great Britain.[49] There are no minimum conditions to be met in relation to the period of employment or the number of hours worked.[50]

The right to seek a remedy under the Act is granted to any person employed under a contract personally to execute any work or labour.[51] This is wider in scope than the Employment Protection (Consolidation) Act 1978 which grants most of the employment rights (for example, maternity rights) and which is limited to employees, that is, those who work under a contract of service. The Equal Pay Act (and the Sex Discrimination Act which has the same definition of those covered)[52] is available both to employees and to certain categories of the self-employed, provided the latter are personally executing work or labour.[53] This extends the anti-discrimination legislation to certain categories of workers who are in special need of assistance, for example home-workers. The practical effect is probably limited, however, since it would be difficult for such a worker to mount an equal pay claim, even one based on equal value, because of the problems of finding suitable male comparators and the likelihood of differences in pay being held to be justifiable.

Whether claiming under the Sex Discrimination Act or the Equal Pay Act, a woman must compare herself to a man in order to establish discrimination. The Sex Discrimination Act, like the Equal Pay Act, requires like to be compared with like, but at least allows the use of a hypothetical male.[54] The Equal Pay Act is more restricted. There are three grounds on which an equal pay claim may be brought (see pp. 118–125) but in each case the drafting of the legislation requires the woman to point to an actual man 'in the same employment'. The male comparator under the Equal Pay Act must, therefore, be employed at the same time as the female complainant. The obvious result is that a woman appointed to succeed a man in a particular job and paid less than her predecessor simply on grounds of her sex is not covered by the Act. Article 119, however, is not restricted to contemporaneous employment. This was decided in *Macarthays Ltd* v *Smith*[55] where the ECJ held that Mrs Smith could compare herself to her male predecessor who had left three months before she arrived.[56] This is a useful widening of the net, but it does not, of course, guarantee success: it may be that the employer can account for the difference in pay on grounds other than the sex of the worker, for example where business is declining and financial stringency is called for.[57]

The claimant under the Equal Pay Act must ensure that her comparator is in the same employment. That phrase is defined in the Act:[58] the comparator must be employed by the same employer or an associated employer[59] and must be employed either at the same establishment[60] or at a different establishment belonging to the same (or an associated) employer where common terms and conditions of employment are observed either generally or for the relevant classes. This provision came before the House of Lords in *Leverton* v *Clwyd County Council*[61] where a nursery nurse employed by the Council chose to compare herself to a number of male clerical officers employed at different establishments.

On the question of whether Leverton shared common terms and conditions of employment with the clerical officers, the majority of the Court of Appeal agreed with the Employment Appeal Tribunal that the radical differences between the contract of a nursery nurse and those of clerical officers meant that the terms and conditions were not common and that she was not, therefore, in the same employment. May LJ dissented, pointing out that such an approach is tantamount to a requirement that the terms and conditions should be the same, and that it is not the individual contracts which should be compared but the conditions of service observed generally by local authorities.

Although the House of Lords decided that Leverton was not entitled to equal pay, on the issue of common terms the views of May LJ were adopted, and it was held that the comparison required is that between the terms and conditions observed at the different establishments which are applicable *either* generally *or* to a particular class or classes to which the men and women belong. The provision necessarily contemplates terms and conditions applying to a wide range of employees whose individual terms will vary significantly. Terms and conditions negotiated in a collective agreement covering a variety of groups, as in the present case, represented the paradigm of what was contemplated by the statute. The appropriate test is not whether the complainant nursery nurse has a similar contract to the comparator clerical officer, but whether someone doing the job of a nursery nurse would enjoy significantly different terms and conditions if she were employed at the comparator's establishment.

Assuming that a woman can find a man whom the Act allows as a comparator, she must present her claim on one of the grounds set out in section 1, namely that she is engaged on like work, or work rated as equivalent or work of equal value. Like work is defined in section 1(4) which provides that a woman does like work if it is of the *same or a broadly similar nature* and any differences there may be are not of practical importance. There are two separate aspects to like work: the broad similarity of the work and the question of how significant are any differences between the two jobs. In relation to both aspects, however, tribunals have been encouraged to take a broad, rather than a detailed approach. A good example of this broad approach is *Capper Pass Ltd* v *Lawton*,[62] where a cook in the directors' kitchen compared herself with assistant chefs in the factory canteen. She served between ten and twenty lunches, they provided 350 meals throughout the day in six sittings. She worked forty hours, they worked forty-five and a half hours and one Saturday in three. Taking into account the kind of work and skills called for, Mrs Lawton was held to be doing like work.

In assessing the similarity of work it should be stressed that the Act requires consideration of the nature of the work, not the precise terms of the contractual job title, nor indeed when it is done. This is particularly relevant to shift work, as is seen in *Dugdale* v *Kraft Foods Ltd*[63] in which female quality control inspectors sought equality with their male counterparts. The women worked two alternate shifts and were paid about £8 per week less on basic rates than the men, who worked three rotating shifts and could volunteer for Sunday working. Since the women were prevented by law, at that time, from working the same shift system, the Industrial Tribunal held that they were not doing like work. The Employment Appeal Tribunal, however, pointed out that the wrong question had been asked. It is simply a question of *what* the women do, not *when* they do it.[64] This decision does not mean that night shift workers can never be paid more than the day shift: a differential which is based on overtime or unsocial hours may well be a difference between the cases which falls within the section 1(3) defence.[65]

Since the work need be only broadly similar there may be differences between the applicant and her comparator. The question is whether these are such that they justify the difference in pay. Having first decided that the work is broadly similar, the tribunal must then consider whether any differences are of practical importance and it is here that notice must be taken of the different range of tasks required, different skills or different responsibilities. Again, however, it is not simply a question of examining the terms of the contract. The tribunal must investigate what is actually done by those involved.[66] Where, for example, a male counter clerk at a betting shop was paid more than a female colleague and the employer claimed that the man had additional responsibilities because he was there partly to deter trouble, it was found that there was no evidence that the man was skilled or trained in this extra function, or that in fact he had ever been called on to perform it. The only real difference between the two was their sex.[67]

There are many cases, however, where the differences between the two have been adjudged to be real and therefore to rule out a finding of like work, even though this may defeat a claim to which the tribunal is sympathetic. This happened in *Maidment and Hardacre* v *Cooper & Co*

119

(Birmingham) Ltd,[68] where Mrs Maidment, a packer/clerk, compared herself with Mr Sanders, a packer/storeman. He was paid a sum of £2 per week, as part of his higher wages, for his storekeeping. Mrs Maidment was happy to discount that £2 and claim parity with a notional equivalent. It was held, however, that, despite the fact that the employer was trying deliberately to evade the Act, she could not succeed because she was not engaged on like work. One may discount extra pay for shift premium, for example, which relates to when you work, but not for additional kinds of work, such as the storekeeping.

Differences may result from different degrees of responsibility, as happened in *Eaton Ltd v Nuttall*[69] where a male production scheduler looked after items which, though fewer in number than those looked after by his female counterpart, were considerably more expensive, and thus his job carried greater responsibility. The same issue of responsibility had the odd effect in *Waddington v Leicester Council for Voluntary Services*[70] of defeating a claim where the female applicant was found to have greater responsibility than her male colleague and was thus not employed on like work. It was therefore lawful to pay her less.[71]

The question of whether there are significant differences between the two so as to rule out like work is sometimes difficult to distinguish in practice from the quite separate legal point of whether the employer can establish a defence to the claim on the ground that the difference in pay stems not from sex but from some other material factor.[72] Logically this defence, contained in section 1(3), only arises on the assumption that there is like work (or work of equal value or work rated as equivalent). It is therefore important to distinguish the two issues. A woman may be doing like work and so make out a case for equal pay even where there are some differences between her and her male colleague because these have been adjudged insignificant under section 1(4). If that is so, then those differences are irrelevant under section 1(3) in proving a reason for differential pay.

On the other hand, a finding of like work is not an automatic route to equal pay because there may well be extraneous factors justifying a difference. The classic example is shift working. In *Dugdale*[73] it was stressed that in assessing like work the court must look at the nature of the job, not when it is done. Thus basic rates should be equivalent. After that, however, section 1(3) could allow premium rates to be paid for overtime or shift working, provided that such rates are not themselves discriminatory, that is that a woman working the same hours would be entitled to the same rates. An example is *NCB v Sherwin*[74] in which two female canteen workers working day shifts claimed the same basic pay as a man who worked in the canteen on permanent nights. The Tribunal first held that the fact that the women waited on table and the man did not was not a difference which prevented a finding of like work. Having established like work, the question was what pay the women were entitled to. The Employment Appeal Tribunal were of the opinion that outlawing pay differentials based on *sex* 'does not mean that men, or women, cannot be paid extra for working at night or weekends, or at other inconvenient times'. This allows for shifts but not for a different basic rate and so it was permissible for the Industrial Tribunal to 'adjust the woman's remuneration...so that it is at the same rate as the man's discounting for the fact that he works at inconvenient hours, and she does not'.[75] The women were allowed an increase in pay to bring their basic rate to within 20 per cent of the night shift rate – a level which the Employment Appeal Tribunal considered to be 'reasonable'.

Before considering the section 1(3) defence in more detail, it is necessary to look at the other two grounds for a claim in section 1(2). A woman may claim equal pay with her male comparator if she is employed on 'work rated as equivalent'. According to section 1(5) this means that the jobs 'have been given equal value, in terms of the demands on a worker under various headings (for instance effort, skill, decision)'. Where a job evaluation study exists that will normally dispose of the case since, if the jobs are rated differently, it is unlikely to be profitable to argue like work and even less to argue for equal value. In the light of this it is clearly of paramount importance to know precisely what will constitute a valid job evaluation study. This is not, however, entirely clear. Job evaluation is traditionally a means of providing a wage structure which, in taking account of the different demands of different jobs under various headings, allows for a hierarchical grading of those jobs and the maintenance of wage differentials. Because the initial purpose of such schemes was to operate as part of the voluntary system of collective bargaining, the translation of job evaluation into the pursuit of the elimination of discrimination is not an entirely satisfactory one.[76]

Collective bargaining is not immune from discriminatory assumptions about the value of women's work and the use of traditional factors for comparison offers little in the way of recognition of the bias against women. Thus, although in selecting the criteria for evaluation it is possible to balance the number of attributes seen as female (for example, manual dexterity) as against the male attributes (for example, physical strength), if the value then given to the 'female' factors is lower than that given to the 'male', sexual bias is not only perpetuated but even given a veneer of authoritative approval.[77]

The Equal Pay Act gives very little guidance as to what is required to achieve a gender-neutral job evaluation scheme. The Employment Appeal Tribunal for its part has made it clear that a job evaluation study must be accurate and objective. In particular it has been held that '[section 1(5)] can only apply to what may be called a valid evaluation study. By that, we mean a study satisfying the test of being thorough in analysis and capable of impartial application.'[78] Although the Employment Appeal Tribunal has allowed for the possibility of a wide variety of job evaluation studies, including systems which are not strictly analytical, the Court of Appeal has more recently reaffirmed that section 1(5) does require an objective analysis within a job evaluation study of the value, in terms of demand under various headings, of each worker's job.[79] Further, if a scheme is to be valid it must be capable of being applied objectively to the job in question.[80]

One factor is specifically mentioned in section 1(5), namely that, even where a study rates the job differently, an equality clause will operate if the jobs would have been given an equal value but for the fact that the job evaluation study is itself sexually discriminatory. If the job evaluation study is based on discriminatory assumptions or concentrates exclusively or mainly on criteria which favour one sex, it will be overridden. The question of sex discrimination in job evaluation has been considered by the ECJ. The Court was asked whether the use of criteria based on muscular strength contravened the requirement in the Equal Pay Directive that an evaluation must be fair. It was held that their use does not necessarily contravene the Directive provided the criteria apply regardless of who is doing the work and provided there are other criteria which take account of the particular skills of the other sex, so that the system as a whole is fair.[81]

Once a valid job evaluation study exists, the value of the two jobs being compared is thereby conclusively established and the tribunal cannot simply ignore it, on the ground, for example, that neither employer nor union were satisfied with it.[82] More problematic is what happens where the employer undertakes a job evaluation study but then does not implement it. It would be enormously frustrating if the woman knows her job has been rated as equivalent but cannot take advantage of that fact. Section 1(2) provides that in a job evaluation claim the equality clause operates in respect of 'any term determined by the rating of the work'. This could be interpreted broadly, to include an existing but unused job evaluation study, or narrowly, to exclude any scheme which does not in fact govern terms and conditions. The broader approach was adopted by the House of Lords in *O'Brien* v *Sim-Chem Ltd*[83] where the implementation of a job evaluation study was delayed because of government pay policy. It was held that Mrs O'Brien could claim equal pay from the date she was told of her new grade.[84]

Job evaluation as a means of eliminating discrimination is an idea which promises more than it delivers and will continue to do so until account is taken of the particular problems of achieving not only gender-neutral evaluation criteria but also the gender-neutral weighting of those criteria, and of the different skills which women bring to their work, which sometimes appear to be regarded as unworthy of recognition.

The whole question of job evaluation is even more crucial in the light of the equal value claim, which is the third of the three ways in which a woman may claim equal pay, and which was introduced in order to comply with the requirements of European law.[85] As originally drafted, the Equal Pay Act allowed a woman to complain of discrimination only where she was doing like work (that is the same or similar work) with her male comparator or work rated as equivalent under a job evaluation study. The United Kingdom conceded[86] that under the Act a woman could not initiate a job evaluation study without the employer's consent and the ECJ therefore concluded that the Act did not comply with Article 119 and the Equal Pay Directive which requires that a woman can claim her work is of equal value.

The reluctance of the government to introduce the amendment is mirrored in the tortuous drafting of the provision which appears to say that a woman may claim that she is entitled to equal pay with a man who is doing work of equal value only as a last resort, if and only if, there is no man doing like work and no job evaluation study. This unfortunate and probably unlawful result[87] arises from the precise words used in section 1(2)(c), under which an equality clause will operate:

> where a woman is employed on work which, *not being work in relation to which paragraph (a) or (b) above applies*, is, in terms of demands made on her (for instance under such headings as effort, skill and decision), of equal value to that of a man in the same employment. (emphasis added)

A literal construction of the italicised words in *Pickstone* v *Freemans plc*[88] led the Employment Appeal Tribunal and the Court of Appeal to conclude that a woman could not proceed under section 1(2)(c) even if her work was of equal value to that of a more highly paid male, if there was a man doing like work with her and getting paid at her rate. The facts in *Pickstone* were relatively straightforward. Mrs Pickstone was employed by Freemans as a warehouse operative. She claimed to be entitled to equal pay with a checker warehouse operative on the ground that her work was of equal value. Warehouse operatives were not, however, exclusively female and the men and women were paid equally. The Industrial Tribunal, the Employment Appeal Tribunal and then the Court of Appeal were all agreed that section 1(2)(c) plainly indicated that Mrs Pickstone was debarred from claiming work of equal value because of the presence of men doing like work. This was quite plainly contrary to the purpose of the amendment. It meant that, provided an employer could persuade one male to accept lower 'female' rates for a job, women were destined to remain at that rate – subject to extra-legal remedies. The Court of Appeal acknowledged this and went on to point out that, as a result, the United Kingdom was still in breach of Article 119, which is not so limited. The Court then allowed Mrs Pickstone a direct remedy under Article 119.[89]

The House of Lords, in what may turn out to be an historic judgment, also found in favour of Mrs Pickstone but by a different and, to English lawyers, radical route. It has always been accepted that judges, in interpreting an Act of Parliament, may have recourse only to the legislation itself and they have not been allowed to refer to the parliamentary debates recorded in Hansard which would give an indication of what the legislature actually intended. In this case, however, the House of Lords, taking into account the special nature of obligations under the Treaty of Rome, held that it was permissible to discover what Parliament intended by examining what was said about the equal value amendment when it was introduced into Parliament. Having done so, their Lordships concluded that section $1(2)(c)$ does not reflect what was intended since it was never suggested that the mere fact that men were employed on the same work would defeat an equal value claim against a man employed on another job. The amendment had simply intended that an equal value claim should not proceed if the *actual comparator chosen* was on like work or work rated as equivalent. This was in line with European law and Parliament could not possibly have intended to fail to comply with it.

In order to make the provision apply in the way which had been intended, the House of Lords held that it should be read in such a way that a woman is prevented from bringing an equal value claim only if the man actually chosen for comparison is doing like work or work rated as equivalent. Mrs Pickstone had not chosen such a man for the purposes of her claim and she was, therefore, successful under the Act, rather than under Article 119.

The actual decision may seem so obviously what was intended that one might be forgiven for overlooking the way in which it was reached. It is, however, a decision which could have far-reaching consequences for the way in which conflicts between United Kingdom legislation and European Community obligations are resolved. The House of Lords is currently setting the pace in anti-discrimination decisions – a pace which lower courts sometimes struggle to match.

Pickstone's victory should not be allowed to obscure the problems presented by the procedure to be followed in equal value claims.[90] This is complex, protracted and likely to deter all but the most determined of applicants. The procedure centres on the report of an independent expert who advises as to whether the work is of equal value.[91] Whatever the criticisms to be made of job evaluation under section $1(2)(b)$ in its failure to acknowledge bias in assessing the value of women's work, the same may be said here, but the problems are further aggravated by the lack of guidelines as to how an expert should approach an equal value claim. The Act stipulates only that a review should be made in terms of demand under such headings as effort, skill and decision.[92] Presumably the report should be analytical rather than impressionistic,[93] but otherwise the expert has a remarkably free hand, which may allow a less stringent approach.[94] Since so much rests on the expert's report this lack of precision is unfortunate.

The first step in an equal value claim, subject to adjournment for conciliation,[95] is for the industrial tribunal to decide whether or not to call for an expert's report. The tribunal is allowed to decline to refer the matter to an expert if it is satisfied that there are no reasonable grounds for determining the work is of equal value.[96] The industrial tribunal is not allowed to refer the issue to an independent expert if the jobs in question have already been rated differently under an existing job evaluation study. There is, however, an exception to this where the job evaluation study is itself sexually discriminatory,[97] in which case the industrial tribunal has the usual discretion as to whether to refer to an independent expert. Finally, it would be a waste of time and money to refer the case to an independent expert only to find later that, despite jobs being of equal value, the employer can justify the pay differentials under the defence in section 1(3). Accordingly, the Rules of Procedure allow the employer to ask that the industrial tribunal listen to his defence at the preliminary hearing,[98] and the industrial tribunal may (but need not) permit that.[99] Subject to these exceptions, an equal value claim must be referred to an expert and the hearing adjourned.[100] The expert's report is not conclusive, but assuming the industrial tribunal accepts it,[101] it will form part of the basis on which the industrial tribunal decides whether the work is of equal value.

Defence to a claim

Once a woman has shown in the industrial tribunal that she is employed on like work, work rated as equivalent or work of equal value, an equality clause will modify the less favourable terms of her contract of employment unless the employer can establish a defence justifying the differential. In other words, even where she is, for example, doing work of equal value, a woman may still find she is not entitled to equality of pay and other conditions.

Prior to the equal value amendments, the defence in section 1(3) required the employer to show[102] that the difference resulted from a genuine material difference other than sex between the two cases. As far as like work and work rated equivalent are concerned, the provision remains unchanged in substance.[103] That defence is also available to an equal value claim but the employer may use not only a material difference between the woman and the man but also any other material factor – apart of course from sex.[104]

In relation to the first limb of the defence, it is clear that the difference between the woman and the man must not be based on sex, but it may be based on differences of skill, experience, merit, seniority or any of a host of factors which indicates that, though there may be like work or work rated as equivalent or work of equal value, there is a difference between the employees so that like is not compared with like.[105] It may be as simple as a matter of geography, as with the London weighting given to many jobs,[106] or it may be that there is a difference in hours or length of holidays, so that the comparators are paid more because they work more hours in a year.[107] The defence does not always succeed. First, it may not be possible to divorce the differential from the sex of the applicant.[108] Secondly, the employer's explanation may prove to be inadequate. Again, what matters is what the employees do, not simply how their jobs are described.[109]

The most complex aspect of the defence under section 1(3)(a) arises in relation to the requirement that both cases must be considered. The employer must show not only why the man is paid more, but also why, in that case, the woman continues to be paid less. This may sound pedantic, but it is crucial in terms of eradicating discriminatory assumptions about the value of women's work. The question arises not so much in relation, say, to skill or expertise where it is easier to see why there is a differential, but, in particular, where market forces raise troublesome and contentious issues.

In 1979 the Court of Appeal held in *Clay Cross (Quarry Services) Ltd* v *Fletcher* that an employer cannot avoid the Equal Pay Act simply 'by saying, "I paid him more because he asked for more" or "I paid her less because she was willing to come for less." If any such excuse were permitted the Act would be a dead letter.'[110] The Court stressed that what mattered was the 'personal equation' of the woman compared to the man. External, market forces were irrelevant. This trenchant view survived until a decision of the House of Lords in 1987, *Rainey* v *Greater Glasgow Health Board*,[111] in which outside economic factors were allowed to justify pay differentials. The dispute concerned prosthetists employed by the Greater Glasgow Health Board. When the prosthetic service was set up in 1980 it was decided that remuneration should be related to the NHS Whitley Council scale. Mrs Rainey, who was recruited directly into the service was therefore paid the NHS rate. The Board could not staff the prosthetic service, however, without recruiting from the private sector, since, until 1980, prosthetists were employed by private contractors. Mr Crumlin was one of twenty who transferred to the NHS on terms identical to the ones they had been enjoying previously. As a result, at the date of the hearing he was earning £10,085 and Mrs Rainey was on £7,295. All of the twenty who joined from the private sector were men. All but one on NHS rates were women.

At all stages, including the House of Lords, it was held that the difference between Rainey and Crumlin resulted from their different entries into the profession, not from their sex. The House of Lords considered *Clay Cross* too narrow since consideration may well extend beyond the personal equation and include economic factors relevant to the efficient management of the business.[112] Rainey's case was dismissed on the basis that she was not paid less, it was simply that Crumlin was paid more than the normal rates. That arose only because, in order to recruit from the private sector, the Board was forced to pay him at a higher rate. After the initial block transfer in 1980, all new entrants were paid NHS rates.

There are aspects of the decision in *Rainey* which are of positive value to women seeking equal pay, in particular, the insistence that an employer seeking to justify unequal pay for equal work must do so on objectively justifiable grounds. The special market conditions obtaining in 1980 were such grounds, which allowed for the protected salaries paid to the private sector recruits who happened to be men. This meant the men were over-valued and not that the women were under-valued: the latter would be unlawful sex discrimination. The Board was able to show, therefore, not only why the men were paid more but also why the women were paid less. Such an approach to market forces may effectively limit their use because it rules out conventional assumptions about the lower value of women's work.

It is one thing, however, to assert that objectively justifiable grounds relating to general economic or non-economic factors beyond the personal qualifications of the particular workers may permit pay differentials. It is quite another to allow such factors to disguise examples of historical bias, conscious or otherwise, against women in a particular profession. It should be noted that in *Rainey* the special arrangements were temporary: there was no obvious intention to perpetuate a two-tier system. There are circumstances however where suspicions of inherent bias are difficult to dispel.

The apparent acceptance of such inherent bias was evident in the decision of an Industrial Tribunal in *Clark v Bexley Health Authority*[113] which dismissed the claims of speech therapists on the express basis that the differential in pay was due to bargaining structures and their history. Two senior NHS speech therapists claimed their work was of equal value to that of male pharmacists and clinical psychologists, also employed in the NHS, whose salaries exceeded theirs by about 60 per cent. Denying that the work was of equal value, the employers argued also that, in any event, there was a defence under section 1(3) because the different pay for the relevant professions was decided by separate negotiating structures. The applicants drew attention to the fact that in the past speech therapists were regarded as medical auxiliaries and that such auxiliaries were predominantly female and they further argued that whether or not it was possible to show a deliberate, overt intention to discriminate, such 'female' jobs attract low salaries.

The applicants' arguments were dismissed on the basis that the differences were attributable to existing collective bargaining structures and the historical differences within them. The decision is questionable on a number of grounds, not least being how negotiators could justify the astonishing differential. Furthermore, whatever may have been the historical reasons, these cannot determine that work which might now be adjudged of equal value (an issue which was not decided) should continue to be subject to this kind of difference in pay, particularly since the original, historical reasons may themselves be based on discriminatory assumptions.

The danger implicit in decisions such as *Rainey* and *Clark* is that superficially gender-neutral salary structures may stem, in reality, from inherent, hidden discrimination which permeates a whole profession or sector of employment (for example the health services).There is a risk that such institutionalised discrimination can become locked into grading schemes. Different pay due to different grades is justifiable provided the grading is not done on the basis of sex.[114] Scales must be applied irrespective of sex[115] and not be a method of discriminating.[116] Some cases involve obvious examples of discrimination but others may involve more subtle issues of the kind to which the Tribunal in *Clark* appeared blind. In *Reed Packaging Ltd* v *Boozer*,[117] for example, the applicant clerk, paid on the staff pay scale, chose as her comparator in an equal value claim, a clerk paid on the scale for hourly paid workers, who earned £17 per week more than she did. The Employment Appeal Tribunal held the difference was due to the separate pay scales which were an objectively justified administrative reason which had nothing to do with the sex of the workers. Such an approach is plainly superficial: the fact that each pay structure operates internally without bias does not explain why there were two scales nor why she was on one and he on another.

The ECJ, on the other hand, has shown itself to be aware of the possibility of discrimination lurking within pay scales. In the *Danfoss* case,[118] the ECJ was faced with a claim from a Danish trade union that a pay system based on a collective agreement was sexually discriminatory. Danfoss paid the same basic minimum pay to workers in the same pay grade, the grading being decided according to job classification. Within the grade, however, the collective agreement allowed for additional pay on the basis of employee 'flexibility' (defined by reference to such factors as quality of work and responsibility) and on the basis of training and seniority. The trade union pointed out that within a pay grade women earned on average less than men and thus the system discriminated on the basis of sex contrary to the Equal Pay Directive. In relation to the extra pay for 'flexibility', the ECJ held that, if it related to the quality of work, the criterion was, on the face of it, gender-neutral. If in practice, however, it resulted in systematic disadvantage to female workers, that had to be because it was used in a discriminatory manner, since it cannot be the case that work done by women will be of a generally lower quality. In other words, the criterion of quality of work cannot be used by the employer to justify a *systematic* pay disadvantage to women. Irrespective of intent, a system based on merit which fails consistently to reward women is unlawful. If, on the other hand, flexibility refers to the adaptability of a worker to variable schedules and locations, that may still indirectly discriminate against women workers who, as a result of household and family duties, may have greater difficulty than male workers in organising their time flexibly. In these circumstances the employer must demonstrate that adaptability is important to the specific duties of the particular worker, using the test outlined by the ECJ in *Bilka-Kaufhaus GmbH* v *Weber von Hartz*,[119] that is, a real business need in relation to which the requirements imposed are appropriate and necessary, and the same reasoning applies to additional pay for vocational training. In relation to the use of the criterion of seniority, however, it was held that, since this betokens experience, the employer may use it as a basis for reward without having to justify it.

The potential effects of this decision should not be underestimated. Employers would be wise to examine the statistical effects of existing pay structures and, wherever there is an adverse impact on women, should be prepared to justify that on grounds that have nothing to do with the sex of the worker.

The most that may currently be said for apparently unbiased grading and pay structures is that they may well be neutral in form but may nevertheless derive from a discriminatory assumption or be operated in a discriminatory fashion. The latter fact was acknowledged by the Court of Appeal in *Benveniste* v *University of Southampton*.[120] Universities operate a salary scale applicable equally to men and women who may be placed anywhere on the scale at the discretion of the employer, but subject in normal circumstances to the age and qualifications of the employee. When Dr Benveniste was first appointed, financial constraints operating on the university meant that she was placed at a point below that commensurate with her age and qualifications. Once the financial problems eased, Dr Benveniste's salary was increased by more than the usual annual increment but that did not bring her up to the point she regarded as appropriate. She brought proceedings claiming work of equal value with four male comparators. The Court of Appeal held that, whatever might have been the case when she was appointed, any material difference between her case and that of her male comparators disappeared with the removal of the financial constraints, and thus there was no longer any justification to pay her less.

This decision is vital in restricting the extent of section 1(3) since it suggests that simply because an inequality could be justified in the past, does not mean it will go on being justifiable for ever. So, in the speech therapists' case, though their negotiating structures and resulting pay differentials may be shown to have been appropriate in the past, it does not inexorably follow that they are now justifiable, irrespective of sex. The same is true of grading schemes and, presumably, market forces. *Benveniste* is the converse of *Rainey* since Benveniste was paid less than normal and in *Rainey* the men were paid more. The decision in *Rainey* lays down that the higher rate went on being justifiable for the initial recruits after the event. Assuming that those higher wages are protected, it is still important to recall that, once the labour shortage eased, future private sector recruits could not justifiably be paid a higher rate.

The idea of protecting wages has been used in many earlier cases to show that a difference in pay is genuinely due to a material difference, other than sex, between the two cases. If an employer decides to regrade or reorganise the workforce, a group of workers may find, as a result, that their pay would decrease. That group may be 'red circled' or put into a special category so that their original salary is protected either temporarily or permanently. Whilst such a red circle may qualify as a material difference under the section 1(3)(*a*) defence, the tribunal must be alert to the possibility that the red circle derives from historical sex discrimination. If the men placed in the red circle in order to protect their higher wages were paid more in the first place because of gradings which were based on sex, the red circling would merely perpetuate that discrimination and will not be allowed.[121]

The defence under what is now section 1(3)(*a*) has been the subject of litigation in one other specific and very important area: the part-timer. Since the vast majority of part-timers in the United Kingdom are women, to pay them a lower rate than full-timers raises immediately the suspicion of sex discrimination. The part-time employee who proceeds under the Equal Pay Act has two hurdles to surmount: first, to show that her work is, for example, like work with that of a male full-time colleague and, secondly, to meet the allegation which may be made under section 1(3) that shorter hours constitute a material difference. Although the first of these hurdles may present practical problems,[122] the courts have been ready to accept that a difference in hours worked does not preclude a finding of like work under the Act. The second obstacle has proved more of a problem. Initially it seemed that the mere difference in hours might amount to a material difference between the two jobs being compared, based on lower productivity and greater over-heads.[123] That suggestion did not survive, however, being finally laid to rest by the Employment Appeal Tribunal in *Jenkins* v *Kingsgate (Clothing Productions) Ltd (No. 2)*.[124] The case was referred to the ECJ in an effort to ameliorate the effects of the earlier English case law. The ECJ was cautious in its decision, seeming to suggest that whilst a lower rate for part-timers is capable of amounting to indirect discrimination against women,[125] it is open to the employer to justify the different rates by reference to the history of the case and the intention of the employer.

Having failed to get clear assistance from Europe, the Employment Appeal Tribunal, when the case came back to it, took the view that English law was in fact more stringent in this regard and that the employer had to show an objectively justifiable economic reason for paying the women less than the men. This view was subsequently supported by the ECJ in *Bilka-Kaufhaus GmbH* v *Weber von Hartz*, where the Court held that in order to avoid a breach of Article 119 an employer must show that differential rates affecting more women than men 'correspond to a real need on the part of the undertaking, are appropriate with a view to achieving the objectives pursued and are necessary to that end'.[126]

It is ironic, perhaps, that the same effort to tighten up the defence to an equal pay claim, which could be said to benefit part-timers, has also led to the acceptance of economic or market forces as a potential justification for discrimination. Even though in *Rainey* it was clear that the House of Lords were aware that market forces could not be allowed to justify paying women less than the normal rate, this does not satisfactorily address the problems created by long-established sex bias in working practices which may have led, for example, to the situation in the speech therapists' case.

In an equal value claim, as opposed to like work or work rated as equivalent, the employer may use as a defence not only a genuine material difference between the man and the woman, but also, under section 1(3)(*b*), 'some other material factor'. The question then arises as to how this differs from section 1(3)(*a*) and whether and to what extent it enlarges the defence. The idea behind the amendment is to allow consideration of market forces as is apparently allowed by European Community law, but, since the decision in *Rainey*, it must be unlikely that there will be any significant difference between the two limbs of the defence.[127] Whichever is used, tribunals should have in mind that whilst market forces may justify an inequality at a particular time, that does not mean the inequality may be continued nor indeed that those market forces should be allowed to disguise the sex discrimination which is built into segregated jobs and traditionally low-paid jobs which tend to be filled by women.

The equality clause

A successful applicant is entitled to have her contract of employment modified so that it is no less favourable than that of the male comparator. This leaves the question of how the contract is to be modified and in particular whether it should be considered term by term to ensure that none is less favourable than those in the man's contract or whether it is permissible to look at the contract as a whole. In an early decision it was held that the former was the correct approach. If a woman is paid a lower hourly rate, then that must be increased even though her contract may contain a more beneficial term, for example, in relation to holidays or sick pay.[128]

That approach means, logically, that the men could then demand improvement in their holiday and sick pay, since it has already been decided that it is like work, of equal value or rated as equivalent. The fear of this 'leap-frogging' which could lead to 'widespread chaos in industry and inflict grave damage on commerce'[129] influenced the Employment Appeal Tribunal and Court of Appeal in *Hayward* v *Cammell Laird Shipbuilders Ltd*[130] to decide in favour of comparing not individual terms but rather the total remuneration package. Miss Hayward, a canteen cook, had been held to do work of equal value to that of male joiners, painters and thermal insulation engineers. Although her basic and overtime rates were lower than those of her male comparators, she did have a paid meal break and better holidays and sickness benefits. The employers argued that, looking at her contract as a whole, she was actually better off than the men. The Employment Appeal Tribunal and Court of Appeal accepted this approach, relying in part on the wide interpretation given to pay under Article 119, which was held to have the effect that it is wrong and artificial to look only at basic pay and to ignore such matters as hours, bonuses, holiday pay and other benefits which now form part of the remuneration of many employees. The equality clause was therefore not to apply to raise her pay, since section 1(2)(*c*) did not require term by term comparison.

This interpretation of the Act received short shrift from the House of Lords who were noticeably unmoved by threats of the economic disaster which would be the result of leap-frogging. The Act provides in section 1(2)(*c*)(i) that 'if...any term of the woman's contract is....less favourable to the woman than a term of a similar kind in the contract under which that man is employed, that term of the woman's contract shall be treated as so modified as not to be less favourable'. It was held that the natural meaning of those words requires a comparison of her basic pay with his, taking into account the hours worked, so as to arrive at a comparable hourly rate. As far as their Lordships were concerned, if she is paid less, that is a less favourable term. Perhaps that common-sense approach will lead to leap-frogging, or as Lord Goff put it 'mutual enhancement', but, for his Lordship at least, such a result seems to be the very philosophy underlying the provision. On this basis, Hayward was entitled to have her pay and overtime rates brought up to as favourable a level as that of the men.[131]

A final point raised by *Hayward* remains to be resolved, and that concerns the extent to which an employer faced with a similar set of facts might take advantage of the material difference defence in section 1(3) to justify the different rates of pay. Cammell Laird had not used the defence and so any comment on it by the judges in *Hayward* is incidental and not binding in future cases. Is it possible for an employer to argue that lower basic pay is offset by other benefits or perks? It has already been seen how different salary structures may justify the difference[132] provided they are not based on sex, but if section 1(3) could be used in a case such as Hayward's it could widen the defence. Remarks in the judgment suggest that whereas such a defence is theoretically possible, it would be applied very narrowly.[133]

Low wages

Despite the Equal Pay Act, there is a persistent gap between the earnings of men and women. In 1973 women's average, gross hourly earnings were 64.4 per cent of those of men. In 1975, the year the Equal Pay Act came into force, this figure improved to 72.1 per cent but, since then, it has hovered at around the same level, reaching a high of 75.5 per cent in 1977. The gap is actually greater when weekly earnings are considered.[134]

The reasons for this gap have been discussed earlier. They derive from women's segregation at work, the undervaluing of women's work and the influence of childbearing and childrearing. Women returning to work part-time not only lose out proportionally because of their shorter hours but also face generally poorer conditions, including low pay. Because so many women are amongst lower-paid workers, no chapter on women's wages would be complete without discussion of the way in which the law purports to protect the low paid, either by guaranteeing minimum rates or by supplementing income which is below a certain level.

The regulation of wages

Levels of pay and other conditions of employment are normally set by voluntary agreement as a result of bargaining between employers and workers, often on a collective level, that is between employers and trade unions. In circumstances where the workforce is not adequately organised (in trade union terms) or for some other reason finds it difficult to bargain effectively with the employer, it is essential that certain minimum conditions are imposed by law on the employer, to ensure at least a living wage.

Minimum wage regulation is thus a substitute for collective bargaining and it is centred on the Wages Councils. The system was first introduced in the Trade Boards Act 1909 which covered four sweated trades. The Trade Boards were to set legally enforceable minimum rates of pay in those trades where wage rates were exceptionally low as compared with other employment. The Boards developed in time into Wages Councils,[135] whose very existence is from time to time threatened. The government planned in 1985 to abolish the Councils but in the face of hostile response from a range of interests, including trade unions and the CBI, a reprieve was granted and the system survived, albeit in an emasculated form, in the Wages Act 1986. In December 1988 further proposals to scrap the system were made, based on the notion that the Councils lead to inflexible and artificially high rates. In this context artificially high means that, without the statutory minima, workers would be prepared to work for less.

The future of the Wages Councils is of particular importance for women because of the concentration of female workers in certain jobs. As was shown in Chapter 4, women make up the majority of the workforce in the occupational grouping of catering, cleaning, hair-dressing and other services, and also in retailing. It is also the case that these sectors, together with clothing, in which women also predominate, account for the vast majority of Wages Council workers.

When the system was introduced, the idea was to provide a level of wages which could be described as a living wage. Additionally, however, the hope was that a legally guaranteed minimum would encourage the development of voluntary collective bargaining so that eventually there would be no need for the protection of the Wages Councils. The system has not been an enormous success in either respect. On the first count, the Councils have not managed to improve the relative earnings of those covered so that they remain amongst the lowest paid. Furthermore, the number of firms paying below the minimum rates is unacceptably high.[136] On the second count, unions have found it difficult to organise in the Wages Council sector. This stems largely from the nature of the work, which may be based on casual labour (for example, in catering), and from the type of employee, often part-time or even working at home. Staff turnover is high and it is difficult both to recruit and to retain union members. Even where there is a solid membership it is an inescapable fact that these workers are the least able to use industrial pressure to achieve better conditions. A threat to strike is meaningless if the employer is aware that alternative job opportunities are few, whereas there is a ready pool of workers to draw from. It is also possible that the very existence of the Wages Councils makes workers less likely to join a trade union.

Despite the criticisms which may be made of the system, there is nevertheless much evidence to suggest that things would be worse for the workers without them. Women, and especially those working part-time, would face a deterioration in their pay and conditions if the Wages Councils disappeared and, since they form the majority of workers covered by the system, they would be affected disproportionately. The government did not appear, however, to consider that to be a reason for retaining the Councils. In particular, it was said that 'the low paid are mainly young with no family responsibilities, or married women bringing a second income into the home.'[137] Criticism by the government did not centre on the failure to raise levels of pay or the possibly inhibiting effect on the development of collective bargaining. Rather, the government based its attack on the idea that the Councils interfere with the freedom of employers to offer and job seekers to accept jobs at wages which would otherwise be acceptable.[138] In other words, wage regulation interferes with the operation of the market since it effectively prevents wages falling to the lowest level which the market will sustain. Workers, said the government, were pricing themselves out of jobs by adherence to these minimum levels.[139]

The present system is governed by the Wages Act 1986 which restricts the scope of the Wages Councils to such an extent that it was necessary for the United Kingdom to denounce the International Labour Organisation Convention 26 (Minimum Wage Fixing Machinery Convention, 1928). Although at one time there were almost seventy Wages Councils, by 1986 the number had declined to twenty-six. These are now subject to the 1986 Act. A Wages Council is a tripartite body comprising representatives of workers, employers and up to five independent members. The Secretary of State is able to abolish a Wages Council or to vary its scope[140] at any time, after considering wage levels current among workers covered by the Council and consultation with persons and organisations he thinks appropriate. This is a much simplified procedure as compared to the earlier law. There is no longer a power to create new Councils and the government made it clear as the Wages Act was going through Parliament that Wages Councils were contrary to its views on deregulation and the encouragement of enterprise. All workers under twenty-one years of age are removed from the scope of Wages Councils operations.[141] This measure affects about half a million workers and reflects the government's unshakeable, but largely unproven, view that Wages Councils priced young workers out of jobs.[142]

Prior to 1986 a Wages Council could fix not only minimum wages but also other terms and conditions, including holidays.[143] Under the 1986 Act, a Council may only set[144] either a single minimum hourly rate for all workers, irrespective of hours worked, or a single minimum hourly rate for a stipulated number of basic hours plus a single minimum hourly overtime rate. Old-style orders could set multiple wage levels for different categories of workers and could provide differential overtime rates and holiday pay levels. This is no longer possible and will doubtless pose a dilemma for a Council of whether to fix a rate at a level appropriate to the lowest paid grade, or whether to pitch it higher. Since there has to be one rate only, it also means that it must apply nationally. It is significant that a Council setting a minimum rate is instructed to consider the effect that rate will have on the level of employment among the workers to whom it applies, particularly in areas where pay rates are generally below the national average.[145] In other words, too high a minimum rate could lead to job losses. The hourly rate applies equally to full-time and part-time workers. This has an adverse effect on part-timers where a minimum overtime rate is set since the part-timer will presumably never achieve the hours necessary to come within the overtime band.

As before, a Wages Order made by the appropriate Council takes effect as part of the worker's contract and thus she can enforce any underpayment by way of an ordinary action for breach of contract. Failure to pay the minimum rate is also a criminal offence punishable by a fine and, more importantly, the employer may be ordered to pay up to two years' arrears of wages. It is the enforcement of the system which has attracted great criticism from all sides. The body responsible for enforcement is the Wages Inspectorate but there have always been allegations that the Inspectors were too few and too reluctant to prosecute.[146] Certainly illegal payment has always been widespread.

The uncertain future of the Wages Councils, the remnants of a wage regulation system, highlights the vulnerability of the low-paid worker. It is not only in this context, however, that the low paid face particular problems. The social security system is supposed to act as a safety net to prevent individuals, employed or unemployed, from falling below the level at which one is calculated to be able adequately to provide for oneself and family. Because women comprise a significant proportion of those who are low paid, the social security system becomes relevant and it is necessary to consider how this operates.

The impact of social security

The social security system was from its inception based on discriminatory treatment of married women who were assumed not to be gainfully employed.[147] Changes in the system have been gradually introduced, partly as a result of European law,[148] although there is still some way to go to achieve total equality of treatment. The general treatment of women in matters of social security is worthy of detailed scrutiny[149] but, in the context of women's wages, the most relevant issue is the overlap between earnings and benefits. What follows applies, in substance, equally to men and women but since the problems are confined to the low paid, the practical effects are felt especially severely by working women. A summary of the immensely complex structure of social security is best achieved by dividing it into the national insurance system, based on contributions, and what might be termed the benefits system, based on means.[150]

The national insurance scheme includes the state retirement pension and unemployment benefit. Payment of these depends on (a) whether the claimant falls within the relevant category (for example, unemployed and actively seeking work), and (b) that the claimant has a fully paid up contributions record. The claimant is disqualified if either (a) or (b) is not met. This is especially important in relation to women with dependants. First, a woman with children may have difficulty proving a genuine availability for work if she cannot show adequate child care arrangements are available. Secondly, the work patterns of many women involve periodic breaks, which interrupt contributions. Even when a woman is working, if the job is part-time and low paid, national insurance contributions may not be payable.[151]

Means-tested benefits include income support, family credit and housing benefit. The purpose of these benefits is to provide a floor below which the income of a family shall not fall. Entitlement does not depend on contributions, but on the level of income (together with other factors such as the number of children and the cost of housing). As income rises, benefits fall and therein lies the problem.

Income support seeks to maintain a minimum level of income for everyone, working or not. The level is set according to family size and composition. If the family income is below the level, income support makes it up. Effectively, therefore, for every additional £1 of income coming into the home income support is cut by £1, thus creating a so-called marginal tax rate of 100 per cent.

Income support is not payable, in any event, to those who are in paid employment for more than twenty-four hours a week, a fact which may make part-time employment below that level a more attractive proposition, since the earnings from a greater number of hours would not always compensate for the loss of income support. Those people with children who work more than twenty-four hours may, however, find that they are entitled to family credit. This depends on whether net income (after tax and national insurance contributions) is below the set level. Above that level, family credit is cut by seventy pence for every £1 of net income. The final calculation involves housing benefit. If the net income (including child benefit and family credit) is below the income support rate, housing benefit is paid at 100 per cent of rent and 80 per cent of rates with a taper effect as net income rises.

The result is, quite simply, that as earnings rise, benefits fall, imprisoning families in the poverty trap: that is, the paradox of being unable to improve one's standard of living by earning more. A related problem is sometimes termed the unemployment trap in which low-earning families discover that they would be better off with the earner unemployed, because their benefits would exceed their present income. Attitudes to the problems created by the overlap of earnings and benefits have verged occasionally on the hysterical, with much of the criticism being focused on the loss of the incentive to work. It was this kind of headline campaigning that contributed to the reduction in the value of unemployment benefit, the introduction of more stringent conditions to be met before it may be claimed and the abolition of earnings related supplements. Such measures rather ignore, however, the real dilemmas faced by those in the situations which lead to the traps – and indeed by policy makers who must try to eliminate the inequities of the system. Marginal tax rates can be such, depending on the composition of a family and their additional earnings, that every extra £1 of income from paid employment is taxed at almost 100 per cent; a rate which should be compared with current top rate of income tax of 40 per cent. Reforms in recent years aimed at avoiding marginal tax rates of over 100 per cent have meant that although the very highest rates have disappeared, the income range over which the trap operates has actually widened and there is no indication that the government has any current proposals to narrow it.

The structure of the social security system provides a clear illustration of how the pursuit of a particular policy in one set of legal rules can effectively undermine the stated goals of a different piece of legislation. Women may well have won the right, in theory and in law, to equal pay but if that particular right gives merely a chance to earn low wages in a segregated, part-time job which then results in a net loss of income to the household under another piece of legislation, it begins to look a somewhat hollow victory. The impact of the Equal Pay Act on attitudes and on rates of pay cannot be discounted and should not be derided, but it is futile to consider it divorced from the social context in which working women find themselves.

It may be unrealistic to expect the law to revolutionise the working conditions of women. The current law, however, is not necessarily the best that could be achieved. The section on low wages illustrates not only that women are disproportionately affected, but that in some instances the law completely fails to address the relevant issues. The restrictions on and proposed abolition of the Wages Councils, for example, form a conscious, deliberate decision to withdraw support from the low paid. Failure adequately to address the poverty trap is a political decision, since the law is as capable of removing it as retaining it. The law is not distinct from the legislators. Lip-service paid to the idea of equality through the chosen mechanism of anti-discrimination legislation is clearly insufficient. The systematic application of an equal scale to unequal social and economic conditions simply perpetuates inequality.

Chapter seven

Financial implications of work

In Chapter 6 attention was focused on those factors, both legal and non-legal, which can affect the amount that a woman receives as earned income. The Equal Pay Act 1970 has sought to eliminate discrimination in the matter of wages, however unsatisfactory and half-hearted the attempt might be. Yet the amount an individual takes home at the end of the week or month will not depend simply on the rate for the job. In taking on paid employment an individual incurs certain obligations, for example, the duty to pay income tax, and it is those obligations seen from the perspective of a working woman which form the subject matter of this chapter. Four factors can substantially reduce a working woman's disposable income. They are:

(i) income tax;
(ii) national insurance contributions;
(iii) provision for occupational social security, such as sick pay, and for a retirement pension;
(iv) the cost of providing for help with domestic tasks, child care or the care of an elderly relative.

In considering each of these factors certain general points need to be kept in mind. The purpose of levying taxes whether in the shape of income tax or national insurance contributions is to allow revenue to be raised which can be devoted to what are perceived as desirable purposes such as the financing of a national health service. It is a matter of political judgement for an elected government, which will be subjected to lobbying by pressure groups and attacks from opposition parties, how much revenue it chooses to raise, what taxes it uses and how it then decides to allocate that revenue. Recent government decisions to cut income tax, substitute a community charge for rates and 'target' state benefits show how contentious such issues can be. As a rule of thumb, justice might seem to require the greatest contribution from those with the greatest resources, whilst benefits should go to those in the greatest need. Some commentators would regard this as an unacceptable analysis of an exceedingly complex issue.[1] It has been argued that the very notion of the state levying taxes is the fiscal equivalent of forced labour and that each individual should make provision for their own long-term welfare.[2] In the majority of capitalist states a balance is usually struck between self-help and state help with the emphasis varying over the years according to the political complexion of the government in power.

Viewed in this way, it might seem that a person's sex is irrelevant to decisions of this kind. Yet the conclusions a government reaches on the manner in which revenue will be raised and the way in which it will be distributed can have exceedingly important consequences for women. The payment of national insurance contributions, for example, regulates the availability of certain state benefits such as sickness pay. A person who earns less than £46 a week[3] is not required to make these contributions and therefore is not entitled to the benefits accruing from such payments. Since some part-time workers earn below this amount[4] and the majority of these workers are women, it is women who in the main suffer from the lack of availability of benefits. A woman in these circumstances can of course attempt to claim non-contributory benefits, though these are available not as of right but according to a person's means. In determining eligibility for these benefits a partner's income will be taken into account with the result that a married woman or a cohabiting woman may not be able to make a claim. Instead, she is expected to rely on her husband or partner for support.

It is questionable whether the thinking that presently underpins the tax and benefits system in this country reflects the needs of working women. In particular, the system may not be designed to take account of the work patterns of women, especially during those periods when they may withdraw from paid employment. As a consequence, the treatment women receive during the course of their working lives and eventually when they retire may be inferior to that received by a working man.

The taxation of women's pay

April 1990 marks a significant reform of an area which has been a source of glaring discrimination, namely the taxation of husband and wife. This situation has been allowed to continue for some fifteen years after the anti-discrimination legislation came into force because this was one of the issues excluded.[5] When income tax was first introduced in 1799 it took account of the fact that, on marriage, a woman's property automatically passed into the control of her husband.[6] It was therefore logical that a married woman's income was to be 'stated and accounted for by her husband'. This practice has continued with some minor modifications until the present day even though the law relating to married women's property was reformed in the latter part of the nineteenth century.[7] Whilst the aggregation of husband's and wife's income might seem justified at a time when few women earned sufficient in their own right to make the payment of income tax necessary, its continuation into the late twentieth century when a significant percentage of married women are in employment outside the home is anachronistic.[8]

The pre-1990 system can be criticised on a number of grounds and the identification of these is vital in order to determine whether the new system will advance the equal treatment of women. First, the original scheme deprives a married woman of independence and privacy in her financial affairs though she has no corresponding right to obtain details of her husband's earnings. Since her income is deemed to be his, it is her husband who is responsible for paying tax on it, and she must disclose to him exactly what she earns. In social terms the rule perpetuates the myth that a married couple are automatically a social unit, headed by the husband who is presumed to be responsible for his dependent wife. To that extent, the philosophy of the law seems at odds with the policy that underpins the anti-discrimination legislation which is to ensure equality of treatment.

Secondly, the pre-1990 system may discourage a woman who wishes to return to paid employment. Since the income of husband and wife is joint, tax is levied on the aggregated income of the couple. This has the disadvantageous result that in calculating the tax payable a higher rate of tax may be levied than if the couple in question were taxed separately. For example, if a married couple each earn £14,000, their aggregated income could bring them into the higher rate bracket of 40 per cent, which would not be the case if each was treated as a single person. There are ways in which a couple can reduce their liability, but that ignores a very basic point that the treatment of a couple's income as joint income may act as a disincentive to a woman to return to paid employment. Liability to tax and the costs of providing for child care may persuade a woman that she is better off staying at home or taking on a part-time job with all the disadvantages that this involves. Research has shown this to be a definite consideration:

> Where research has shown sensitivity to taxation, however, is for married women. Many are in the position where they are deciding whether to take a paid job and, if so, how many hours to work, balancing the returns from doing so against childcare costs.[9]

Those in paid employment may be able to claim certain allowances which reduce their tax liability. At 1989-90 levels a single person, male or female, may earn £2,785 before their income is taxed. In contrast a married man has an allowance of £4,375. This extra tax allowance is a recognition that a husband is presumed to be providing not only for himself but for a dependent wife. Though this might have been true in the past, the number of households that still consist of a working husband and a dependent wife must be decreasing. In some respects the law has acknowledged this fact by making available other allowances such as the wife's earned income allowance[10] and the additional personal allowance.[11] The former allowance which is equivalent to a single person's allowance is available to a wife who works. It was realised as early as 1942 that without it a working wife's total earnings would be taxed and this would be another disincentive to her obtaining paid employment. The additional personal allowance is available to single parents and consists of the difference between the single and married person's allowance. By making this concession the law acknowledges the increasing number of children born outside marriage as well as the many marriages which end in divorce. Whether this pre-1990 set of allowances represents a fair and non-discriminatory use of resources is open to doubt, as becomes apparent when those allowances are listed.

Single person: £2,785
Married man with wife who does not work: £4,375
Single parent: £4,375
Married man with working wife: £7,160
Cohabiting couple: £5,570

From this it is possible to conclude:

(a) married men are more favourably treated than single men or women;
(b) married men are more favourably treated than married women, since if both earn the same gross pay his income net of tax will be greater than hers because his allowance is greater;
(c) married couples are treated more favourably than cohabiting couples;
(d) married couples where both partners work are treated more favourably than those where only the husband is in paid employment.

The simplest way to solve this discrimination between married and single, and men and women, would be to abolish the married man's allowance. Various objections could, however, be raised to such a proposal. The most convincing would seem to be the inequity in expecting a working spouse whose income has to provide for a dependent partner to pay the same amount in tax as a single person. There are of course ways in which this difficulty could be met. For example non-working spouses could be given an allowance which they could transfer to their working partners whilst they were not in employment. Transferable allowances would ensure that a married couple's tax position remained the same whether one or both partners were working. When this was proposed as a feature of the reformed 1990 system, the suggestion meet with considerable opposition from quite disparate groups.[12] Much criticism was directed at the fact that transferable allowances would discourage married women from working. First, since there would no longer be a married man's allowance, two-earner couples would find themselves worse off because their allowances would fall. The alternative, to increase the allowances to cushion two-earner couples, would have been extremely expensive. Secondly, a non-working wife who had transferred her allowance to her husband might have faced opposition should she have wished to take up paid employment, since the loss of her allowance would decrease her husband's net pay. Thirdly, such a system was seen as offering little to those in need. Increases in child benefit and in allowances to those caring for the sick and for elderly relatives were seen as offering greater advantages than putting extra money in a working person's pay packet, particularly if that person was the husband who might not pass on any additional income to his wife.

The inequities of the pre-1990 system, with the Inland Revenue's treatment of married women as 'non-persons', led to pressure for reform. Since 1980 the matter has been under consideration and, spurred on by a memorandum from the European Community,[13] the Chancellor of the Exchequer announced in 1988 that reforms in personal taxation would come into effect in April 1990.[14] The system is described as 'independent taxation' but it does not go so far as to remove the special treatment reserved for married couples and in particular for married men. A suggestion that this special treatment should be abolished met with considerable opposition. The 'independence' derives from the fact that husband and wife will be taxed separately on their incomes, both their earnings and investment income.[15] The system of personal allowances is revised so that everyone, male or female, married or single, will be entitled to a personal allowance which can be set against all types of income.[16] The level of this allowance will be equivalent to the former single person's allowance.

Additionally, however, there will be a married couple's allowance[17] which will represent the difference between the current single person's allowance and the current married man's allowance. This new allowance will in the first place go to the husband but, if he has insufficient income to use it up, any unused part may be transferred to the wife. Transfer is only possible in the case of the married couple's allowance and not the personal allowance. Thus, if the wife is not earning and has no other income, such as investment income, her personal allowance is 'wasted'.

The new system, though put forward by government as a radical move towards sexual equality in taxation, is really little more than a concession to the demands for privacy and a degree of autonomy for married women. In most instances the new system will make no difference to the tax paid, though there are some exceptions. The move away from aggregation means that each spouse has his or her own tax rate band and thus some couples who are paying higher rate tax will cease to do so. The retention of the married man's allowance in the shape of the married couple's allowance has guaranteed that little else will change. Doubts will remain over whether this determination to 'reward' marriage is the best use of resources. Indeed, the presumption that this allowance will go to the husband[18] rather than letting the couple elect who should receive it appears to perpetuate rather than eliminate discrimination. Yet, for all the criticism that one can direct at the 'new' system, it does at least acknowledge a wife as a separate entity. This new-found freedom is in sharp contrast to the situation regarding the community charge where a wife may be made responsible for her husband's charge, or he for hers, if either fails to pay.[19] Whether the new tax system will make a married woman more inclined to return to paid employment is a matter for conjecture. In practice it should make no difference to the vast majority of women since other factors, such as the costs of child care remain major disincentives. However, the fact that the law now acknowledges that a woman can handle her own tax affairs may make a difference for some couples where a wife may no longer feel obliged to secure her husband's 'permission' before she takes on paid employment. Also uncertain in its effect is the advice currently being given that, where a wife does not work, her husband should consider transferring into her name investments, income from which can then be set against her unused personal allowance. It is an intriguing thought that some wives may gain out of their husband's wish to avoid tax. As one financial adviser commented:

> Thus, the changes will only be of real benefit if there is a large shift of capital from joint accounts, or accounts in the husband's name, into investments in the wife's sole name. The results will be most interesting in the divorce courts....My bet is that there will be no huge shift of capital. Even husbands who think their marriage is stable are not above the odd nagging doubt.[20]

A woman's ability to obtain state benefits

Apart from any income tax that is deducted from her wages, a working woman may find her disposable income further reduced by national insurance contributions. This is another form of tax paid by those in

145

employment in order to finance certain benefits such as sickness pay and the state retirement pension. By building up a record of contributions, an employee may gain the right to claim those benefits if and when the need arises. The emphasis placed on a contributions record may, however, have unfortunate consequences for women workers. Single or married women can find it necessary to take a career break – to care for a child or an elderly relative or to follow a partner who has taken up employment in another part of the country – and thus interrupt their record of contributions. A second factor which may limit a woman's ability to claim contributory benefits in her own right is that those who earn below a certain level[21] are not liable to make contributions or to claim benefit. This may have the additional effect of depressing part-time wages to keep them below this threshold.

The difficulty that some women experience in claiming contributory benefits is not new. Indeed it may well be that the situation is improving as women take fewer career breaks and build up a more complete record of contributions. Various strategies have been proposed over the years to cope with the fact that the working patterns of women may be distinct from those of working men. The fairest solution might be simply to acknowledge this and use a different basis on which to calculate a woman's right to benefits. In practice, the cost of doing so and the possible complexity of such a system rule it out. Nor would the award of concessions to women as a class seem equitable to those men forced to give up work to shoulder domestic responsibilities. Whilst admitting that there is no easy solution to this problem, this in no way excuses the character of the concessions that have been made which presume that a married woman can rely on her husband for support. When the national insurance scheme was originally instituted, the view was that few married women would undertake paid employment. Those who did work and either lost their jobs or became ill were expected to rely on their husbands' income.[22] Married women in work were offered the option of paying a reduced contribution – the married woman's contribution – which did not entitle them to claim benefit in their own right. Indeed, in these circumstances, it seems strange that they were required to make any contribution, leading one commentator to suggest that: 'These payments are more akin to taxes than to contributions for they cannot assist in gaining title to any benefits or to the crediting of contributions during periods of sickness, unemployment or domestic responsibilities.'[23] The option of taking advantage of this far from generous scheme has now ceased, though those women who had already made that choice were allowed to continue with it.[24] Working women are now expected to make a full contribution and in time this will undoubtedly increase the number of women who can claim benefits in their own right. As for the problem posed by career breaks, there has been some attempt to deal with this by making provision for 'home responsibilities protection'.[25] This permits persons who are precluded from working by having to care for a child under sixteen, or a child over sixteen in respect of whom an attendance allowance is received, or who themselves receive supplementary benefit and are not required to be available for work because of the need to care for an elderly or incapacitated person, to have their contribution records protected. In the case of such persons less stringent contribution requirements have to be satisfied in order to gain a pension.

Any concession that acknowledges the domestic responsibilities that women, and indeed men, may have to face is welcome, though when it is recalled how much an individual who is prepared to care for a sick partner or child is 'saving' the state, the concession may appear less generous. Indeed, an individual who is caring for a 'severely disabled person' may qualify for a special payment from the state, namely invalid care allowance. Until recently, however, women living with their husbands or cohabiting were not permitted to claim this allowance 'because they were presumed to be at home caring for families, to have no paid employment and therefore to not require compensation for giving up employment'.[26] Neither does home responsibilities protection assist those women who take a part-time job in order to combine work with domestic responsibilities. The fact that they work prevents them from qualifying, yet their levels of pay may be below the threshold for national insurance contributions. In these circumstances a woman may yet again be forced to rely on her partner and not on her own resources if she is ill or out of work and ultimately in order to claim a state pension.

Women may be unable to work at certain periods, for example immediately before and after the birth of a child. National insurance benefits are aimed at supporting individuals at such times in their lives, when because of maternity, illness or unemployment they may not have an income. Whilst there appears to be acceptance of the principle that maternity is 'a risk appropriate for inclusion in a social insurance system',[27] there is no corresponding agreement on who should benefit and how such a scheme should be financed. This may be an occasion where the paternalistic urge to ensure the health of the next generation should prevail. If so, one would expect every pregnant woman to benefit and the state to bear the cost. Alternatively, the aim might be to maintain the incomes of pregnant women in employment. In these circumstances far fewer women would benefit and the employer might be expected to bear the costs.

After several schemes had been tried and discarded, a far from happy compromise was reached with the introduction of Statutory Maternity Pay (SMP).[28] This is not a benefit which is universally available. Instead, it can be claimed only by working women who satisfy certain conditions.[29] These include the necessity to be an employee, to have average weekly earnings in the eight weeks prior to the 'qualifying week'[30] that exceed the lower earnings limit for national insurance contributions and to have worked continuously for the employer for a specified period prior to the qualifying week. That specified period is either two years for women who work more than sixteen hours a week, five years for those who work for between eight and sixteen hours a week, or twenty-six weeks. The reason for prescribing these different lengths of service is that they determine the rate of SMP. In the case of women who can satisfy only the twenty-six weeks test, their rate of SMP is lower than for those women who can satisfy one of the other tests.

In the light of these complex rules regarding eligibility, it seems certain that some women at least will not qualify for SMP. Women who are not employees are automatically excluded. Therefore women who are self-employed, either by choice or because that is how their 'employer' chooses to describe them, cannot claim. Women who have worked for less than twenty-six weeks are in a similar position. Women who are poorly paid may find that their average earnings are not sufficient to allow them to make a claim. There will also be working women who will find it hard to qualify for the higher rate of SMP, for example women who work for between eight and sixteen hours a week. In short, it might be possible to conclude that the women who are least likely to qualify for SMP are those who most need it.

Those who are unable to claim SMP may still be eligible for State Maternity Allowance (SMA).[31] The availability of this benefit appears to meet some at least of the criticisms made above since SMA is available to the self-employed and those who have not been employed for long enough to claim SMP. Unfortunately, claimants for SMA also have to satisfy a number of conditions, which include the need to have paid national insurance contributions for a specified period.[32] In addition, SMA is paid at a lower rate than SMP and entitlement to SMA can be lost if, for example, a claimant refuses to attend a medical examination.[33]

From the evidence it is apparent that the contributory benefits system discriminates against women. When the system was first instituted it took as its model the stereotypical couple in the expectation that a man would be in full-time employment for much of his life and a woman's primary role was that of wife and mother. It is possible to argue over the accuracy of that model even when it was first used in the 1940s,[34] but with the passage of time such a model has become totally unrepresentative. This has led to adjustments to the system, with the introduction of features such as home responsibilities protection, but it has not received the thorough-going overhaul which it requires. The woman with most to gain from the system is the woman whose working pattern most closely resembles that of a man. Those with least to gain are women who work on a temporary or casual basis or who earn below the national insurance lower earnings limit or who still pay the married woman's contribution.

It is easier to criticise the contributory benefits system than to suggest ways in which it could become less discriminatory. Contributory benefits, as opposed to means-tested benefits, are based on the notion of the employee contributing towards his or her future welfare. An individual is expected to pay into the system in order to be able to draw upon it. When the system was first instituted one exception was a married woman who was to be able to gain from the system by virtue of contributions made by her husband. The implications of such an approach are undoubtedly unsatisfactory and women are now quite legitimately required to play a full part in the system. The difficulty is that for the foreseeable future some women will not be able to establish as complete a contributions record as men and thus discrimination will continue despite the fact that in theory women have equal access to benefits. A woman with a poor contributions record can either be left to manage as best she can, or she can turn to means-tested benefits or, where possible, she can rely on her husband's contributions' record.

Even the European Community has demonstrated an unaccustomed reticence in dealing with the complexities of social security. Reference has already been made to various Directives[35] on this subject which were initiated less out of a sense of altruism than a desire on the part of the Community to ensure no unfair advantages as between member states. The most relevant of those Directives is Directive 79/7 which calls for equal treatment in statutory social security schemes covering such matters as sickness pay and pensions. The interesting feature of this Directive is that it specifically excludes issues such as equal treatment in relation to pensionable age and survivors' benefits. These will be dealt with at greater length in the next section but at this stage it is sufficient to note this implied acknowledgement of the difficulties in eliminating discrimination. The implementation of Directive 79/7 by the United Kingdom in the Social Security Act 1980 is alleged to be mainly cosmetic.[36] The inequalities discussed in this section still exist and no amount of legislation giving women equal access to benefits will alter the fact that women's work patterns are substantially different from those of men.

Means-tested benefits such as income support and housing benefit provide a safety net for the poorest families. The very term 'means-tested' indicates that what is important are the resources of the claimant. The complexity of the system and the range of benefits available make it impossible to describe the system in detail. It might of course be argued that such benefits will have little or no relevance for working women. Regrettably this is far from the truth. A working woman may be forced to rely on means-tested benefits in order to supplement a low income or whilst she is temporarily out of work. Low wages have been discussed in another context[37] and the point was made then that, by reason of the types of employment they take as well as the fact that they work part-time, women are particularly prone to low wages. The Wages Councils have in the past tried to ameliorate the situation by setting minimum rates of pay in industries where low wages are perceived as a particular problem. With the government's continued attempts to abolish these bodies on the basis that they represent an unwarranted interference with the labour market the situation is unlikely to improve. It is ironic, however, that while, on the one hand, the government is advocating deregulation of the market, it is still, for now, prepared to subsidise low wages through the benefits system.

Besides being used to supplement low incomes, means-tested benefits take over when contributory benefits are no longer available or they may be used to supplement such benefits. Contributory benefits are, with the exception of retirement pensions, not long-term benefits and the rate at which they are set is far from generous. A retired person will find it hard to exist solely on the state retirement pension without help from other sources. A single parent who is unable to take employment because of child care responsibilities may also be forced to rely on means-tested benefits. In other words there are certain groups to whom means-tested benefits may represent their only or a substantial part of their income. On closer investigation it becomes clear that to a great extent it will be women who are forced to rely on state help and there are increasing references to that process which is known as the feminisation of poverty. Even if a woman is not a single parent or a widowed pensioner but is married or cohabiting she may still have to rely on means-tested benefits if her husband is unemployed or in a low-paid occupation.

The system of means-tested benefits produces a number of problems for women. Where a couple wish to claim a means-tested benefit either partner can elect to be the claimant. However, the rules regulating these benefits often specify that the claimant has to be available for work. A woman with children may not be able to comply with this requirement, making it impossible for her to claim.[38] Benefit is paid not to individuals but to the family and all the family's resources are taken into account in setting the level of benefit. It also means that if a wife takes a job to improve the family finances, benefit will be lost as a consequence.[39] In addition, if a woman should become unemployed but her husband still has a job, then she is unable to claim any means-tested benefit in her own right without account being taken of her husband's income.

This brief account of the means-tested benefit system demonstrates yet again that the insistence on equal treatment and the legislative force given to that principle by Acts such as the Social Security Act 1980 make little impression on the underlying situation. In the first place the system still forces women to assume the position of a dependant. Secondly, if women are unable to rely on contributory benefits to the same degree as men – and here one would include occupational benefits such as company sick pay – then more and more will be forced to depend on means-tested benefits. It is of course a separate, but no less important point that means-tested benefits have recently been closely scrutinised by government. Changes have been made which are said to have the effect of targeting benefits at those in need. The wisdom of this approach has been closely questioned and some regard it more as an exercise in saving money than improving the system. Whether one likes or loathes the new system, it is undeniable that adverse effects will be felt especially keenly by women since they are forced to make the most calls on it.

Some employers are of course prepared to give their employees additional financial support to supplement any state benefit they might receive. Hence, the level of sickness pay available from an employer might be superior to that available from the state.[40] There may, however, be rules which regulate an employee's access to such additional benefits and these might require full-time employment or service for a minimum period with the particular employer. A recent survey conducted on behalf of the Equal Opportunities Commission revealed that access to many so-called fringe benefits such as company sick pay or private medical insurance depended on length of service and hours worked.[41] Though the companies surveyed had no very definite reasons for imposing such conditions, their effect was undoubtedly to discriminate against women.[42] This is because women will experience the greater difficulty in complying, particularly if they work part-time. The situation may improve with the passage of the Social Security Act 1989. One of the purposes of this Act is to implement Directive 86/378 which applies the principle of equal treatment for men and women to occupational social security schemes.

The concepts of direct and indirect discrimination are now applicable to the conditions governing such schemes. It has been suggested that if a company's sick pay scheme is open only to those who work, say, twenty-five hours a week or more, a female employee can challenge it on the grounds that considerably fewer women than men can comply with that condition and that it is not justifiable irrespective of sex. Should this claim be accepted, it represents illegal indirect discrimination. There is, however, some doubt on this point since the legislation refers to discrimination against members of a scheme rather than against any employee wishing to join it.[43] In a recent case, *Rinner-Kühn* v *FWW Spezial Gebaudereinigung GmbH & Co KG*,[44] the European Court held that conditions regarding eligibility for employment protection rights, here the payment of sick pay, imposed by the state and not by the employer were capable of being discriminatory. Legislative provisions restricting access to benefits may, therefore, constitute discrimination on the grounds of sex contrary to Article 119[45] or the Equal Treatment Directive[46] unless the state can justify their use. In contrast, the extent of the duty imposed on employers by the Social Security Act 1989 to allow equal access to purely occupational schemes appears in doubt because of the way in which the Act is worded. In these circumstances, a part-time worker, for example, excluded from her employer's occupational sick pay scheme, may find that the protection afforded her by domestic legislation is wanting. Instead, if the benefit in question qualifies as pay according to the extended meaning given to that term under Article 119, she may be better advised to rely on the European Court's reasoning in *Bilka-Kaufhaus GmbH* where the concept of indirect discrimination was applied to occupational benefits.

A woman's right to a pension

A passing reference has already been made to the subject of retirement pensions. The topic is an important one, however, and deserves closer consideration because women who retire at sixty can expect, on average, to survive another twenty years. So for a quarter of her lifetime a woman may have to subsist on a pension and the provision that is made during the course of her working life for this eventuality is vital. There are two types of pension. On the one hand, there is the basic state retirement pension, the availability of which is dependent on the payment of sufficient national insurance contributions or alternatively on being the partner or ex-partner of someone who has paid sufficient contributions. On the other hand, there are occupational pensions. These, as the name implies, are pension schemes provided by employers for the benefit of their workers and may enable an employee to retire on a pension that will bear some relation to the amount earned whilst in employment. Clearly not every employer will either wish or be able to offer this facility and unless employees are far-sighted enough to make their own arrangements they run the risk of a less than financially secure retirement.

It is of course possible to argue that the problem would be resolved in part if the basic state pension was set at a realistic level. Instead, schemes have been produced aimed at enhancing the basic pension. Employees earning above a certain level[47] now have to make additional national insurance payments which vary according to their earnings.

The first such scheme of this nature – graduated retirement benefit[48] – was replaced by the state earnings related pension or SERPS.[49] With these attempts to augment the basic pension came the acknowledgement that those who were already members of an occupational scheme should not be expected to contribute twice. Therefore it was made possible for occupational schemes to contract out of the state scheme provided certain conditions are satisfied.[50] Lately the law has been further modified to allow individual employees to make their own personal pension arrangements rather than rely on their employer or the state scheme.[51]

The situation regarding pensions is far from straightforward for anyone. Working women can find themselves at a considerable disadvantage, however, since occupational and state schemes rely on an individual maintaining a consistent record of employment and contributions. Career breaks or the necessity of taking part-time employment can have serious consequences upon a woman's eligibility to receive a retirement pension. The fact that on average a woman's earnings are appreciably lower than those of a man means that the SERPS scheme with its emphasis on earnings may not work to her advantage. If her employer offers an occupational pension scheme it may have features that are not in a woman's best interests. For example, it may have a minimum age for entering the scheme. For men this may not be of particular importance but for women who are likely to take a career break or leave employment completely, a loss of opportunity to build up pension rights may have serious consequences. In addition, some occupational schemes are open only to full-time workers and therefore part-timers, who in the main are women, may suffer disproportionately, though discrimination of this nature may not be unlawful if it is objectively justifiable. Nor does the discrimination cease when a woman worker retires since she may find that her pension is less than that paid to a man since, according to actuarial calculations, she may on average be expected to survive longer. Finally, when a woman dies and her husband survives her, it may emerge that little provision exists for him.[52] In contrast, widows are much better provided for, since they are presumed to be dependent.

These examples would seem to provide proof of discrimination against women employees in access to pensions and the benefits that accrue on retirement. The Sex Discrimination Act and the Equal Pay Act therefore would seem to present the perfect opportunity for eliminating such practices. Unfortunately, the terms of both Acts, as originally drafted, seemed to rule out such a challenge, forcing prospective claimants demanding equal treatment to rely on Article 119 of the Treaty of Rome. This Article provides that men and women shall receive equal pay for equal work and adopts a very broad definition of pay. This encouraged individuals to claim that pensions and pension contributions represented a form of deferred pay and were subject to the article. In *Worringham and Humphreys* v *Lloyds Bank Ltd*[53] women were not required to contribute to the employer's contributory pension scheme until they reached the age of twenty-five. In contrast, men were required to contribute as soon as they were employed and in recognition of this fact received 5 per cent more gross pay to cover this additional cost. The European Court of Justice held that this extra amount constituted pay for the purposes of Article 119. The Court reasoned that:

> Sums such as those in question which are included in the calculation of the gross salary payable to the employee and which directly determine the calculation of other advantages linked to the salary, such as redundancy payments, unemployment benefits, family allowances and credit facilities, form part of the worker's pay within the meaning of...article 119...even if they are immediately deducted by the employer.[54]

The Court also held that a claimant could rely directly on Article 119 when arguing their case before the English courts. In contrast, the decision in *Newstead* v *Department of Transport and HM Treasury*[55] involved a civil servant who received the same gross pay as a female colleague. A greater sum was deducted from his salary, however, in order to provide for widows' pensions under his employer's pension scheme which was contracted out from the state pension provision. Women were not under a similar duty to contribute towards widowers' pensions. He argued that since he was a confirmed bachelor he was being denied access to part of his salary and that as women were not treated in this fashion this was discrimination on the grounds of sex. The European Court held that there was no breach of Article 119. Male and female employees received the same gross salary and the deduction in question had to be made under the rules regulating contracted-out pension schemes. Article 119 is not concerned with payments to social security schemes and, similarly, contracted-out schemes which substitute in part for state provision do not appear to be affected. This at least was one possible interpretation of *Newstead*. Moreover, survivors' benefits under such schemes were not subject to the principle of equal treatment.

In *Bilka-Kaufhaus GmbH* v *Weber von Hartz*[56] a German department store's refusal to allow part-time employees to benefit from its occupational pension scheme unless they could satisfy certain conditions was held by the European Court to constitute indirect discrimination contrary to Article 119. Since the pension scheme was a contractual scheme it was held to represent part of the consideration paid to the firm's employees. The conditions regulating eligibility excluded part-timers, the majority of whom were women, and this was indirect discrimination unless the employer could justify his actions. This decision would seem to indicate that the principle of equal treatment applied to conditions governing access to occupational pension schemes provided by the employer under the contract. *Bilka-Kaufhaus GmbH* still did not decide whether a United Kingdom contracted-out pension was covered by Article 119.

In *Barber v Guardian Royal Exchange Assurance Group*,[57] however, the European Court has unequivocally stated that occupational pensions, even those that are contracted-out, are within the scope of Article 119. As a consequence, men and women in receipt of such pensions must be treated equally. The situation which led to this ruling concerned Mr Barber's redundancy at the age of fifty-two. He received a lump sum payment but, according to his terms of employment, was not entitled to a pension until he reached the age of sixty-two. In contrast, a woman of Mr Barber's age, who had been made redundant, would have been entitled to an immediate pension.

In holding that Mr Barber's treatment was contrary to Article 119, the European Court ruled that the compensation awarded to a redundant employee amounted to pay. It was immaterial whether it was in cash or kind, that payment was immediate or at some future date, or that the obligation to pay was statutory or that a firm had chosen to make an *ex gratia* payment. This wide interpretation given to the term 'pay' as used in Article 119 reflects earlier rulings by the Court. What is exceptional is the clear statement that an occupational pension could be regarded as pay. Past decisions gave no clear guidance on whether occupational pensions which in part were a substitute for state benefits were to be classed as comparable to social security benefits. In *Barber* various features were isolated, such as a firm's control over the terms on which occupational pensions were awarded, which made this comparison erroneous.

Once it was conceded that contracted-out occupational pensions fell within the scope of Article 119, the immediate consequence was that men and women must be treated equally. Therefore the differential in pensionable age which was a feature of the Guardian Royal Exchange scheme was unlawful. The fact that it reflected the difference in state pensionable age was immaterial.

As must be abundantly clear the decision in *Barber* will have far-reaching repercussions, many of which are not yet apparent. The European Court was aware of this when it limited the effect of the decision in order to prevent retrospective claims. Claims, unless already initiated, are effective only from the date of judgment, that is 17 May 1990. What is not certain is whether this decision offers any positive benefits for women. If firms are now forced to equalise pensionable ages women may find that they have to work longer before becoming entitled to a pension. Women may, however, gain in respect of the benefits which accrue from an occupational pension. Since equality is the order of the day, the lower pensions and unequal survivors' benefits which women currently receive may no longer be justified.

The position of the Social Security Act 1989 is also made uncertain by the decision in *Barber*. The Act was designed to implement Directive 86/378 and extended the concepts of direct and indirect discrimination to occupational pension schemes as well as amending the Sex Discrimination Act.[58] The 1989 Act, as it currently stands, deals with conditions governing access to occupational pension schemes. Therefore schemes which are not open to part-timers may be challenged on the grounds that such a condition constitutes less favourable treatment for women. That apart, the Social Security Act sets out various exceptions to the principle of equal treatment. Actuarial grounds can be used to justify differences in the level of pension contributions, since such variations are based on calculations indicating the average life expectancies of men and women.[59] In addition, the Act allows for discrimination in pensionable ages[60] and survivors' benefits.[61] The exceptions in the 1989 Act which reflect the terms of Directive 86/375 may have been overtaken by the decision in *Barber*.[62] Some amendments to the law are certainly required and the current uncertainty may work to women's advantage with firms forced to guarantee women the same advantages as men on issues such as survivors' benefits. What has not changed is the situation in relation to state pensions, including SERPS. Here unequal treatment is still possible since these are most definitely social security schemes. Those women not included in occupational pension schemes and forced to rely on the state may still find themselves the subject of discrimination on matters such as pensionable age.

The vexed issue of state pensionable age – which is sixty for a woman and sixty-five for a man – is not affected by these changes. It is common for individuals to retire at state pensionable age though there is no legislation that requires it. In the past twenty years so-called early retirement has become more common, perhaps in response to rising unemployment or the altered expectations of employees. Nor is it unusual for employers to have a common retirement age for both men and women. The differential pensionable age is, however, a blatant example of sex discrimination either against men in requiring them to work longer or against women in depriving them of the opportunity to enhance their contribution record at a stage in their lives when they might find it easier to work. The explanation for the difference is that, in the past, state pensions were payable to husband and wife only when both had passed the age of sixty-five. Since men married women who tended to be younger than themselves this could cause hardship. This problem was dealt with by lowering the age when a woman might obtain a pension. Even though the law has been further amended so that the passing of pensionable age by either party allows a pension to be paid, the age differential remained largely as a result of pressure from women's groups.[63] The possibility of equalising the pensionable age has been considered on various occasions but it seems that legislation on the point has been avoided because of the costs and resentment involved.[64]

Even the European Community has been ambivalent on the issue of equalising pensionable ages since it has allowed states to defer any action needed to achieve equality of treatment, though currently a draft Directive is in preparation. Where the European Directives do appear to have made some impact is in relation to retirement ages. In *Marshall* v *Southampton and South-West Hampshire Area Health Authority (Teaching)*[65] women employed by the Area Health Authority were forced to retire when they reached the age of sixty. This was held by the European Court of Justice to be contrary to the Equal Treatment Directive. The plaintiff was particularly fortunate in this case since no attempt had been made to give this Directive legislative effect in England. The defendant, however, was a state body and was held to be directly bound by the terms of the Directive, thereby creating an anomaly between the rules governing state and private undertakings. This anomaly was removed by the Sex Discrimination Act 1986[66] which has had the practical effect, where the employer has a differential retirement age, of allowing women workers to choose between retiring at sixty or remaining in employment until whatever age men are expected to retire which is usually sixty-five. The Social Security Act 1989 does not affect this provision to ensure equal treatment as regards retirement age. In contrast, the equalising of the age at which men and women receive their state pensions, equal pensionable age, is likely to be an issue for some time to come. As *James* v *Eastleigh Borough Council*[67] demonstrates, other privileges can depend on this issue. Indeed, there might be the anomalous situation where the differential in pensionable age does not amount to discrimination but its use to govern the availability of other benefits does.

The costs of child care

Besides the deductions made from a working woman's salary in respect of such items as tax, national insurance and pension provision, meeting the cost of child care whilst she is at work may substantially reduce her disposable income. Some women have campaigned for tax relief on payments made for child care. This would mean that a woman who spent £1,000 a year on child care could earn that amount in addition to her personal allowance and not have to pay tax on those sums. This solution is defective in that not every woman pays for her child care, since it may be provided by members of the family such as grandparents or her partner.[68] A more fundamental criticism is that such a scheme favours those women who earn sufficient to pay for a nanny or childminder. In contrast, a woman who cleans part-time in the evenings when she can leave her children with her husband would seem to have nothing to gain. A better solution might be to raise the level of child benefit which is a non-taxable sum paid in respect of children under the age of sixteen.[69] One advantage of child benefit is that it normally goes directly to a mother and payment is not dependent on the making of contributions or means-testing. Therefore the benefit has a high take-up rate. The present government has, despite opposition, frozen child benefit on the basis that it is paid to many individuals who have no need of it. Instead, the government has chosen to enhance benefits that are targeted at those who in its view most need help.[70] Any increase in child benefit and its use to offset the costs of child care seem highly unlikely, which is regrettable, since such a scheme would allow women a choice. Those who choose not to enter paid employment could regard it as a payment by the state for their time spent on child care. Those women in paid employment could use the money towards the cost of child care.

An alternative solution to the problem of child care might be for the state to provide nurseries for pre-school age children. Arguably, this measure would help not only those who choose to work, but all mothers. Such a course of action would involve considerable expenditure and no state has infinite resources at its disposal but has instead to decide on its priorities in allocating public funds. Other European countries, however, do find it worthwhile to provide such facilities and seem to regard them not only as benefiting mothers but as enhancing the development of pre-school age children.[71]

Given the falling numbers of school leavers entering employment in the 1990s and the increasing need to encourage women back to work, child care is currently a topical issue with government being urged to take action on the matter.[72] At present the government's response is to press employers to provide facilities for their employees whilst making little provision itself. The grudging concession in the 1990 Budget that a woman earning over £8,500 a year will no longer pay tax on any contribution her employer makes towards subsidising the cost of workplace nursery places, will benefit few women. Indeed a recent survey of 1.1 million working women discovered that 0.02 per cent (198 women) had had children in employer provided creches.[73] In this manner, the tax and benefit system, far from offering a woman an incentive to work, perpetuates the stereotype of a woman whose place is in the home.

In this discussion of how the taxation system and the benefit system affect the working woman it has emerged that on the whole women are treated poorly. Matters can be improved to some extent by insisting that men and women are treated equally. However, the distinctive working patterns of women ensure that they cannot gain a great deal from simple equality of treatment. What seems to be required is a complete reassessment of the way in which benefits in particular are distributed. Special concessions may also have a part to play but these, such as tax relief on the costs of child care, need not be aimed specifically at women. Some women also need to be convinced of the sense of contributing towards future benefits such as pensions. They may prefer to undertake certain types of work, for example work at home, because there is less likelihood that deductions will be made. In one sense their cynicism regarding the taxation and benefit system may be well founded since as it is presently structured it takes little account of women's needs.

Chapter eight

The mechanics of equality

The laws which demand that working women should be treated equally with men, that men and women should be paid equally and that women should not be prejudiced in their working lives by pregnancy and childbirth are, despite their complexities, merely translating into specific duties and correlative rights the underlying notion of the elimination of discrimination. Leaving aside for the moment the question of whether eliminating discrimination is sufficient to achieve equality of opportunity, or indeed whether it is feasible to do so using the rather blunt weapon of legislation, there remains an issue which is crucial to an assessment of the law's impact on working women. Given the existence of a body of law which, however inadequately, purports in many cases to alter behaviour by imposing a policy of non-discrimination, there must be ways and means of enforcing the rules against the ignorant, the hesitant and the plain unwilling. This chapter aims, therefore, to examine what might be called the mechanics of equality: the structure, operation and efficiency of the system created to facilitate the working of the laws designed to benefit women, with particular reference to the legislation against discrimination.

If the mechanics of equality are defective, the impact of the law is fundamentally undermined. A system of enforcement and sanction is necessary for the implementation of law. Those who actively oppose the law and those who would prefer to ignore it must be compelled into obedience by processes which may range from education and conciliation, through to negotiation, litigation and punishment in the form of compensation to a successful complainant. Those who are willing to comply with the law may not need punishment as a spur to obedience but do need to know what, precisely, the law requires. From the victim's point of view this raises a number of issues.

Access to remedies should be readily available, well publicised and straightforward. The injured party should have access not only to the institution able to grant redress but also to someone with the expertise necessary to give advice where needed.

The procedure or process whereby remedies are granted should also be as straightforward and as cheap and speedy as possible. Again, the victim of the alleged discrimination should have access to assistance and support.

The remedies available to a successful complainant should not only be aimed at compensating the victim in a way commensurate with the injury suffered but should also deter a repetition of the unlawful act. One way to achieve deterrence is to ensure a level of compensation which is more than nominal and a system of enforcement which provides for further significant sanctions against non-compliance.

Finally, it is arguable that the special nature of discrimination cases (including race discrimination), in which the individual manifestation is evidence of a wider institutional prejudice, calls for the availability of a class action which removes both financial and emotional burdens from the individual complainant.

These requirements are the minimum for an adequate rather than an ideal system of enforcement of anti-discrimination law. In examining how far the access, process and remedies currently available meet these standards, it is apparent that the machinery making up the system is crudely divisible into what Gregory has termed first the individual route and secondly the administrative route to equality.[1] Thus, in a case of allegedly unlawful sex discrimination, two aspects must be examined: the individual right to equal treatment and, also, the interest that various regulatory institutions have in the enforcement of the law. The principal example of institutional interest is the Equal Opportunities Commission though it is possible to identify other interested institutions such as the trade unions and local authorities. In order to reflect this the chapter is divided into individual complaints and institutional enforcement.

Individual complaints

The enactment of legislation requires decisions as to how the new laws are to be enforced and, in particular, whether responsibility for seeking enforcement should fall on the individual citizen or on a regulatory institution, whether that be a public body, such as a local authority, or a 'quango' such as the Equal Opportunities Commission, or indeed the state itself, as is the case with the criminal law. In general, in the civil law, enforcement and the pursuit of a remedy are left to the individual plaintiff. There are many cases where the justification for this is clear, particularly, say, in the general law of contract where one party to the agreement is in breach and the other is seeking redress. In other areas, however, the focus on the victim seeking an individual and personalised remedy is less readily explicable. This may be seen in the law of tort where a group or class of individuals has been injured in a rail disaster, for example, or as a result of the prescribing of a particular drug. In such cases it may be argued that it would be administratively more efficient and, from the point of view of the injured individual, less costly in terms of finance, time and emotional commitment if a remedy could be sought on behalf of the class or group.

There is no provision in English law, however, which allows for a group remedy by resorting to a 'class action'.[2] This is a general rule and is not peculiar to discrimination cases, but it is in precisely this context that a group or class action would prove invaluable. On a very basic level, it would relieve some of the burden of individual litigation as well as making victimisation less likely after a complaint. Equally important, however, the possibility of a group of women complaining of discrimination would emphasise that, although the effects of the discrimination are felt by the individual, it is the result of systemic values which operate in an essentially collective fashion. In a class action, as the concept has been developed in the United States of America, one court case disposes of the dispute between each member of the class and the defendant, thus avoiding numerous claims and reducing costs. Each member of the class is bound by the result and liable for an equal share of the costs. The concept of a class action is far from a complete answer to the inadequacies of the present English system. Nevertheless, the possibility of a system which places less emphasis on the individual is an attractive option, and would strengthen the role of the Equal Opportunities Commission, since it is via such a body that class actions would have to be instituted.

The enforcement of the anti-discrimination legislation currently depends to a large extent on the individual's willingness to complain. The Sex Discrimination Act 1975 creates a statutory tort for which damages are payable to the victim.[3] A woman who alleges discriminatory treatment, whether it falls under the Sex Discrimination Acts 1975 and 1986, the Equal Pay Act 1970 or the Employment Protection (Consolidation) Act 1978, must be prepared to take her case to an industrial tribunal and to withstand the response this may well provoke not only from the defendant employer, but also from others more peripherally involved, such as workmates, family and indeed the general public. In the context of the Race Relations Act 1976, which introduced the individual complaints procedure into that particular area of discrimination, one writer commented that:

The mind boggles at the almost lunatic kind of courage an ordinary black citizen would need to go into court on his own against lawyers employed by a large institution on which his future may depend.[4]

The same is, of course, true in the context of sex discrimination, as is graphically illustrated by the studies carried out into the operation of the industrial tribunal system.[5] Not only is there often an inequality of representation and resources between the individual complainant and the employer who is frequently a corporate body,[6] but the individual, even when represented, has to be prepared to challenge the opponent organisation. The choice of the 'individual route to enforcement' was a deliberate policy decision.[7] Legislation outlawing racial discrimination pre-dated the Equal Pay and Sex Discrimination Acts.[8] In particular, the Race Relations Act 1968 provided that an aggrieved individual could not pursue a remedy by going directly to a tribunal. The initial step was to complain to the Race Relations Board and the decision as to whether, first, the law had been infringed and, second, what action to take was for the Board alone. Critics of this administrative or institutional method of enforcement focused on the denial of access to the law suffered by the individual and on the unsatisfactory settlements and, by the time the Equal Pay Act was passed in 1970, it had been decided to adopt an individual complaint system under which the law was enforceable by the victim of the discrimination. Of course this too has its drawbacks, the most obvious being that, in relying on the individual, the system for eliminating discrimination depends on individual initiative: if nobody complains, nothing happens.

The haphazard nature of such individual initiative was recognised in the White Paper which preceded the Sex Discrimination Act 1975, and which attempted to make the best of both the institutional and the individual mechanisms by allowing individuals direct access to tribunals and establishing the Equal Opportunities Commission (EOC) which could assist and represent complainants but which also had a much wider role in the elimination of discrimination. The success or otherwise of the EOC will be examined in the next section, but it is important in this context to note that, even where the EOC does adopt a case, the woman remains on the front line, as the complainant seeking compensation against the employer. The EOC has itself pointed out the deficiencies of the individual complaints procedure. In a 1989 Consultative Document, *Review of the Equal Pay Legislation*, it proposes a power for tribunals to hear representative cases to avoid the need for multiple applications.

The individual route to the enforcement of equality was a legislative compromise, as was the forum within which these cases should be heard. It would have been possible to set up special tribunals to deal with issues of discrimination but instead the decision was to use the existing system of industrial tribunals, and so bring discrimination within the mainstream of employment law. Industrial tribunals first appeared in 1964[9] and were envisaged as an ideal mechanism for dispensing accessible, speedy, informal and cheap justice. They are comprised of a legally qualified chairman (*sic*) and two lay members, drawn from the two sides of industry (management and labour). Once created, the industrial tribunals became the repository for more and more employment cases as the explosion of legislation in that field continued through the 1960s and 1970s. Tribunals now hear cases ranging from unfair dismissal, redundancy, maternity rights and, of course, cases of race discrimination, sex discrimination and equal pay. Since so much depends on the individual right to a remedy under the various pieces of equality legislation, it is instructive to ask how appropriate a forum the tribunals are, before examining the particular problems faced by complainants using them.

The industrial tribunals

It has been argued that keeping discrimination cases in the general body of employment law has certain advantages. In 1987 a report on the workings of the industrial tribunals by Justice[10] noted that the Commission for Racial Equality had proposed a specialist discrimination division within the tribunals. Apart from the practical drawbacks (for example, applicants having to travel further to specialist centres or specialist members travelling around the country), the report suggests that such specialisation could lead to the marginalising of discrimination, as has happened with immigration appeals. It could also encourage sensationalism in the media, according to the report, with an adverse impact on race relations and equality.

Whilst there is force in these reservations the advantages of keeping discrimination in the mainstream may yet be outweighed by the very real disadvantages. Investigations into tribunal procedures and decisions have uncovered ignorance of the law, errors in decisions, lack of expertise in tribunal personnel and over-reliance on concepts which are peculiar to unfair dismissal rather than discrimination. Applicants, even when successful, have recorded levels of dissatisfaction with procedures and awards such that one has to question whether the law is even beginning to address the problems faced by many working women.

It is part of the thesis of this book that the laws which affect working women should be seen not only in a social context but as different strands making up a single, if rather tangled, web of legal rules. On that basis, the separation of equal pay cases or of discrimination in recruitment from a case where a pregnant employee is unfairly dismissed or otherwise penalised is not necessarily an attractive or logical solution. Nevertheless, the interests of working women are not best served by the system of industrial tribunals as they are currently comprised and conducted. Some of the most damning indictments of the tribunals are contained in two studies by Alice Leonard.[11]

In *Judging Inequality*[12] Leonard analysed tribunal decisions relating to sex discrimination and equal pay during the three-year period 1980-82 and interviewed the whole range of people who are involved in such cases, including the parties, lawyers, chairmen of tribunals, panel members and experts from the EOC. The findings were depressing in the extreme, showing incomprehension or even ignorance of the law leading inevitably to wrong decisions. Apart from errors relating to the scope of the legislation or the types of compensation available, Leonard found a misunderstanding as to the irrelevance of motive in discrimination claims, with tribunals commenting not on the fact that a woman had been treated less favourably but rather on the benevolent nature of the employer's intentions and questioning why the claimant had seen fit to bring the claim in the first place. The influence of the unfair dismissal legislation could be seen in the substantial number of cases where the tribunals were not concerned simply with less favourable treatment but with whether the employer had acted reasonably as would be the case in a complaint of unfair dismissal. The use of the wrong legal standard, and indeed the general misapplication of the law, underlined one of Leonard's principal findings which was that the lack of expertise apparent in the tribunals could be attributed to a lack of opportunity to develop the necessary specialist knowledge. In England and Wales cases are assigned at random. As a result, over the three-year period the 215 hearings under the anti-discrimination legislation were distributed amongst 116 different chairmen and only seven chairmen heard more than one case a year. Amongst the lay members of the panel the situation was even worse: only five individuals sat on as many as one case each year. As Leonard points out, this kind of contact with what is complex legislation makes it virtually impossible to build up meaningful expertise through experience.[13]

The composition of tribunals has also been the subject of criticism. The tribunal always comprises a legally qualified chairman and two lay members, chosen for their experience of industrial relations from lists compiled by the TUC on the one hand and, on the other, by the CBI, local authorities, the NHS and the Retail Consortium. As is pointed out in the Justice Report:

The vast majority of Chairmen of tribunals and industrial members have never experienced discrimination on grounds of sex or race. They tend to be white, male, middle-aged and middle-class. Many of

165

them make traditional assumptions about the role of women in society and sometimes make unfortunate remarks about women or ethnic minorities in the course of proceedings.[14]

There is, currently, no legal requirement that in discrimination cases there should be a tribunal member of the same sex as the applicant.[15] In practice a tribunal administrator might aim to ensure the presence of a woman member, but this is far from the norm. Leonard found that, in England and Wales, one in ten sex discrimination cases and one in four equal pay cases were heard by all-male panels. That this does have a bearing on the ultimate decisions can be seen by contrasting results in cases heard by all-male panels with those which included a woman member. Thus, Leonard found that in equal pay cases in England and Wales, success rates were noticeably higher where there was a woman on the panel, both with full-time chairmen (40 per cent compared to 25 per cent) and with part-time (25 per cent compared to 8 per cent). In Scotland, where every panel has a full-time chairman and a woman, the success rate was 42 per cent.[16] The importance of having at least one woman on the panel stems from the fact that this is more likely to result in the tribunal as a whole having a greater understanding of the issues involved and of the very real distress caused by discrimination.[17] There is, however, another problem in relation to the way in which tribunals are constituted, again highlighted by the Justice Report:

> The expertise of the tribunals in industrial relations may actually run counter to the policy of discrimination law. The desire of industrial members to uphold existing norms, collective agreements and pay structures...can easily lead them to deny claims for equal rights which appear to threaten those norms, agreements and structures. The applicant may be challenging both the employer and the union.[18]

This would suggest that a tribunal as currently comprised is not the best forum in which to deal with discrimination and equal pay claims. A woman who seeks to rely on the legislation may be said to be challenging the status quo, not only generally, in terms of women's traditional roles, but also specifically in her profession or industry. This is a threat to the very institutions which the panel members represent. It is not clear, however, that women would fare any better in front of 'impartial' judges in a specialised tribunal. It may be that the answer is to keep the cases in the industrial tribunals but to ensure that both chairman and lay members are properly trained and appropriately experienced.[19]

The general problems which result from lack of expertise in the law and the composition of tribunals contribute to the poor handling of equality cases. There are, however, more specific difficulties that a woman may face and these may be considered in relation to access, procedure and remedies.

Access

The legislation depends on there being an individual ready to pursue her claim through the tribunal and possibly the appeal courts, and it is therefore essential to ensure that the individual has ready access to the machinery which will process the complaint. Here too the picture is somewhat gloomy. The first sign that the system may be failing is to be found in the statistics for the number of claims that are made to tribunals. There was a marked decrease in the number of equal pay claims, which numbered 1742 in 1976 (just after the Act came into force) and then fell steadily to a few dozen in 1983. The introduction of the 'equal value' claim saw another rise in the number of claimants but many of these stem from the same dispute and represent multiple applications against the same employer.[20] The number of claims under the Sex Discrimination Act have not shown quite the same dramatic changes, though the numbers have been on the increase in recent years.[21]

Given what is known about the persistent gap between the earnings of men and women and the continuing discriminatory practices in many areas (as examined in Chapters 5 and 6), these figures cannot be explained in terms of the success of the legislation in removing discrimination. A number of causes have been pinpointed both for reluctance to use the law and for the difficulties encountered by those who do choose that route. In a study entitled *Pyrrhic Victories*[22] Leonard investigated a number of successful tribunal cases brought under the Sex Discrimination Act 1975 and the Equal Pay Act 1970. Her earlier study, *Judging Inequality*,[23] had already established the importance of representation for claimants: those who were legally represented won considerably more often than those who were represented by trade union officials, lay people or those who represented themselves. In the later study the importance of expert advice and assistance also figures prominently and there was some evidence that lack of advice may discourage applicants at a very early stage, some of them commenting on the lack of general information about the legal process.[24] Since legal advice and representation appear to confer a significant advantage on the individual applicant, this raises the question of the availability and – inevitably – the cost of such representation.

The tribunal hearing is adversarial and it has been suggested that the system works best 'where both parties are well represented and have equal access to resources'.[25] Employers are more likely to have access to legal representation than are claimants, leading to 'unequal representation'. The results of this inequality are striking. According to

Leonard,[26] where both parties had legal representation, the applicant success rate was 46 per cent, but where the employer was represented and the employee self-represented, the applicant success rate fell to 23 per cent. It has been calculated that legal advice and representation at a one-day hearing outside London could cost up to £700.[27] When compared to the level of compensation commonly awarded, this figure puts such help out of the reach of many – unless, that is, legal aid were to be available. The Benson Commission on Legal Services in 1979[28] recommended that, where legal representation is needed, legal aid should be available. Apart from some limited assistance prior to the hearing under the so-called 'green form' scheme, legal aid is not available in tribunals.[29] Even if legal aid were available, not many applicants would benefit because of the capital and income limits. Married women in particular would be unlikely to qualify since family income is used to decide eligibility.[30] Access to legal aid would not, in any event, guarantee access to lawyers with the necessary expertise in a very complicated area of law.

Legal representation or self-representation is not the only choice. The other principal sources of assistance are trade unions and, of course, the EOC. In the case of trade unions, Leonard's research suggested that the availability and quality of assistance varied considerably,[31] but where the union was supportive this seemed to make a real and positive contribution to the applicant's pursuit of a remedy. Those applicants with experience of the EOC also gave a variety of responses, though perhaps most worrying are those who did not even approach the EOC. Adoption of a case by the EOC can involve assistance ranging from the giving of advice to the provision of legal representation including the assumption of costs. Such support is not, however, available universally. The EOC is not in a position to help all potential applicants and many requests for assistance are rejected. Unfortunately, there is no statutory obligation to explain such rejections and a discouraged complainant may assume the case is weak, whereas help may be denied for some other reason, for example, lack of EOC resources.

Apart from the lack of information as to how to proceed, the cost of bringing a case is daunting to many potential applicants. In this context one can only despair at the provision in the Employment Act 1989 which allows for an extension of powers in relation to pre-hearing reviews. Originally, it was most unlikely that an unsuccessful applicant to a tribunal would have to pay the 'costs' of the hearing. Such awards were made only in 'vexatious and frivolous cases'[32] but in 1980 this was extended to cover a party who acted 'unreasonably' – a charge which some judges and chairmen might feel able to make about 'trivial' complaints of discrimination. Also, pre-hearing reviews were introduced to allow for a preliminary consideration of the case.[33] If the case is considered to have no reasonable prospect of success, the party concerned may be warned that continuing could result in an award of costs being made against them at the full hearing. Even as it stood that procedure was criticised, but the Employment Act 1989 goes further and makes it possible in section 20 to ask a party who wishes to continue after an unfavourable decision in a pre-hearing review to pay a deposit of up to £150. Access to the law is thus made even more subject to one's ability to pay.

A final comment on access to the tribunal hearing concerns the influence of the Advisory, Conciliation and Arbitration Service (ACAS). In claims under the Sex Discrimination Acts, the Equal Pay Act and the Employment Protection (Consolidation) Act 1978, the parties have access to the services of ACAS conciliation officers. Because of the relatively small number of claims brought under the anti-discrimination legislation, the ACAS personnel are more used to the kind of conciliation which is appropriate in unfair dismissal cases. The task of the conciliation officer in those circumstances is to be absolutely impartial and to attempt, by exchanging information and stressing the common ground between the parties, an agreed settlement which in practical terms means a compromise. There is considerable evidence to suggest that such conciliation is inappropriate in discrimination cases, not least because such compromises dilute the absolute standards required by the legislation:

> Equal pay means equal pay and not a bargained reduction in the current differential between men and women, yet the latter, if attainable, will occasionally form the basis for a settlement....[T]here is a central contradiction within the discrimination legislation in this respect which arises when undilutable standards are demanded on the one hand and out-of-court settlements on the other, channelled through officers whose working habits are determined by other employment legislation of a very different colour.[34]

By and large the role of ACAS in this area is seen as a negative rather than a helpful one. Leonard noted[35] that most comments about ACAS were uncomplimentary and some of the claimants (and, it must be remembered, these were successful) stated that the ACAS officials were discouraging. Similar criticisms of ACAS have been made elsewhere,[36] not only in relation to sex discrimination, and it underlines yet again that the applicants who get as far as a tribunal hearing are clearly only a small proportion of those suffering from discrimination – they are the most determined, the most committed and, in the majority of cases, the best supported and assisted by lawyers, union or the EOC.

A further problem with the attempt to conciliate prior to hearing is one which applies beyond the context of discrimination. Since conciliation officers are charged with a duty of impartiality, it is not part of their function to advise on the merits or otherwise of proposed settlements. As a result, the involvement of ACAS does nothing to restore the inequality of representation as between the parties and thus the 'relative disadvantage of the...applicant is perpetuated, not ameliorated, by the neutral stance required by ACAS in conciliation'.[37]

The overall picture of access to the law for a victim of discrimination is far from encouraging. Some brave souls do, however, find themselves in the tribunal hearing. What fortunes await them there?

Procedure in the tribunal

It was always intended that industrial tribunals should be a quick, cheap and informal system of enforcing the law.[38] The very fact that legal representation seems now to be so crucial is an indication that, quite apart from time and cost, tribunal proceedings can be far from informal. A criticism often heard is that industrial tribunals have become overly 'legalistic'. In so far as the tribunals are part of the legal system and are called upon to interpret and apply highly complex legislation, it is perhaps inevitable that a degree of 'legalism' is present in the arguments and in deciding the case.[39] This is a somewhat different issue from the legalism or formality which may manifest itself in the way the proceedings are conducted. There are, of course, rules regulating tribunal procedures, but for applicants what may matter most is the atmosphere in the tribunal, particularly to self-represented applicants who may be faced by the respondent employer plus legal adviser(s). Much can depend, therefore, on the attitude and behaviour of the chairman and whether he or she is sympathetic to an often bewildered and intimidated applicant. In Leonard's study, *Pyrrhic Victories*, several of the applicants were favourably disposed to the tribunals: 'Attending the tribunal was nerve-racking although the committee were very patient and listened to both sides with equal attention.' Others were not so impressed: 'The tribunal is intimidating, legalistic and patronising.'[40]

It may be that specialist chairmen and members who build up experience in discrimination cases could ameliorate the excesses of a formal and over-legal atmosphere. There are, however, certain aspects of procedure which would require legislation if they were to be changed.

Burden of proof and discovery of documents

The phrase 'burden of proof' refers to who has to prove what in a court of law. In unfair dismissal cases for example, it is for the employer to prove to the tribunal that there was a reason for the dismissal and that it falls within the specified permissible reasons. It is then the role of the tribunal to decide whether in all the circumstances the dismissal was fair. Where the allegation is that the employee has been dismissed for a reason which makes the dismissal automatically unfair – for example, dismissal on grounds of pregnancy – the burden is again on the employer to show either that it was for some other reason or that the employee fell within one of the exceptions to the provision (for example, that she was incapacitated by her pregnancy).[41]

In contrast, in discrimination cases the 'formal burden of proof lies on the applicant'.[42] The position is not entirely clear-cut, however. In equal pay cases, for example, once equal pay for equal work has been established, the burden shifts to the employer to establish the defence that the differential is not based on sex. Similarly, in claims of indirect discrimination, once a requirement or condition with disparate impact has been shown, it is for the respondent to show that the discrimination is justified. In cases of direct discrimination, however, the burden of proof rests squarely on the applicant to prove less favourable treatment on grounds of her sex.[43] The problems which this creates in practice relate once again to the inequality between the parties, this time in relation to evidence. The EOC has stated that:

> Questions of proof are crucial to the outcome of many claims under [the] Act. Only in very rare cases will the complainant have clear proof of unlawful sex discrimination (or victimisation). More often, complainants will need to rely on circumstantial evidence to lead the tribunal to draw inferences that the respondents treated them less favourably on the ground of their sex.[44]

Recognising that the burden of proof is a daunting prospect for unaided applicants and is likely to discourage the tribunal from inferring discrimination, the EOC has recommended that once the applicant proves less favourable treatment in circumstances consistent with discrimination on grounds of sex, a presumption of discrimination should arise which would require the respondent to prove there were other grounds for that treatment. The likelihood of this proposal being accepted may be gauged from the attitude of the United Kingdom government to the proposed Directive from the European Commission which would modify the burden of proof in equality cases. The proposal, already weaker than in its original form, would shift the burden to the employer to prove 'objective reasons, not connected with a person's sex, justifying a difference in treatment' where, and only where, the complainant establishes facts from which it appears probable that there has been direct or indirect discrimination. The United Kingdom government has blocked this proposal, which requires unanimous support, by use of the veto. It is unlikely, therefore, to respond sympathetically to the EOC proposals.[45]

171

The burden of proof is not a mere legal technicality. It is a very real problem facing an applicant, particularly one who is unaided, to adduce, marshall and present the kind of evidence which will persuade the tribunal. Matters are not helped by the reluctance of the courts to give guidance as to the kind of evidence which would be both helpful and admissible. Only recently, for example, has the Court of Appeal accepted that a complainant in a race discrimination case was entitled to discover and present to the tribunal the total number of applicants for promotion, classified by race, in the two years before his own unsuccessful attempt.[46]

This raises a further but connected issue: if the applicant is to prove her case, how does she get hold of the material to do so? At this point lawyers begin to talk about the rules relating to 'discovery' or the disclosure of documents. Even a moment's thought will reveal that in discrimination cases, perhaps more than any others, the respondent (employer) holds all the cards. The woman refused a job or promotion needs to be able to find out what went on in the process which led to her rejection. The equal pay claimant may need details of job descriptions and wages structures. To obtain such information the applicant may need the disclosure of sensitive, personal or even confidential information.

There is a procedure under the Sex Discrimination Act 1975, section 74,[47] where a person who thinks she may have been unlawfully discriminated against may use a questionnaire to gauge whether she has a worthwhile case. Responses are admissible in evidence and failure by the respondent to answer the questionnaire may be adversely interpreted by the tribunal even to the extent of inferring unlawful discrimination under the Act. Such a questionnaire can be helpful in providing a basis for a claim, since it can elicit a good deal of general information, but the questionnaire procedure cannot be used as a back door method of obtaining confidential information since in that respect it is governed by the normal rules of discovery. These rules are interpreted restrictively and therefore to the prejudice of the applicant. The principle is, simply, that either party may apply for discovery of documents but the tribunal may order discovery only if it is necessary to do so for disposing fairly of the proceedings.[48] The exercise of this power is subject to a decision of the House of Lords in *Science Research Council* v *Nasse* in which the importance of confidentiality was stressed and it was held that 'relevance alone, though a necessary ingredient, does not provide an automatic sufficient test for ordering discovery'.[49] Nevertheless, the House of Lords at least allowed that 'the Tribunal should inspect the documents. It will naturally consider whether justice can be done by special measures such as "covering up", substituting anonymous references for specific names, or, in rare cases, hearing in camera.'[50]

Such a discretion vests crucial power in the hands of the tribunal and adds a further obstacle to those strewn in the path of the applicant. Many cases depend on the disclosure of confidential information and it is certainly arguable that little damage would be done to notions of confidentiality if sensible steps were taken to preserve anonymity.

The problems associated with proof and discovery apply equally to sex discrimination and equal pay cases. There is, however, one specific aspect of procedure which has excited adverse comment from a range of sources. The introduction of the 'equal value' claim in 1984[51] brought with it a tortuous and complex procedure which threatens to defeat the purpose of the provision. Since the equal value regulations came into force in January 1984 there have been almost 4,000 applications, yet only about twenty have gone through the full procedure. The average time between requiring an expert's report and final determination is sixteen and a half months, though that seems to be increasing and one case took fifty months.[52] Apart from the length of time taken to decide the cases (blamed by the experts on the parties and by the parties on experts), the costs in these cases are frightening. The EOC estimates[53] that the applicant's costs in a relatively straightforward equal value complaint in an industrial tribunal, including solicitor, barrister and expert are around £7,500. The speech therapists' case went to the High Court on a preliminary point and, even before the tribunal considered referral to an expert, the applicants' costs were £60,000. Not surprisingly, applicants in these cases are far more likely to seek and to need the support of a trade union or the EOC.

The complexities, delays and costs of the equal value procedure have resulted in a number of recommendations for its reform. The EOC has made various suggestions, for example that the expert should be dispensed with and the claim decided solely by the tribunal or that claims should be removed from the industrial tribunal and referred to arbitration or to a specialist sitting as a judge. Another, alternative suggestion from the EOC is to use the expert as an adviser to the tribunal rather than simply a fact-finder. For its part, the Justice report echoes these options but recommends finally that independent experts should be removed from the procedure, each party being able to call their own expert. To counter problems of unequal representation, funds saved by abolishing the present system of publicly funded experts should be allocated to the EOC so that it could pay the costs of an applicant it was supporting. There is no guarantee, however, that this would shorten the time taken, nor would it benefit all applicants, since presumably not all would be EOC supported. The EOC may be tempering the ideal with the practicable when it finally suggests refining the present procedure, by, amongst other things, ensuring greater availability of experts and improving access to information.[54]

Most commentators seem to agree that the present procedures in tribunals, particularly in relation to over-formality, proof, discovery and the equal value claims have numerous drawbacks. Nevertheless, some applicants weather all of this and are, eventually, successful. But is it, in the end, worth the trouble?

Remedies

A discussion of the remedies available to applicants has to be seen against the background of the number of successful cases that are actually brought and this is, relatively, very few.[55]

The remedy for a successful equal pay applicant is, in theory, uncomplicated. Her contract is modified to take account of the finding[56] and arrears of pay may be claimed going back no more than two years.[57] The glaring defect, however, is that it is an individual remedy and here, as with indirect discrimination, it would make a good deal of sense if, instead of an individual employee bringing an individual claim, a claim could be made on behalf of a class of employee, thus providing a class or group remedy.[58]

Unlawful discrimination under the Sex Discrimination Act constitutes a statutory tort and, as far as the individual victim is concerned, the remedy is simply an award of damages to compensate for the wrong. Leaving other considerations aside, the potential inadequacies of such a remedy are obvious. A dismissed employee who claims under the employment legislation (including a woman dismissed because of pregnancy or denied the right to return after maternity leave) may likewise claim compensation but, importantly, the industrial tribunal may, if the complainant wishes, order re-employment. A woman who fails to get a job, or loses her job but claims under the Sex Discrimination Act, is largely confined to a monetary award since the employer cannot be ordered to employ or re-employ the successful applicant. These awards are rarely of a level which could be described as truly compensatory, which only serves to highlight the relative weakness of the sanction.

There are three orders that a tribunal can make in a sex discrimination case decided in favour of the applicant: a declaration which simply declares the rights of the woman; an order that the employer pays compensation, which may include compensation for injury to feelings; and a recommendation that the employer takes action within a specified time to obviate or reduce the adverse effects of the discrimination to which the complaint relates. The tribunal may make one or more of these orders as it considers just and equitable. If the employer fails without justification to comply with a recommendation, compensation may be awarded or, if already awarded, it may be increased.[59]

Compensation

The range of remedies available to the tribunal means that not all successful applicants are financially compensated, and indeed between 1980-84 only half of successful applicants received compensation.[60] The amount of compensation which may be awarded is subject to a statutory maximum, currently £8,925,[61] though most awards come nowhere near that. Leonard found for example that the average award in recruitment cases was £291.[62] A survey carried out by the Equal Opportunities Review showed that in 1987 the average award in sex and race discrimination cases was under £450: 'not a level likely to deter employers from discriminating'.[63] An effort to achieve a more realistic level of award was made by an industrial tribunal in *Marshall* v *Southampton and South-West Hampshire Area Health Authority (Teaching) (No. 2)*.[64] The successful applicant was awarded over £19,000, the tribunal having decided that the Sex Discrimination Act was in breach of Article 6 of the Equal Treatment Directive in that it did not provide an adequate remedy. The tribunal therefore ignored the statutory maximum and also awarded interest on the damages which amounted to over £7,000. In arriving at its decision the tribunal relied on a decision of the ECJ in which it was held that in order to comply with the Directive the member state must provide a sanction for unlawful discrimination which has a real deterrent effect.[65] The employers in *Marshall* appealed, but chose only to query the award of interest. The Employment Appeal Tribunal[66] refused to allow that award and, since the reason was that the existing remedy under the Sex Discrimination Act was sufficient to comply with the Equal Treatment Directive, it must be assumed that, if the Employment Appeal Tribunal had been asked to decide on the lawfulness of the statutory maximum, it too would have been held to be lawful.

The damages awarded for sex discrimination are meant to compensate the victim for foreseeable damage which causes loss, including pecuniary loss and future loss. If that were the whole story, the low level of awards would have to be explained on the basis of a low level of loss and it is true that Leonard found that recruitment cases (failure to be appointed) attracted lower awards than did cases of dismissal on grounds of sex, where presumably the loss was both more obvious (in recruitment, even a non-biased employer *might* have appointed someone else) and easier to calculate. However, the Sex Discrimination Act 1975 makes provision for damages to include compensation for injured feelings and these may be awarded whether or not compensation has been ordered under any other head.[67]

The assessment of compensation for pecuniary loss, including future loss, should be reasonably straightforward. The rules applied are the same as if the claim had been an action for damages in tort in the County Court.[68] Thus, if a woman has lost her job she will recover loss of wages to the date of the hearing plus an element for future loss based on a tribunal estimate (or guess) as to how long she will continue to suffer financially because of the discrimination. Where she has failed to get promotion the tribunal may estimate what would have been the likelihood of her being successful and how long she will now be in her present grade. This allows for a lump sum to be assessed which reflects the money she will lose over the period during which her lost chance is operative.[69]

No compensation at all is payable where there has been a finding of indirect discrimination but the discriminator did not apply the requirement or condition with the *intention* to discriminate. The discriminator may be aware of the effect of the practice, but will not have to compensate those affected if the intention was not to discriminate on grounds of sex. This provision,[70] mirrored in the Race Relations Act 1976,[71] has provoked a good deal of criticism since, as is pointed out by Ellis, 'the present law conveys the impression that, for some unexplained reason, the legislature condones unintentional indirect discrimination and it deprives the claimant of an essential remedy in a very significant class of cases.'[72] Ellis also suggests that intentional indirect discrimination is difficult to distinguish from direct discrimination where women are treated less favourably than men. This should perhaps be considered in the light of the reasoning in *James* v *Eastleigh Borough Council*,[73] where the Court of Appeal decided that direct discrimination depends on the employer acting overtly on the basis of sex or having a desire to treat one sex less favourably than the other. Where there is neither an overt reason based on sex nor a covert reason relating to the desire to discriminate there is no direct discrimination. According to the Court of Appeal there may, however, be indirect discrimination. Apart from the fact that such discrimination may be justified, even a successful claim will attract no compensation because by definition there will have been, on the court's reasoning, no intention to discriminate in the sense that the reasons for applying the criteria in question were divorced from the question of sex. It is fortunate that the House of Lords disagreed with the reasoning of the Court of Appeal and found direct discrimination. If upheld, the effect of the Court of Appeal's decision would have been not only to narrow the scope of direct discrimination but also to highlight the absurdity of refusing compensation to individuals who have felt the prejudicial effects of discriminatory policies whatever might be the motives behind those policies. There is no reason why, in the pursuit of the elimination of long-standing and sometimes unconsciously sex-biased practices, the victims should not be compensated. Among those calling for such a change is the EOC which now advocates that compensation should be payable in indirect discrimination cases irrespective of intent.[74]

Compensation for injury to feelings is expressly specified in the Act as a potential head for the award of damages.[75] Even though the attention of the tribunals is thus focused on the possibility of such awards it has taken a long time for them to approach anything like a worthwhile level, though usually some award is made. In *Hurley* v *Mustoe*, for example, the mother of four children who was unlawfully sacked from her waitressing job was awarded £100.[76] The victim of the discrimination must show she did suffer some injury to her feelings as a result of the discrimination. This is not often difficult since, because of the very nature of what happens, few tribunals would deny at least a degree of injured feelings. The problem, therefore, is to assess the extent of the injury and this assessment, it must be recalled, is done primarily by male, middle-aged and middle-class white tribunal members. Cases of sexual harassment provide graphic illustrations of the problems encountered. It is revealing to find a tribunal commenting adversely on the fact that a woman managed to put up with the harassment for quite some time,[77] but the nadir was reached in *Snowball* v *Gardner Merchant Ltd*[78] where the Employment Appeal Tribunal held that the woman's attitude to sex (her behaviour, her mode of dress) was relevant in deciding on the degree of injury sustained. As was pointed out in Chapter 5, this confuses, quite wrongly, a woman's attitude to consensual sex with her right not to be molested and harassed in her working environment.

In arriving at a figure for these awards the Court of Appeal has suggested that tribunals should try to steer a middle road:

> Awards should not be minimal because this would tend to trivialise or diminish respect for the public policy to which the Act gives effect. On the other hand, just because it is impossible to assess the monetary value of injured feelings, awards should be restrained. To award sums which are generally felt to be excessive does almost as much harm to the policy and the results which it seeks to achieve as do nominal awards.[79]

In a study carried out by the Equal Opportunities Review of cases decided between 1985-87,[80] it was found that in sex discrimination cases the average award for injury to feelings was £400. The lowest was £25 but, more encouragingly, the highest was £3,000 awarded on two occasions, each involving sexual harassment.[81] In a race discrimination case, *Noone* v *North West Thames Regional Health Authority*,[82] the Court of Appeal awarded £3,000 for injury to feelings, describing it as at the top end of the bracket. Isolated examples do not, however, predict a trend and the overall impression of the levels of compensation is that the awards continue to be low and in some cases derisory.[83]

One possible route to the award of higher damages, albeit within the statutory maximum, is via exemplary or aggravated damages. These are damages awarded in exceptional circumstances where the defendant has behaved in a particularly outrageous manner. Aggravated damages reflect the manner in which the tort was committed, for example, where the defendant has acted in a malicious or insulting way and has thereby 'aggravated' the plaintiff's injury. Such damages were awarded in *Alexander* v *Home Office*,[84] a race discrimination case in which a black prisoner in Parkhurst prison was awarded £500 for injury to feelings by the Court of Appeal. It was accepted that in arriving at a figure which will properly compensate the victim of discrimination, damages might include an element for aggravated damage which reflects the nature of the injury to the individual. Such an approach is welcome, though it should also be noted that, in discussing injury to feelings, the Court was of the opinion that it is likely to be of relatively short duration and be less serious than physical injury to mind or body. The transient nature ascribed to the injury to one's personal worth and dignity caused by such discrimination is questionable, to say the least.

The Court went further, however, in *Alexander* and held that, in appropriate cases, there is no reason why exemplary damages should not be awarded. These are not compensatory, but are meant to punish the defendant and indicate abhorrence of the behaviour and, of course, to deter further such conduct. The punitive nature of such damages blurs the distinction between criminal and civil law and this has caused judicial unease to the extent that their use has been restricted to three specific cases.[85] One of these is where the defendant's act has been calculated by him to make a profit which could exceed the damages that may be payable. This seems particularly relevant to discrimination where the employer might well calculate that the level of compensation payable to a female worker is so low that breaking the law is the lesser and cheaper of two evils. Unfortunately, the Employment Appeal Tribunal did not take the same view in a case which involved both race and sex discrimination, *City of Bradford Metropolitan Council* v *Arora*.[86] The Tribunal found, though not very convincingly, that the case did not fall within any of the permitted examples where exemplary damages may be awarded and, moreover, seemed concerned to indicate to industrial tribunals that exemplary, as opposed to aggravated, damages were not appropriate in discrimination cases. Accepting that such damages must always be rare, and must be awarded with a degree of circumspection, it still seems unfortunate, given the level of awards, that such a discretion should be removed from the tribunals. It is also not clear how the remarks of the Employment Appeal Tribunal can be reconciled with the views of the Court of Appeal in *Alexander*.[87]

The EOC has suggested[88] that, in an effort to promote consistency as between different tribunals and to achieve a realistic standard of award, there should be a basic minimum award in all cases where there is a finding of unlawful discrimination. The amount proposed is £500 (or in the case of employment, £500 or four weeks pay, whichever is higher). A compensatory award, including injury to feelings, should be additional to the basic award. Whilst this proposal would avoid the kind of nominal award which is all that some tribunals see fit to make, it would not necessarily deal with problems at the other end of the scale. Whilst the maximum level of compensation is set at £8,925[89] some deserving claimants will fail to be adequately compensated. This figure cannot be exceeded[90] and must, therefore, encompass not only financial loss but also non-pecuniary injury. It places constraints on what a tribunal may award for injury to feelings since there has to be room for 'actual' loss. This was expressly stated in the Court of Appeal in *Noone*[91] where £5,000 had initially been awarded for 'severe injury to feelings'. The Court of Appeal set the award at £3,000 since, given that at the time the maximum available compensation was £7,500, and given that it had to include not only injury to feelings but also actual loss and any compensation payable because of the respondent's failure to comply with a recommendation, £5,000 was outside the appropriate range. Quite apart from all the heads of damage that have to be accounted for within the £8,925 maximum, it is quite possible that the claimant's actual loss (that is financial loss) could exceed the £8,925 maximum if she is a highly paid employee who has lost her job or failed to be appointed.

Few would argue with Leonard's conclusion in *Pyrrhic Victories* that 'it is now clear beyond doubt that the level of many tribunal awards is grossly insufficient either to compensate the victims of discrimination or to deter its perpetrators'.[92] In her study she asked the successful applicants if they felt fully compensated. Of the sixty who responded only sixteen said the money had fully compensated them. The remainder commented on the low level of awards for injury to feelings, the disparity between the amount of the award and the distress and stress occasioned by the case and, significantly, the absence of any deterrent effect on the employer as to future conduct. It is true that despite the inadequacy of compensation 87 per cent of respondents nevertheless felt that bringing their cases had been worthwhile, either because it was a matter of principle or because it helped others or because they felt they had triumphed as individuals in the face of concerted opposition. Whilst this might suggest that applicants in discrimination cases are a particularly resilient and principled set of individuals it does not excuse the equivocal response of the legal system to their proven injuries. The inadequacy of compensation is, moreover, compounded by two further factors, also identified by Leonard: victimisation and enforcement.

The EOC has stated that 'the fear of victimisation, particularly fear of dismissal, is a major deterrent to many individual victims of discrimination taking proceedings to enforce their rights'.[93] Though the respondents in Leonard's study had clearly not been deterred they experienced deterioration in relationships with employers and fellow workers, some to such an extent that they left their jobs. Others were dismissed. Difficulties continued, in that a proportion of those looking for new jobs experienced problems which they attributed to the case they had brought. The 1975 Act specifically provides[94] that victimisation is unlawful discrimination. The EOC has argued that in cases of victimisation the basic award (in addition to any compensatory award) should be £1,000. This could require a woman to complain first that she has been discriminated against and then, later, to complain about victimisation. Such a remedy may not be sufficient to encourage women to bring complaints of discrimination to tribunals in the first place nor to deter employers from victimising them for doing so.

One of the most serious shortcomings of the present system is undoubtedly the procedure for enforcing an award. In Leonard's study,[95] 46 per cent of respondents reported difficulty or delay in enforcing the tribunal's decision. Less than half had received their compensation within two months of the decision. In England and Wales, tribunals have no power to enforce their judgments. If an employer delays or even refuses to pay, the applicant must again resort to law, but this time to the County Court. At this stage, the applicant is unaided, since the EOC does not pay for assistance in collecting the compensation. The applicant may need legal representation and will have to pay the fees incurred in the County Court proceedings. Bearing in mind the adverse levels of compensation this is quite clearly not only unjust but invites disrespect for the law. The EOC has proposed[96] that decisions of industrial tribunals should be treated as County Court judgments, which would mean that they could be enforced without a fee and that after fourteen days they would start to accrue interest, which might encourage earlier payments. Compensation is in many ways the most tangible and immediate of the potential remedies. The weaknesses of the enforcement system are, however, such as to make some applicants wonder why they bothered. The two other remedies do not, therefore, hold out much attraction to a potential complainant.

Declarations and recommendations

The industrial tribunal may, apart from awarding compensation, make an order which simply declares the rights of the applicant or may recommend that the employer takes action to deal with the discrimination. If the employer fails without reasonable justification to comply with that recommendation, the amount of compensation awarded to the applicant may be increased.[97] A declaration or recommendation may accompany compensation but, bearing in mind that a significant number of successful applicants are awarded no compensation, it is clear that for some successful applicants in sex discrimination cases their rewards appear meagre. In practice, certain individuals could derive considerable benefit from the non-pecuniary remedies since they should, in appropriate cases, see an improvement in their working conditions. The importance of this is underlined by what Leonard found to be the motivation of many applicants, who tended to be more concerned with establishing a principle and setting a precedent than with levels of compensation. Some applicants, however, are less likely to benefit in any real sense from a declaration or recommendation, because they are not *in* the workplace (for example, in recruitment and dismissal cases) and there is no power to order employment or re-employment.

Overall, the remedies available in sex discrimination cases are unsatisfactory and contribute significantly to the limitations on the role of the law in achieving equality. Not all the faults are exclusive to discrimination cases since some, for example delay in payment of awards, are found also in unfair dismissal complaints. At least in unfair dismissal, the tribunal has a discretion to order re-employment, even though this is rarely used, and there is always a basic minimum award of compensation.[98]

Institutional enforcement

Given the haphazard nature of individual complaints and what must now be acknowledged to be the inadequacies of the tribunal system and the remedies available, it is essential that there should be an alternative route to equality. From the outset it was envisaged that, as part of the machinery of enforcement, there would be a public body charged with the administrative task of promoting and securing equality between sexes. That body, the EOC, was to have 'a major role in enforcing the law in the public interest'.[99] A dual system was thus created which, whilst it allowed for individuals to be directly involved in the enforcement of the law and to receive compensation for injuries suffered, also provided for the possibility of a more coherent and far-reaching movement towards equality. Certainly the new body was given an inspiring list of powers and functions, but the success or otherwise of the EOC must be judged against the limitations imposed by judicial interpretation of those powers and the uneasy relationship between publicly funded bodies and their paymaster, the government.

The role of the EOC

The Sex Discrimination Act 1975 defines the duties of the EOC:[100] to work towards the elimination of discrimination;[101] to promote equality of opportunity between men and women generally;[102] and to keep under review the working of the 1975 Act and the Equal Pay Act 1970 and, when so required by the Secretary of State or when they otherwise think it necessary, to draw up and submit to the Secretary of State proposals for amending the legislation.

In order to fulfil these duties, the EOC is granted a number of statutory powers which relate to both the individual and the administrative aspects of the legislation. The EOC is, for example, empowered to provide assistance to individuals who bring complaints under either the 1975 or 1970 Acts, and that assistance may include advice and legal representation.[103] On the other hand, the EOC alone has the power to take action in respect of a variety of matters covering discriminatory advertisements, discriminatory practices, instructions and pressure to discriminate and also in relation to 'persistent discrimination'. More generally, the Commission is charged with carrying out the research and education necessary to further its objectives, with the review of discriminatory statutory provisions and with the issuing of codes of practice in so far as they relate to employment. The final power granted to the EOC appeared potentially to offer a positive opportunity for the Commission in the promotion of equality and the elimination of long-established discriminatory practices. The Act provides for the EOC to conduct formal investigations either at its own discretion or as requested by the Secretary of State, and as a result of such investigations it may issue non-discrimination notices which are legally enforceable. The history of the EOC's use of such formal investigations has not, however, proved to be a happy or productive one and the initial fears of certain politicians and judges that the EOC had been granted powers which were akin to those of the Inquisition seem in retrospect to have been grossly exaggerated.[104] Experience has shown that the powers which, on the face of it, appeared to be wide are in practice complex and drafted in such a way as to allow for judicial interpretation which effectively negates much of their potential usefulness. The judges are a crucial element in the success (or failure) of any legislative policy. The decisions in relation to formal investigations provide a classic example of the damaging constraints which the judiciary can so easily impose on the law. The major decisions are based not on the Sex Discrimination Act but rather on the Race Relations Act 1976 which, however, contains directly analogous provisions and suffers from the same complexities.

Apart from a formal investigation requested by the Secretary of State, the EOC may institute two other kinds of investigation. The first may be described as general in that there is no specific allegation of unlawful discrimination but the EOC may wish simply to examine a particular industry or profession. The second type of formal investigation depends on there being a named person or organisation where the EOC believes that discrimination contrary to the legislation has occurred or is occurring. Although this distinction appears unproblematic, difficulties begin even in the earliest stages of the investigation.

At all times the EOC must satisfy the requirements of the Act as they are interpreted by the judges. Section 58 of the Sex Discrimination Act 1975 provides that a formal investigation cannot take place until terms of reference have been drawn up and notice has been given of the investigation. In the case of a 'general' formal investigation, general notice is sufficient, but where the investigation relates to a named person, the EOC must notify those named. Furthermore, in the named person investigations where the EOC believes that unlawful discrimination is occurring or has occurred, the named person, in addition to the right to notice of the investigation, has the right to make oral or written representations, with legal representation if desired. In *R v Commission for Racial Equality ex parte London Borough of Hillingdon*,[105] the House of Lords held, on the analogous provision in the Race Relations Act 1976, that a named person must have a full opportunity to be heard before the full formal investigation can begin. The same case also established that the terms of reference of the formal investigation were invalid if they were wider than the Commission's actual belief or suspicion. The terms of reference must, therefore, be narrowly drawn to cover only those operations suspected at the outset as being unlawfully discriminatory, and must not be widely phrased so as to allow for a more general investigation into other aspects of the named person (or organisation or authority). Subsequently, the House of Lords held in *R v Commision for Racial Equality ex parte Prestige Group plc*,[106] relying on the *Hillingdon* decision, that, where a person is named, the Commission cannot conduct a general, exploratory formal investigation but it must have a belief that unlawful discrimination is present. In other words, once a person is named, the investigation must accuse that person of something. Not only does this necessitate a preliminary inquiry, thus causing lengthy delays, it also plainly flies in the face of the spirit of the law since it drastically curtails the scope and the usefulness of formal investigations. Both the EOC and the CRE have protested strongly against this interpretation of the law. The EOC has stated that the purpose of named person investigations was to allow an investigation into the possible causes of unequal treatment or barriers to equal opportunity in a named organisation, irrespective of a belief that the organisation might be committing unlawful acts: 'inequality is not necessarily the result of unlawful activity; it may simply be the result of ignorance or misunderstanding.'[107]

The current interpretation of the law seriously weakens the efficacy of the formal investigation. Recognising the crippling effects of the *Prestige*[108] decision, the EOC has stated that:

> one of the main purposes of an investigation is to establish whether or not unlawful acts have in fact occurred, not to confirm a preconceived conclusion. There are many situations which give rise to concern that equality of opportunity is being denied, for example where a high degree of job segregation between men and women occurs, but where in advance of an investigation, there is no evidence as to the reasons why this has come about on which a belief relating to unlawful acts could be based....The Commission proposes an amendment to make clear that the Commission can carry out an investigation into a named person or organisation for any purpose connected with the carrying out of its duties and reverse the Prestige decision.[109]

In the light of the recommended reversal of *Prestige*, the EOC is content to retain preliminary inquiries in named person investigations, since these allow clarification of the issues. Since the major disadvantage in the present preliminary hearing procedure is delay, the EOC has suggested a time limit of twenty-eight days.[110]

Once the preliminary stages are over, the EOC may move to the full formal investigation. Ironically, the legislation has less to say about how the full investigation should be conducted. In a named person investigation the EOC has the right to require information and evidence and this can be enforced by court order.[111] Again, in a named person investigation, that person has the right to make representations. The EOC is under an implicit general duty, as with all quasi-judicial bodies, to comply with the rules of natural justice which, simply stated, insist that everyone is entitled to a fair hearing before an unbiased tribunal. On that basis, the named person must at least have the opportunity to be heard.[112] Apart from such considerations the conduct of the formal investigation is not laid down by statute.

Once the investigation is complete the EOC must produce a report which is published or made available for inspection.[113] In the light of the findings the EOC may make recommendations to named persons as to changes in their policies or procedures with a view to promoting equality between the sexes and may also recommend changes in the law to the Secretary of State.[114]

If, during a formal investigation, the EOC finds that a person has committed, or is committing, unlawful discrimination contrary to either the 1975 Act or the Equal Pay Act 1970, it may serve a non-discrimination notice on that person under section 67 of the Sex Discrimination Act.[115] At this point the law yet again becomes complex and restrictive. The non-discrimination notice must be made in the prescribed way.[116] It requires the person not to commit further unlawful acts, and if, for example, this involves changes in practices, these changes may have to be notified to the EOC and other relevant persons. It may also require information to be supplied to enable the EOC to check compliance with the notice.[117]

Before serving the non-discrimination notice, however, there are a number of conditions the EOC must meet. First, the EOC must warn the person to be named in the notice that it is 'minded' to issue it and why. Secondly, that person must be given the chance to make oral or written representations within twenty-eight days and the EOC must take note of those.[118] If the EOC then decides to go ahead and issue the notice, the named person then has a right to appeal within six weeks against any requirement in the notice and, in the employment field, such appeals are to the industrial tribunal. If the appeal succeeds the requirement is quashed, though it may be replaced by another.[119] It was originally argued (in the context of race discrimination) that such appeals, coming at the end of such a lengthy and careful inquiry in which the 'accused' has had several opportunities to put his case, must be taken to be appeals against the precise requirements of the notice rather than the notice itself and therefore the findings of fact on which the notice is based. Nevertheless, the Court of Appeal held in *Commission for Racial Equality* v *Amari Plastics Ltd*[120] that a person served with a non-discrimination notice may challenge in court all the facts found by the Commission, which involves the CRE or EOC having to outline to the court the facts used to justify serving the notice. The recipient of the notice may then dispute those facts in a further hearing. The notice may then be quashed but, even if it is not, the whole procedure from preliminary inquiry to final notice is appallingly lengthy. In a frequently quoted remark in *Amari Plastics*, Lord Denning commented that he was 'very sorry for the Commission, but they have been caught up in a spider's web spun by Parliament from which there is little hope of their escaping'.[121] As Ellis pertinently states, the practical outcome of the right of appeal is that the Commission is sometimes better advised not to issue a non-discrimination notice 'but instead to rely simply on the publication of the report and its attendant publicity, which may well cause embarrassment to those named in it' since there is no appeal against the report.[122]

The EOC must maintain a register of any non-discrimination notices issued and allow public inspection of this.[123] Within five years of a non-discrimination notice becoming final, if it appears to the EOC that the person concerned is likely to commit more unlawful acts of discrimination, it may apply to the County Court for an injunction to stop such acts.[124] In the context of employment, even if the EOC suspects breaches of the notice, it cannot seek an injunction without first applying to an industrial tribunal for a finding of unlawful discrimination.[125] The injunction must be very carefully worded: one that is too wide will be overturned by the appeal courts.[126]

Thus, the formal investigation procedure ends as it began in tortuous complexity. Moreover, at the end of this 'cumbrous and unsatisfactory procedure'[127] all the EOC can do is to make recommendations, not orders,[128] and even if there have been individuals injured by discrimination there is no power to order that they be compensated.[129] It is not surprising, then, that the EOC has made very little use of its powers of formal investigation, nor that, even where it has embarked on such an exercise, the results have been mixed.[130] Only three non-discrimination notices have been issued, although the EOC would point out that these are not always necessary since the organisation concerned may agree to measures which eliminate discrimination. The drawback in such cases is that the lack of publicity afforded to such negotiated informal settlements fails to achieve a wider educative or deterrent effect.

In its 1988 proposals *Strengthening the Acts* the EOC made it clear that it wishes to retain the right to conduct formal investigations rather than (as the CRE suggested) transfer decision-making powers, as opposed to evidence gathering, to an independent body. This must be seen, however, in the context of the amendments which the EOC proposed. Without those changes, such as the reversal of *Prestige*, and given the restrictions on the EOC's power to bring legal proceedings in its own name, the EOC appears to be an organisation charged with a whole range of duties by a legislature not prepared to grant it realistic powers to carry out those obligations.

Apart from formal investigations, the EOC has a variety of other functions,[131] one of the most important being assistance to individual complainants. Under section 75 of the 1975 Act, the EOC may assist individuals either where the case raises a question of principle or because it is unreasonable to expect the applicant to deal with it unaided or because of any other special consideration. The assistance may range from advice, trying to settle a case, providing for advice from lawyers or providing for legal representation. Money spent in this way may be reclaimed from a successful applicant's compensation. This power has proved valuable, not only for those individuals who have benefited but also because it has allowed for clarification of difficult or complex points of law which in turn has clarified the EOC's task of the promotion of equality and reform of the law. Of course, the numbers who can be assisted are limited both financially and administratively and a good many applications have to be rejected. Nevertheless, by pursuing 'test cases', the EOC, under section 75, has made a real contribution both to the development of the law and to general awareness of its requirements.[132] It is rather ironic that section 75 which was initially seen as an adjunct to the major weapon of formal investigation has become, because of the drawbacks of the investigatory procedures, a relatively important means to enforcement.

The EOC's role in the institutional or administrative route to equality is beset with problems. Some of these undoubtedly result from the way in which the judges have seen fit to interpret the law and so constrain the powers of the EOC. On the other hand, the EOC shares many of its difficulties with the CRE and it is certainly a possibility that at least some of the defects currently identifiable stem from the nature of the institution itself. The EOC is a quango: a quasi-autonomous non-governmental organisation. Such bodies have a number of advantages from a government's point of view. They are seen to be separate from government which means that, having set them up, the government can deny involvement in unpopular policies adopted by the quango in pursuit of its functions. On the other hand, real control is retained by the government via funding arrangements and the power to control personnel.

The composition of the EOC and the way its Commissioners are appointed has attracted a good deal of criticism. There are usually fourteen or fifteen Commissioners, a number which must militate against consensus and the identification of a coherent strategy. Of the Commissioners, three are nominated by the CBI and three by the TUC. Perhaps inevitably, these two groups have tended, at least in the past, to retain some loyalty to their 'constituency' above their commitment to equality.[133] The other Commissioners may be described as 'independent' but have not generally been noted as leaders in women's issues. The 1975 legislation provides for the appointment of a chairman (*sic*)[134] and deputy chairman by the Secretary of State, and the EOC may itself appoint officers and staff subject to consultation with the Secretary of State and the Minister's approval as to the numbers employed, their remuneration and terms and conditions of employment. Despite this ministerial involvement the EOC is not a servant, agent or emanation of the Crown and the Commissioners and other staff are not civil servants as such.[135]

The EOC is funded by central government and must account annually to the Secretary of State,[136] though the Commission decides, subject to certain limitations, how the money should be spent. The relationship between the EOC and central government is a rather uneasy one. The EOC owes its funding to the government and the appointment of its personnel is overseen by government. It is subject, as are other quangos, to periodic governmental review. This does not mean that the EOC is always uncritical of the government and its policies (whatever the precise policies may be) but it is very easy for the government to ignore criticisms made by the EOC, particularly if the Commission itself lacks clear direction from within.

The picture that emerges of the 'mechanics of equality' judged from both the individual and the institutional standpoint is not an optimistic one. The laws are themselves inadequate in several respects but, additionally, the legislation has been interpreted in a way which seems quite contrary to any avowed policy for the elimination of discrimination. Reform of the EOC has been suggested as one way of improving the institutional aspects, for example by reducing the number of Commissioners and making more use of the legal powers which it now has. More importantly perhaps, it has been pointed out that while individual remedies remain unsatisfactory and while formal investigations are so ineffective, it is essential to *extend* the powers of the EOC so that it can act in its own name against those suspected of breaking the law, whether or not there has been an individual complaint. Giving the EOC direct access to the courts would lessen the burden on individuals while at the same time having the advantage of exposing in public the continuing discrimination which women face.

Extra-legal regulation

The EOC is the body most closely involved and identified with the promotion and enforcement of equality between men and women. There are, however, other institutional sources of persuasion and regulation, which, though they may lack legislative sanctions to coerce the unwilling, nevertheless can exert considerable pressure on those within their spheres of influence. This can be seen from the response to the calls for reform and the changes in policies which have emanated from the trade union movement and from local government.

The influence of the trade union movement has both an internal and external dimension. Internally, trade unions need to examine their own structures, rules and practices to encourage fuller participation by women at all levels of union organisation. Externally, when negotiating with employers over terms and conditions of employment, the unions must be astute in ensuring that discriminatory practices are not perpetuated and that the particular needs of women workers are recognised. In fulfilling their more general role as the representatives of the labour movement, unions have an important part to play, largely through the TUC, in the area of law reform and the campaign for changes in the working environment which will benefit all workers and women in particular.

Internally, the trade unions themselves acknowledge that there is still a long way to go before women can be said to have equal representation at various levels of union influence. In 1979 the TUC published its *Charter for Equality for Women within Trade Unions*, a ten-point plan for affiliated unions to help ensure equality of representation.[137] Recent surveys[138] have found, however, that women remain 'hopelessly under-represented' particularly at the level of national executive committees, conference and full-time officials. Moreover, representation was especially poor where women were in low-status jobs and particularly where their status was lower than that of the men in the union. The TUC has recommended that in order to deal with these findings positive action should be taken to encourage women to become full-time officers and that reserved seats should be established for women on committees where their representation is low.[139] Apart from this kind of general exhortation to do better, it has been recognised for some time that significant improvements are possible by attention to detail. It is, for example, not surprising that women's attendance at union meetings is low if those meetings are held at times or venues which make attendance impossible for women workers with domestic commitments. Such considerations, as well as the campaigning issues of equal opportunities, must be on the agenda of internal union reform. If working women cannot achieve real equality within their 'own' organisations it must severely weaken the seriousness with which employers would treat unions demanding equal rights for female workers.

When considering the record of trade unions in the struggle for equality between male and female workers, it is apparent that it is not unblemished. A trade union may find itself in a dilemma when the insistence on equal rates for women undermines well-established job hierarchies based on wage differentials. This is not an excuse for inaction but it is, undoubtedly, a problem which some unions have had to face.[140] Nevertheless, trade unions have recently been using the law with some success, and indeed in the midst of calls from both sides of industry for changes in the law following decisions such as *Hayward* and *Pickstone* only the unions have called for the law to be *strengthened*. The law on equal pay for work of equal value has been used by trade unions both directly, in terms of supporting claimants in tribunal cases,[141] and indirectly, as a lever in collective bargaining.[142] There is little doubt that constructive union assistance in such cases makes a vital difference to the individual claimant both financially and in terms of 'moral' support.

Clearly, if the trade unions mean what they say, they must carry this forward into collective bargaining with employers. This means not only negotiating for improved maternity rights, workplace creches, equal pay, job-share schemes and whatever else might be appropriate to their membership, but also ensuring that collective agreements already in existence and those that are negotiated in the future are themselves free from sex discrimination. The EOC has published a report[143] alleging that sex discrimination is widespread in collective agreements. Legislation to deal with this was included in the Sex Discrimination Act 1986, following a decision of the European Court of Justice that the United Kingdom was in breach of the Equal Treatment Directive because it failed to provide that provisions in collective agreements which are contrary to the principle of equal treatment are to be declared void or are to be amended.[144] The relevant law prior to 1986 was that contained in the Equal Pay Act 1970, section 3, which provided that discriminatory terms in collective agreements could be referred to the Central Arbitration Committee for amendment. That section was repealed by the 1986 Act and there is now no way of amending rather than striking out offending provisions. Moreover, the drafting of the relevant section in the 1986 Act (section 6) means that the remedy in respect of discriminatory collective agreements is now an individual and not a collective one. Apparently, the idea is that the union will have to rely on the threat of individual complaints to persuade the employer to negotiate a new agreement which does not discriminate. This ignores not only the problems inherent in the individual complaint system but also seems an unlikely solution to what is, after all, a *collective* not an individual problem. Under section 6 of the 1986 Act, sexually discriminatory provisions in collective agreements[145] are void and therefore of no effect.

In the light of what the EOC identified as widespread sex discrimination in collective agreements, particularly against part-timers, it is unfortunate that the collective machinery for dealing with this should have been dismantled. It is true that, while the Central Arbitration Committee was operating in this area, the courts circumscribed its powers in a fairly conclusive fashion, yet there is no reason why the Central Arbitration Committee procedure should not itself have been revised to take account of European requirements. Without such collective machinery the task for the unions who are disposed to act against discrimination in collective agreements is made more difficult.

There are many areas in which the trade union movement has paid more than lip service to equality, though it is as well not to get carried away by the rhetoric. As the composition of the workforce changes, unions are forced to look for support and for membership from different quarters. Unions which traditionally may not have recruited many women members are now instituting programmes to attract part-time and even casual employees. The growing participation of women in the labour market combined with the effects of the free market and deregulation make it more important – and more difficult – for the unions to recruit, retain and properly represent their membership, which is increasingly a potentially female membership.

The increasing involvement of trade unions in the promotion of equal opportunities has positive benefits for working women, not least because it lends collective strength to calls for an end to discriminatory practices and the reform of the working conditions enjoyed or endured by women. Trade unions which adopt these strategies will meet, of course, with different responses from different employers on these as any other issues. Certain sectors of employment have been more willing than others to adopt equal opportunity policies and to advertise themselves as equal opportunity employers (not only in relation to women, but also in the context of race and disability).[146] One sector of employment that adopted (or was advertised as adopting) such policies was the public sector and in particular local authorities. Press reports of what were alleged to be examples of local authorities going to extreme lengths to promote the interests of minority groups provided easy targets for a whole range of opponents.[147]

Apart from the equality policies which a local authority may choose to follow in relation to its own employees, it is possible for such large public bodies to have a significant impact on *other* employers by imposing conditions on those with whom it chooses to contract, and this is of growing importance as authorities increasingly use outside labour, on a contracted-out basis. Where a local authority decides that it will no longer employ cleaners to clean local authority premises but will use an outside contractor who will employ its own workforce, the local authority may decide that any firm which wishes to tender for the contract must provide evidence that it promotes equality between the sexes by ensuring, for example, equal pay and equal promotion chances. The loss of a chance to tender for lucrative public sector contracts will have an impact, in theory, on the practices of relevant employers.

The ability of local authorities to promote equal opportunities has, however, been drastically curtailed by the Local Government Act 1988, which effectively prohibits local authorities from taking into account 'non-commercial matters' when making decisions about the award of contracts, including drawing up approved lists of contractors, inviting tenders and making or terminating contracts. Non-commercial matters are defined to include 'the terms and conditions of employment by contractors of their workers or the composition of, the arrangements for the promotion, transfer or training of or the other opportunities afforded to, their workforces'.[148] The Department of Environment issued a circular in 1988 giving other examples of non-commercial matters including rates of pay and number or proportion of women to be employed. The effect is to make it impossible for local authorities to monitor contractors' policies or even to ask about them. An amendment to the Act as it went through Parliament allows authorities to operate certain vetting functions to enable them to comply with their duties under the Race Relations Act 1976[149] but no such amendment was permitted in relation to sex (or disability). Such restrictions are clearly destructive of any positive influence local authorities could have on employers who come into their sphere of influence. In the context of industrial relations and industrial disputes 'contract compliance' has undoubtedly been a thorn in the present government's side (for example, a refusal by local authorities to contract with non-union firms under threat of strike action from their own employees). Whatever one's views on the legitimacy of using economic pressure to further industrial or trade union influence, the arguments for or against the promotion of equal opportunities appear quite different. The law demands equality of opportunity and to forbid a public body to use its economic leverage to further the objectives of the law serves to underline the low priority given to sex equality – especially in the light of the exception made in relation to racial discrimination.

Chapter nine

Conclusions

This book set out to examine the laws which are of particular relevance to women in paid employment. There will always be debate between those who are sceptical about the power of the law to change society[1] and those whose legal training makes them reluctant to acknowledge the law's limitations or to dismiss the law entirely.[2] Nevertheless, it is worth attempting to assess how, in practice, the present laws impact on the lives of working women. If it appears that the law has little relevance or if it is found to be defective in its structure or operation, this has major repercussions, since much of the movement towards equality has been based to a greater or lesser extent on the existence of a programme of reform in which the law has an important supporting or indeed central role. This immediately raises at least two questions: is it realistic to rely on the law to achieve such change, and has the law been used as efffectively as possible?

Taking the latter point first, it is central to the arguments in this book that those who have created the legislative aids to achieving equality have confused or have at least given insufficient thought to their precise goals. The term equality is protean and complex. Eliminating discrimination and outlawing different treatment between men and women does not represent equality of opportunity because it does not and cannot address the fundamental disadvantages that women experience throughout their lives. To aim simply to eliminate discrimination and ensure equal treatment, as opposed to equality of opportunity, is tantamount to asserting that the Ritz is open to all – the availability of a facility does not mean that everyone has the wherewithal to take advantage of it. Thus, an employer who espouses an equal opportunities policy and advertises jobs accordingly is doubtless to be commended, but the policy is meaningless if no woman is in a position to apply because of the age limits imposed or the qualifications demanded or if the hours required rule out those with domestic commitments. Even the current law recognises this by allowing for the concept of indirect discrimination which has the potential to deal with wider, more complex

193

issues of equality, but which has never realised that potential because of problems of interpretation and application. Equal treatment, which is the guiding principle of the Sex Discrimination Act 1975 and the Equal Pay Act 1970, merely ensures that all may, theoretically, enter the race, but does nothing to recognise the handicaps carried by some entrants, some of which may be so severe as to prevent them reaching the starting line.

Neither equality of opportunity nor indeed equal treatment is possible where the law adopts a traditionally paternalistic or protective approach which entails that the protected individual or class is treated in a worse or more constraining fashion than those who are not so protected. Few obvious examples of such laws now remain but it might be argued that the attitude lingers on. In contrast, special treatment for women in the form of additional rights, positive action or positive discrimination might be said to advance the cause of equality of opportunity, but this is at the cost of equal treatment. In such circumstances the argument that according special treatment to women implies discrimination against men is clearly one that has to be faced. Certainly, where women are granted specific additional rights, which relate to the particular ways in which a woman's biology may be said to handicap her in the context of employment (that is, in relation to pregnancy, childbirth and connected matters), the measures are designed to recognise and to compensate for the handicaps. To a certain extent, programmes of positive action which are targeted at women to encourage them to undertake training or to participate in specific areas of employment where women have been traditionally under-represented do not have to work to the prejudice of men if women are simply encouraged to take advantage of what is offered. Full-blown positive discrimination which sets out to treat women more favourably, to the prejudice of appropriately qualified men, faces more difficult problems on both theoretical and practical levels, but in reality, given the present government's adherence to deregulation, the prospect of any kind of positive discrimination is unthinkable.

Even if a consensus were to be reached as to what might be attainable goals, the question still remains as to whether in practice the law can ever be a successful instrument of social change. The limits to the law were recognised and rehearsed in Chapter 2. In *Feminism and the Power of Law*,[3] Carol Smart provides a sustained, thought-provoking, but ultimately negative critique of the power of law. She sets out, in her own words, to 'marginalize law and to challenge law's over-inflated view of itself'.[4] Smart believes that 'it is important to think of non-legal strategies and to discourage a resort to law as if it holds the key to unlock women's oppression'.[5] Such antipathy to law as a possible route to change is overly dismissive. On the one hand, it is, admittedly, difficult to challenge the statement that 'there is a substantial and well-founded fear that legal power works better for (white, middle-class) men than for anyone else'.[6] On the other hand, neither can it be denied that the law has, in the past at least, contributed positively to the improvement of women's position in society in general and in the particular sphere with which this book has been concerned, that of paid labour. As Smart concedes:

> although second-wave feminists may be critical of first-wave liberal feminists for their emphasis on formal legal equality, and their apparent attempts to have women admitted to the male order, it is unlikely that we would willingly give up any of the legal reforms they achieved.[7]

The caveat that Smart attaches to this statement is that initially it was important to use the law to achieve 'equal rights' and thus remove the overt and legally imposed impediments which discriminated against women, for example in relation to access to the professions. Since the law no longer discriminates in this overt way, however, 'the rhetoric of rights has become exhausted, and may even be detrimental'.[8]

Our contention is that, whilst equality of opportunity is not achievable solely through the medium of the law, there is still an essential function for the law in the pursuit of that goal. The law purports to represent the values and mores of society at a given time. It is debatable whether the law merely reflects or actively promotes changing social beliefs through laws which permit or require certain behaviour, and which impose sanctions on those who do not comply. For present purposes, however, what is more significant is the belief that the law remains a valuable weapon in the wider armoury of those who campaign on a range of issues as diverse as abortion, divorce, freedom of association and sexual and racial equality.

There are two consequences which flow from an assertion of the importance of law as an indicator of what is regarded as 'proper' in society. First, laws should be comprehensible to as many people as possible and, secondly, they should be comprehensive enough to cover the widest range of factual situations which fall within the intended ambit of the law, without being so vague as to permit deviation from the goals. Even accepting the limitations of the law, however, the present legislation does great harm to the perception of law as a possible means for progress. The answer to the question of whether the law has been used as effectively as possible must be no. The legislation is prone to excessive technical complexity, while its application has demonstrated a defective realisation of potentially valuable concepts. There is no excuse for the horrendous complexities of the provisions which relate to maternity rights nor the protracted and labyrinthine procedure for equal value claims. Such provisions fail to assist those whom they are intended to benefit and, equally importantly, encourage the belief that the law is not 'user-friendly'. The way in which the legislation deals with indirect discrimination is an example of how the drafting of laws and their interpretation can provide opportunities to limit the usefulness of a particular idea. Permitting the employer to 'justify' such discrimination has narrowed the scope of what might have been an effective method of attacking long-established institutional bias. It took years for the courts to arrive at an 'objective' test for justification, which even now leaves scope for the forces of the market place to override the social good of equality.

Indirect discrimination has been particularly, though not exclusively, susceptible to the prejudicial effects of unsympathetic judicial interpretation which has been another constraining influence on the usefulness of the law. Not all judges and tribunal chairmen (*sic*) are unsympathetic to or ignorant of what the law could be achieving, but those who are can do immeasurable damage, not only to the individual in the case before them, but also to later applicants when subsequent decisions follow the earlier one (because of precedent) and even to potential applicants who are advised not to proceed on the strength of earlier decisions. The judges, however, could and occasionally do advance the cause of equality. This can be seen in cases such as *Pickstone* v *Freemans plc*[9] (equal value); *Hayward* v *Cammell Laird*[10] (equal value) or *Hayes* v *Malleable Working Men's Club*[11] (dismissal because of pregnancy). The converse is apparent in cases such as *Clymo* v *Wandsworth Borough Council*[12] (job-sharing); *James* v *Eastleigh Borough Council*[13] (sex discrimination) and *Reed Packaging* v *Boozer*[14] (equal pay).

If the law is not currently being used effectively, it has to be asked what changes would improve matters. Many of the proposals for reform have been noted in the relevant chapters but there are certain general points which are so fundamental as to bear repetition. The first is that the structure of the law is unnecessarily complicated. Whatever might have been the historical and political reasons for separating equal pay and sex discrimination, there is no longer any justification for this. The Equal Opportunities Commission has proposed a single Equal Treatment Act which would combine the two pieces of legislation. This would encourage a greater harmonisation of the concepts now used in both the present Acts, the most obvious being indirect discrimination, which is not expressly mentioned in the Equal Pay Act. It would also allow equal pay to take its place in the wider context of sex discrimination, if only to underline the deep-seated sex bias that women continue to face in many apparently neutral contractual terms and conditions.

Structure apart, there are legal procedures which are in great need of overhaul. A single, but important example is that which relates to the burden of proof which remains on the applicant in sex discrimination cases and which, given the present rules as to discovery of documents, can have a fatal effect on a claim. This could be changed. In other cases, for example where someone is dismissed because of trade union membership or non-membership (in other words discriminated against), the burden of proof is on the employer to show that there was some other reason for the dismissal. It is a serious defect in the Sex Discrimination Act that applicants must discharge the burden of proof, but it is one which the government seems intent on maintaining. The importance of simplifying procedures can be seen in relation to equal value claims. If such claims are ever to be a realistic remedy for the greatest number of women, it is essential to reappraise the role of the independent expert and to allow, if not class, then at least representative actions. It is vital that the individual route to equality is made more accessible and less protracted. Accessibility also depends on a recognition that tribunal proceedings should be eligible for legal aid at a realistic level, otherwise many potential claimants will be denied recourse to the law.

The legal profession itself is not immune from the need for reform, if only to ensure sufficient expertise in a difficult area of the law. Industrial tribunals hearing discrimination cases should include a specialist in the anti-discrimination legislation, though such a reform would not alter the composition of the higher reaches of the judiciary which remain almost exclusively white, male and middle-class.

A final important practical change that could be made relates to remedies. These should be re-examined in terms of the levels of compensation awarded and in respect of those occasions where a discretion to order re-employment or employment could prove a more convincing sanction. The question of remedies also raises the role of the EOC which requires not only a more sympathetic judiciary but also powers to bring cases in its own name.

These points relate generally to the question of whether the present law is the best that can be hoped for. There are, however, rather more fundamental issues that have to be addressed. Ultimately, the most essential requirement for the pursuit of equality in its widest sense is a genuine political will to achieve that goal as a matter of basic civil liberties. Without this will there can be very little progress.[15] The consequences of downgrading issues of equality are not all as obvious as underfunding of the relevant bodies or a reluctance to provide for proper child care facilities. When the government makes clear its attitude to equality by its repeated reluctance to take measures to bring this country into line with other European states, and when the changes that are imposed via Europe are enacted grudgingly, piecemeal and in the narrowest possible way, the message is quite clear that equality of opportunity or even equal treatment is not a social priority. When the system of minimum wage regulation is threatened and when contract compliance is outlawed it becomes quite clear that social welfare has given way to *laisser faire* and that the market rules through the mechanism of deregulation. The whole concept of equality of opportunity depends on a recognition that, left to its own devices, society does not organise itself in a truly egalitarian, non-discriminatory fashion. Women and others who face discrimination and prejudice can achieve true equality only if there is a sustained determination to order society in a way which facilitates that equality. The mood of the 1960s and the early 1970s has changed radically. Those who saw the passage of the first equality legislation have also witnessed the restrictive and negative implementation of those laws.

Behaviour and attitudes are not changed by the mere presence of laws on the statute book, but change is much more unlikely in the absence of a coherent comprehensive code, backed by sanctions that make law-breaking an unattractive option. The law could play a part in the improvement of the lives of working women. That it currently appears to do so little is due not simply to the inherent limitations of the law, but also to the indifference of those who formulate the laws and those who interpret them.

Notes

Chapter one   Women in work: law in a social context

1 See, for example, Wedderburn, K. W., *The Worker and the Law*, Penguin, 3rd ed., 1986.
2 On the maleness of law see Smart, C., *Feminism and the Power of Law*, Routledge, 1989, pp. 86–9.
3 Other organisations would include Women Law Teachers and the Women's Caucus of ECCLS.
4 O'Donovan, K., and Szyszczak, E., *Equality and Sex Discrimination Law*, Blackwell, 1988, Ch. 6.
5 Stang Dahl, T., *Women's Law*, Norwegian University Press, 1987, p. 29.
6 Ibid, p. 35.
7 See, for example, Leonard, A. M., *Judging Inequality*, Cobden Trust, 1987.
8 Pascall, G., *Social Policy: A Feminist Analysis*, Tavistock, 1986, p. 32.
9 Smart, op cit, p. 160.
10 Ibid, pp. 88–9.
11 See Ch. 7. Also Szyszczak, E., 'Employment protection and social security', in Lewis, R. (ed.), *Labour Law in Britain*, Blackwell, 1986, Ch. 13.

Chapter two   Theory and practice: the realisation of an ideal

1 HMSO, Cmnd 5724, 1974.
2 Ibid, para 21.
3 Pascall, G., *Social Policy: A Feminist Analysis*, Tavistock, 1986, p. 32.
4 David, M., and Land, H., 'Sex and social policy', in Glennerster, H. (ed.), *The Future of the Welfare State*, Heinemann, 1983, p. 144.
5 Coyle, A., 'Continuity and change: women in paid work', in Coyle, A., and Skinner, J., (eds), *Women and Work*, Macmillan, 1988, p. 8.
6 For a review of a range of these theories regarding the nature of law see Lord Lloyd of Hampstead and Freeman, M. D. A., *Lloyd's Introduction to Jurisprudence*, 5th ed., Stevens, 1985.
7 On the meaning of the term 'society' see the discussion in Allott, A., *The Limits of Law*, Butterworths, 1980, p. 24 and pp. 51–67.
8 For a consideration of this question see Roberts, S., *Order and Dispute: An Introduction to Legal Anthropology*, Penguin, 1979.

9 Hart, H. L. A., *The Concept of Law*, Oxford University Press, 1961, p. 89.

10 Cain, M., and Hunt, A., *Marx and Engels on Law*, Academic Press, 1979, p. 52. This gives the relevant extract from Marx's Preface to a *Contribution to the Critique of Political Economy*.

11 See the account in Collins, H., *Marxism and Law*, Oxford University Press, 1984, p. 22.

12 For an explanation of this theory and a detailed consideration of its application see Collins, H., op cit.

13 This is the so-called natural law approach which asserts that there are certain discoverable human goods and considers the relationship between them and law. For example, does a law which is in breach of one or more of these human goods cease to be binding? The most authoritative twentieth-century account of the natural law doctrine is to be found in Finnis, J., *Natural Law and Natural Rights*, Clarendon Press, 1980.

14 Cain, M., and Hunt, A., op cit, pp. 163–4, quoting the extract from Engels' *Anti-Duhring*.

15 The Soviet jurist Pashukanis suggested that law would disappear but would be replaced by administration. See Warrington, R., 'Pashukanis and the commodity form theory', in Sugarman, D. (ed.), *Legality, Ideology and the State*, Academic Press, 1983.

16 The idea is that a capitalist state is based on conflict whilst a communist state is based on consensus.

17 See, for example, Breugel, I., 'Women as a reserve army of labour' (1979) *Feminist Review* 12.

18 Though see Engels, F., *The Origin of the Family, Private Property and the State*, 1884.

19 In other words, law reform will achieve little and instead society needs reorganising on a totally different basis – that of communism. It is a separate issue whether those countries which purport to operate on this basis are true communist regimes and whether the communist system has more to offer women in the way of equal opportunities. In addition, the political changes currently being experienced by some communist states raise fundamental questions about the nature of communism, but not perhaps about the validity of Marxist theory.

20 Routledge, 1989.

21 Employment Protection (Consolidation) Act 1978, s. 64.

22 Stang Dahl, T., *Women's Law*, Norwegian University Press, 1987, advocates the construction of a feminist jurisprudence.

23 The most obvious example must be the Nazi regime in Germany. This has provoked a great deal of argument among lawyers over whether such 'laws' are in fact true laws. See Hart, H. L. A., 'Positivism and the separation of law and morals' (1958) *Harvard Law Review* 71, pp. 593–629; Fuller, L., 'Positivism and fidelity to law – a reply to Professor Hart' (1958) *Harvard Law Review* 71, pp. 630–72.

24 Fuller, L., *The Morality of Law*, Yale University Press, 1979.

25 Aristotle, *Nichomachean Ethics*, translated by Rackham, H., Heinemann, 1962.

26 Lukes, S., 'Marxism, morality and justice', in Parkinson, G. H. R. (ed.),

Marx and Marxisms, Cambridge University Press, 1982, p. 177.

27 Alternatively, it might have its own concept of justice. Much recent debate has focused on whether rights and socialism are incompatible. Campbell, T., *The Left and Rights: A Conceptual Analysis of the Idea of Socialist Rights,* Routledge & Kegan Paul, 1983.

28 Rawls, J., *A Theory of Justice,* Oxford University Press, 1973.

29 Ibid, p. 22.

30 Writers such as Jeremy Bentham used the utilitarian platform to point out that law was not 'mystical'. Instead, it was the product of human activity and could just as easily be changed by human activity.

31 Rawls, op cit, Ch. 2.

32 Rawls, op cit, Ch. 3.

33 Rawls, op cit, p. 302.

34 Rawls, op cit, p. 284 *et seq.*

35 Rawls, op cit, p. 285.

36 Rawls, op cit, pp. 83–90.

37 Rawls, op cit, p. 84.

38 Bedau, H., 'Inequality, how much and why?' (1975) *Journal of Social Philosophy* 6, p. 25.

39 See the essays in Daniels, N. (ed.), *Reading Rawls,* Blackwell, 1975, particularly those in Parts 1 and 2.

40 Lord Lloyd of Hampstead and Freeman, M. D. A., *Lloyd's Introduction to Jurisprudence,* 5th ed., Stevens, 1985, p. 419.

41 Though Rawls in his *A Theory of Justice* does concede that extra resources can be devoted to a specific group in order to improve their position.

42 Edwards, J., *Positive Discrimination,* Tavistock, 1987, p. 37.

43 Stang Dahl, T., op cit.

44 Ibid, p. 90.

45 *Chorlton* v *Lings* (1868) 4 CP 374.

46 *Bebb* v *Law Society* [1914] 1 Ch 286.

47 O'Donovan, K., *Sexual Divisions in Law,* Weidenfeld & Nicolson, 1985, pp. 29–30.

48 With Acts such as the Factory Act 1848 which limited women's working hours to ten a day.

49 See, for example, the speech of Lord Neaves in *Jex-Blake* v *Senatus of Edinburgh University* (1873) 11 M 784.

50 See, for example, the Report of the Committee on the Employment of Women and Children in Mines and Collieries 1842. This appeared immediately before the passage of the Act to Prohibit the Employment of Women and Girls in Mines and Collieries 1842.

51 One group who organised resistance to the protective legislation was the Women's Rights Opposition Movement. See Creighton, W. B., *Working Women and the Law,* Mansell, 1979, p. 25.

52 O'Donovan, K., op cit.

53 See, for example, the rules governing the availability of Income Support in the *National Welfare Benefits Handbook,* 20th ed., Child Poverty Action Group, 1990.

54 On the powers possessed by various agencies to intervene in the family if children are believed to be neglected or ill-treated, see Cretney, S. M., *Elements of Family Law*, Sweet & Maxwell, 1987, Ch. 18. The whole position is, however, about to change with the passage of the Children Act 1989.

55 It is possible, for example, for any person, including a social worker, to apply for a place of safety order under the terms of the Children and Young Persons Act 1969, s. 28. This order, if granted, allows a child to be removed from the home. When the Children Act 1989 comes into force this order will disappear and will be replaced by an emergency protection order.

56 See the views on this issue advanced in Taub, N., and Schneider, E., 'Perspectives on women's subordination and the role of law', in Kairys, D. (ed.), *The Politics of Law*, Partheon, 1982, Ch. 6.

57 Sex Discrimination Act 1986, s. 7.

58 See Ch. 6, p. 134–136.

59 As outlined in Coyle, A., 'Going private' (1985) *Feminist Review* 6.

60 The Fair Wages Resolution was passed by the Labour Government in 1946. One of its purposes was to ensure that those contractors employed by government paid wages 'not less than those paid by the best employer in the trade'.

61 Bowers, J., *A Practical Approach to Employment Law*, 3rd ed., Blackstone Press, 1990, Ch. 3.

62 *Wilsons & Clyde Coal Ltd* v *English* [1938] AC 57.

63 Fontana, 1986.

64 See Dworkin, R., *Taking Rights Seriously*, Duckworth, 1978.

65 Ibid, pp. 116–17.

66 Dworkin, op cit, Ch. 2.

67 Ibid, Ch. 7.

68 Ibid, p. 236.

69 Though Dworkin does provide a rejoinder to this argument: ibid, p. 260.

70 Ibid, p. 265.

71 Ibid, p. 265.

72 Hart, op cit, Ch. 7.

73 Ibid, pp. 138–44.

74 Griffith, J. A., *Politics of the Judiciary*, 3rd ed., Fontana, 1985, Chs 1 and 3.

75 A good example of an 'unsympathetic' interpretation of the anti-discrimination legislation can be found in *Turley* v *Allders Department Stores Ltd* [1980] IRLR 4. Note, however, the dissenting judgment in this case delivered by the female member of the tribunal. The decision in *Turley* was reversed in *Hayes* v *Malleable Working Men's Club* [1985] ICR 703.

76 Dworkin, op cit, pp. 118–23.

77 Whether it will act as a complete counterweight is a matter for argument. See McCluskey, J. H., *Law, Justice and Democracy*, Sweet & Maxwell, 1987.

78 For an account of the doctrine of precedent see Cross, R., *Precedent in English Law*, 3rd ed., Clarendon Press, 1977; Goldstein, L., *Precedent in Law*, Clarendon Press, 1987.

79 [1981] ICR 299.

80 This section has been amended by the Employment Act 1989, s. 3.

81 This subject is considered in greater detail in Ch. 5, pp. 74 and 90–92.

82 [1986] IRLR 134.

83 Equal Pay Directive 75/117; Equal Treatment Directive 76/207; Social Security Directive 79/7. For a more detailed account of how the law of the European Community affects women in employment see McCrudden, C. (ed.), *Women, Employment and European Equality Law*, Eclipse, 1987.

84 See, for example, *Marshall* v *Southampton and South-West Hampshire Area Health Authority (Teaching)* [1986] ICR 335. As a result of this decision the United Kingdom was obliged to amend its law in s. 2 of the Sex Discrimination Act 1986. Some uncertainty still remained, however, regarding the true state of the law. See *Duke* v *Reliance Systems Ltd* [1987] IRLR 139 CA; [1988] ICR 339 HL.

85 Health and Safety at Work Act 1974, s. 33.

Chapter three   Policy and prejudice: the tangled web

1 'There is now an elaborate machinery to ensure her equal opportunity and equal rights; but I think we ought to stop and ask: where does this leave the family?' Statement made by Patrick Jenkin in 1977 when Conservative social services spokesman. Quoted in Pascall, G., *Social Policy: A Feminist Analysis*, Tavistock, 1986, p. 196.

2 For a twentieth-century exposition of these ideals, see Finnis, J., *Natural Law and Natural Rights*, Clarendon Press, 1980.

3 Circulars are a form of guidance or advice issued by a government department such as the Department of Social Security. It is not usual for them to have the force of law though undoubtedly the advice they contain influences the behaviour of other bodies such as local authorities. For a detailed account of the legal significance of circulars see Baldwin, R., and Houghton, J., 'Circular arguments: the status and legitimacy of administrative rules' (1986) *Public Law* 239.

4 On the grounds, for example, that the terms of the legislation are contrary to community law; *MacMahon* v *Department of Education and Science* [1982] 3 CMLR 91.

5 Such as the coal-mining industry: An Act to Prohibit the Employment of Women and Girls in Mines and Collieries 1842.

6 See, for example, An Act to Limit the Hours of Labour of Young Persons and Females in Factories 1847, Factories Act 1961.

7 Mill, J. S., *On Liberty* (1859), Penguin, 1983.

8 Ibid, p. 68.

9 Hart, H. L. A., *Law, Liberty and Morality*, Oxford University Press, 1968: Devlin, P., *The Enforcement of Morals*, Oxford University Press, 1968.

10 Stephen, J. F., *Liberty, Equality, Fraternity*, London, 1874.

11 Devlin, P., op cit.

12 A society's morals are seen by a writer such as Devlin as a seamless web which holds it together. He does, however, concede that the individual should be given as much freedom as is compatible with society's well-being.

13 Dworkin, G., 'Paternalism', in Wasserstrom, R. (ed.), *Morality and the Law*, Wadsworth, 1971, p. 107.
14 Ibid, pp. 122–3.
15 Ibid, p. 123.
16 Ibid, p. 124.
17 Quoted in Dworkin, G., op cit, p. 115.
18 See O'Donovan, K., *Sexual Divisions in Law*, Weidenfeld & Nicolson, 1985, pp. 163–70.
19 Dworkin, G., op cit, p. 108.
20 Creighton, W. B., *Working Women and the Law*, Mansell, 1979, pp. 19–26.
21 (1873) 11 M 784.
22 Ibid, p. 833.
23 Male workers were never subject to restrictions on their hours of work. However, legislation relating to health and safety to which may be attributed a paternalistic motive, such as the Health and Safety at Work Act 1974, does apply to them.
24 See, for example, the Sex Discrimination Act 1986, s. 7. This measure removes restrictions on the employment of women at night in industrial undertakings and other curbs on their hours of employment and Sunday working in factories. The Employment Act 1989 also repeals legislation which conflicts with the principle of non-discrimination (s. 1), though provisions designed to protect women as regards pregnancy, maternity or other circumstances giving rise to risks specifically affecting women are expressly retained (s. 3).
25 Married Women's Property Acts 1870 and 1882.
26 Infant Custody Act 1839 (which allowed women custody of their children under seven, but subject to numerous conditions), Guardianship of Infants Act 1886. Men and women did not obtain equal rights over their children until the passage of the Guardianship of Infants Act 1925.
27 Sex Disqualification (Removal) Act 1919.
28 *Equal in the Law*, Law Society, 1988. This report points out that the number of women admitted to the legal profession has increased dramatically from 1973 onwards. In that year women accounted for 13 per cent of the solicitors admitted. In 1986 that percentage had risen to 44 per cent and currently shows no sign of declining.
29 *Wilsons & Clyde Coal Ltd* v *English* [1938] AC 57.
30 For example, Factories Act 1961.
31 [1981] ICR 299.
32 It was assumed in this case that DMF was a danger only to women of childbearing age, though there was some suggestion that it could cause other damage to men and women alike. In concluding that a man could continue to make deliveries of DMF but a woman could not, and that, therefore, she had been the object of discrimination, the Employment Appeal Tribunal's reasoning appears mistaken. Instead, consideration should have been given to how the employers would have treated a man whose reproductive capacity was threatened by the cargo he was carrying. If they would have treated him as they treated Mrs Page there would appear to be no discrimination.

33 222/84, [1987] ICR 83.
34 Directive 76/207.
35 Ibid, Article 2(3).
36 [1987] ICR 83, 105.
37 Dworkin, G., op cit, p. 126.
38 (1989) *Equal Opportunities Review* 23, p. 35.
39 Ibid, p. 36.
40 Ibid, p. 35.
41 Ibid, pp. 35–6.
42 This was the opinion of the European Commission.
43 Section 3. For an account of the Act see (1990) *Equal Opportunities Review* 29, p. 27.
44 S. 1(1).
45 S. 1(4).
46 Dicey, A. V., *An Introduction to the Study of the Law of the Constitution* (1885), 10th ed., Macmillan, p. 193.
47 Beginning with the Reform Act 1832 the franchise was gradually extended. Adult male suffrage for parliamentary elections was achieved in 1918 and female suffrage in 1928.
48 Mill, J.S., in 'The subjection of women' (1869) in Mill, J.S., and H.T., *Essays on Sex Equality*, University of Chicago Press, 1970, pp. 129–30.
49 Ibid, p. 130.
50 *Short v Poole Corporation* [1926] 1 Ch 66; cf *Roberts v Hopwood* [1925] AC 578.
51 *Price v Rhondda UDC* [1923] 2 Ch 372.
52 O'Donovan, K., and Szyszczak, E., *Equality and Sex Discrimination Law*, Blackwell, 1988, p. 3.
53 Ibid, p. 4.
54 Ibid, p. 4.
55 Edwards, J., *Positive Discrimination*, Tavistock, 1987, p. 79.
56 Ibid, Foreword, p. x.
57 David, M., and Land, H., 'Sex and social policy', in Glennerster, H. (ed.), *The Future of the Welfare State*, Heinemann, 1983, p. 138.
58 Cmnd 5724, para 39.
59 Ibid, para 39.
60 Sex Discrimination Act 1975, ss. 6(4), 7. S. 6(4) has now been amended by the Social Security Act 1989, Sched. 5, para 14(2),(3),(4).
61 'Genuine occupational qualification' (1988) *Equal Opportunities Review* 18, p. 24.
62 Ellis, E., *Sex Discrimination Law*, Gower, 1988, p. 107.
63 Ibid, p. 107.
64 Such behaviour could, however, amount to discrimination. See *Hurley v Mustoe* [1981] IRLR 208.
65 Tavistock, 1987.
66 Ibid, pp. 17–18.
67 Ibid, p. 167.
68 Ch. 5, pp. 75–76.
69 Employment Protection (Consolidation) Act 1978, ss. 45, 60.

70 Sex Discrimination Act 1975, s. 47.
71 Edwards, J., op cit, p. 209.

Chapter four   Patterns of employment

1 Beechey, V., *A Matter of Hours: Women, Part-Time Work and the Labour Market*, Polity Press, 1987. For a challenge to this view, see Hakim, C., 'Employment rights: a comparison of part-time and full-time employees' (1989) *Industrial Law Journal* 18, pp. 69–83, but note also the response by Disney, R., and Szyszczak, E., 'Part-time work: reply to Catherine Hakim' (1989) *Industrial Law Journal* 18, pp. 223–8 and finally the comment on that by Hakim, C. (1989) *Industrial Law Journal* 18, pp. 228–9.
2 Hakim, C., 'Employment rights: a comparison of part-time and full-time employees', above, n.1, at p. 82 and also in her Reply, above, n.1, at p. 228.
3 The definition of which has produced a good deal of litigation. Casuals and homeworkers have been particularly vulnerable to classification as self-employed: *Mailway (Southern) Ltd* v *Willsher* [1978] ICR 511. Cf. *Nethermere (St Neots) Ltd* v *Gardiner* [1984] ICR 612.
4 The image of the *male* worker: Beechey, V., *Unequal Work*, Verso, 1987, p. 209.
5 With certain exceptions, e.g. if the employee has worked for five years between 8 and 16 hours: Employment Protection (Consolidation) Act 1978, Sched. 13.
6 Daniel, W. W., *Maternity Rights: The Experience of Women*, Report No. 588, Policy Studies Institute, 1980; Daniel, W. W., *Maternity Rights: The Experience of Employers*, Report No. 596, PSI, 1981. The EOC has recommended the abolition of the two-year qualifying period in relation to maternity leave and dismissal because of pregnancy, *Legislating for Change*, EOC, 1986.
7 In addition, of 2.8 million self-employed, one-quarter were women. Numbers of women entering self-employment are expanding rapidly. More than half of self-employed married women work part-time: *Women and Men in Britain 1989*, EOC, HMSO, 1989, p. 6.
8 *Women and Men in Britain 1987* EOC, HMSO, 1988 Table 3.4, based on *Employment Gazette* (1988) 96, No. 3, Labour Market Data. By March 1989, of the 22 million in employment, women numbered over 10 million, of whom 4.3 million were part-time: *Employment Gazette* (1989) 97, No. 8, Labour Market Data, 59 Table 1.1.
9 *Employment Gazette* (1989) 97, No. 4, Table 1, pp. 160–1. Ninety per cent of the projected increase in the labour force is among women. It is predicted that by the year 2000 the activity rate for females of working age will be only 13 percentage points below the male rate, as compared with 18 points in 1988 and over 30 in 1971. The labour force comprises people 16 or over with jobs and those seeking work whether or not they claim benefit.
10 *Women and Unemployment*, Employment Institute Economic Report, Vol. 4, No. 5, May 1989.
11 It is difficult to assess the real extent of female unemployment. Department

of Employment figures exclude women who are not eligible for or not claiming benefit.

12 Martin, J., and Roberts, C., *Women and Employment: A Lifetime Perspective*, HMSO, 1984, based on the Women and Employment Survey (W.E.S.) 1980 by Department of Employment and Office of Population Census and Surveys. Evidence from WES appeared in *Employment Gazette* (1984) 92, Nos 5, 6, 9.

13 Elias, P., and Main, B., *Women's Working Lives: Evidence from the National Training Survey*, University of Warwick, Institute for Employment Research, 1982.

14 See above, n. 12. See also Dex, S., *Women's Occupational Mobility*, Macmillan, 1987.

15 For example, Hakim, C., *Occupational Segregation*, Department of Employment Research Paper No. 9, London: HMSO, 1979; Hakim, C., 'Job segregation: trends in the 1970s', *Employment Gazette* (1981) 89, No. 12; Dex, S., *Women's Occupational Mobility*, Macmillan, 1987 (based on the WES); Yeandle, S., *Women's Working Lives: Patterns and Strategies*, Tavistock, 1984.

16 See above, n. 12, *Employment Gazette* (1984) 92, No. 5, p. 208.

17 Martin, J., and Roberts, C., 'Evidence from the Women in Employment Survey', *Employment Gazette* (1984) 92, No. 5, p. 201.

18 Seventeen per cent of husbands felt a woman's place was in the home as compared with 11 per cent of all wives. By 1987, less than half of women of working age thought that mothers of children under school age should stay at home: *Women and Men in Britain 1989*, EOC, HMSO, 1989, p. 35.

19 Of female employees in spring 1988, 40 per cent were part-time. Forty-nine per cent of married female employees worked part-time: 1988 Labour Force Survey, *Employment Gazette* (1989) 97, No. 4, Table 3, p. 184. It is estimated that by 1995, 27 per cent of all employees will work part-time. Most of the new entrants to part-time work are likely to be women: *Women and Men in Britain 1989* EOC, HMSO, 1989, p. 6.

20 *Women and Men in Britain 1989* EOC, HMSO, 1989, p. 11.

21 Children under the age of 16, or between 16 and 18 in full-time education, living with the family.

22 OPCS, General Household Survey 1985: Table 3.18, taken from *Women and Men in Britain 1987* EOC, HMSO, 1988.

23 *Employment Gazette* (1989) 97, No. 4, Labour Force Survey 1988, Table 5, p. 185: nearly 71 per cent of part-time employees did not want a full-time job but this begs the question, why not?

24 Above, n. 5. Note Hakim, C., above, n. 1.

25 Vast majority made self-assessments consistent with the Department of Employment's 30 hour rule. See Ballard, B., 'Women part-time workers: evidence from the 1980 Women and Employment Survey', *Employment Gazette* (1984) 92, No. 9, p. 409 at 410.

26 Unpublished data from Labour Force Survey 1986, taken from Table 3.17, *Women and Men in Britain 1987*, EOC, HMSO, 1988.

27 New Earnings Survey 1987, Part E, Table 138. See Table 3.12, *Women and Men in Britain 1987*, EOC, HMSO, 1988.

28 Table 3.5, *Women and Men in Britain 1987*, EOC, HMSO, 1988. See also Labour Force Survey 1988, *Employment Gazette* 97, No. 4, p. 185.
29 Ballard, B., op cit, p. 411.
30 Dex, S., above n. 14, p. 87.
31 Hakim, C., *Home-Based Work in Britain*, Department of Employment Research Paper No. 60, HMSO, 1987, p. 43.
32 Ibid, p. 242. The majority of homeworkers were said to be satisfied with the levels of pay.
33 OPCS, General Household Survey 1980, HMSO, 1982.
34 Hakim, C., above n. 31, p. 199.
35 OPCS, General Household Survey 1985, with unpublished statistics from OPCS (GHS Unit): see Table 3.19, *Women and Men in Britain 1987*, EOC, HMSO, 1988.
36 OPCS, General Household Survey 1985, see Table 3.20, *Women and Men in Britain 1987*, EOC, HMSO, 1988.
37 Single mothers as a group are most dependent on social security benefit.
38 See Ch. 6.
39 For example, *Childcare and Equality of Opportunity*, Report of the European Commission, 1988.
40 Above, n. 29 at p. 413.
41 Ibid.
42 Elias and Main, above, n. 13, found that one part-timer in twenty-five with a teaching qualification is in the low-skilled catering or cleaning occupations, as is one part-timer in twelve with a nursing qualification.
43 Taken from IDS Study 402, January 1988, p. 3, based on *Employment Gazette* (1987) 95, No. 11.
44 The New Earnings Survey 1987, which shows distribution by occupation, shows the same clustering effect. In catering, cleaning, hairdressing and other personal services, e.g., women formed 75 per cent of the workforce, but only, e.g., 11 per cent in general management. NES 1987, Part E, in *Woman and Men in Britain 1987*, EOC, HMSO, 1988, Table 3.12.
45 *Commission of EC* v *United Kingdom* 61/81 [1982] ICR 578 ECJ and see Ch. 6.
46 New Earnings Survey 1988. See *Employment Gazette* (1988) 96, No. 11, 601 at pp. 604, 605. Of female manual workers, 79.4 per cent earned less than £150 a week. Of female non-manual workers, 45.5 per cent earned less than £150 per week.
47 NES 1987, Part A, Tables 8 and 9; Part D, Tables 86 and 87. See *Women and Men in Great Britain 1987* EOC, HMSO, 1988, Table 4:3.
48 WES 1980, see *Employment Gazette* (1984) 92, No. 5, p. 205.

Chapter five   Women's rights at work

1 [1976] IRLR 198.
2 This should now be covered by the equal value amendment provided there is a man in the same employment. See Ch. 6, pp. 123–125.
3 *Equal Treatment for Men and Women: Strengthening the Acts*, Equal Opportunities Commission, 1988.

4 Byre, A., *Indirect Discrimination*, Equal Opportunities Commission, 1987. See the discussion at p. 68. The situation may perhaps be improved by the introduction of the National Curriculum.

5 An Equal Opportunities Commission formal investigation in 1987 considered that the restricted access to craft subjects afforded to girls in certain West Glamorgan schools amounted to sex discrimination.

6 Collinson, D., *Barriers to Fair Selection*, Equal Opportunities Commission, 1986, p. 51.

7 Curran, M., *Stereotypes and Selection*, Equal Opportunities Commission, 1985.

8 Ibid, p. 29.

9 'Age discrimination: over the hill at 45?' (1989) *Equal Opportunities Review* 25, p. 10.

10 Ibid, p. 12.

11 For a discussion of the importance of geographical mobility in relation to recruitment practices see Collinson, D., op cit, p. 22.

12 Ibid, Chs 5 and 6.

13 Ibid, Ch. 8.

14 Robbins, D., *Wanted: Railmen*, Equal Opportunities Commission, 1986, p. 34.

15 Collinson, D., op cit, p. 27.

16 Cf. *Vaux & Associated Breweries* v *Ward* (1968) 3 ITR 385.

17 For example, Baroness Phillips unsuccessfully introduced a Private Members Bill – the Employment (Age Limits) Bill – to outlaw discrimination on the grounds of age.

18 See the examples quoted in 'Equal opportunity horizons: 1. American State laws' (1989) *Equal Opportunities Review* 25, p. 23. Michigan outlaws discrimination on the grounds of height or weight, the District of Columbia on the grounds of personal appearance.

19 Quoted in 'Harassment at Work' (1985) Equal Opportunities Review 4, p. 8.

20 Interview quoted in Collinson, D., op cit, p. 22.

21 Ibid, p. 29, again quoting from an interview.

22 Ch. 4.

23 Quoted in *Positive Action: Equal Opportunities for Women in Employment*, Commission of the European Communities, 1988, p. 23.

24 'Achieving equal opportunity through positive action' (1987) *Equal Opportunities Review* 14, p. 13.

25 Sex Discrimination Act 1975, s. 47(3).

26 As was the case in *Watches of Switzerland Ltd* v *Savell* [1983] IRLR 141.

27 Interview quoted in Collinson, D., op cit, p. 39.

28 Employment Protection (Consolidation) Act 1978, ss. 45 and 60.

29 Employment Protection (Consolidation) Act 1978, s. 33(3)(*b*), Sched. 13.

30 For a definition of what constitutes part-time work, see Ch. 4, p. 52.

31 Social Security Act 1989, Sched. 5, extends the concept of discrimination to occupational benefits. See Ch. 7, pp. 151–152 and 155–156.

32 See, for example, *Clarke* v *Eley (IMI) Kynoch Ltd* [1982] IRLR 482 (successful claim of discrimination); *Kidd* v *DRG (UK) Ltd* [1985] IRLR 190 (unsuccessful claim of discrimination).

33 Ch. 4, pp. 62–64.
34 For example, the rights granted to pregnant employees under the Employment Protection (Consolidation) Act 1978, ss. 45, 60. This is not the case with the Sex Discrimination Act 1975.
35 This need not be an actual man, a hypothetical man will suffice.
36 S. 6 of the Sex Discrimination Act defines the circumstances where s. 1 discrimination is unlawful in an employment context.
37 [1986] IRLR 134.
38 Ibid, p. 137.
39 [1989] IRLR 173.
40 Ibid, p. 175.
41 [1989] 2 All ER 914.
42 [1990] 2 All ER 607.
43 Ibid, n. 42 at p. 612, per Lord Bridge.
44 It is not, for example, contrary to the rules of natural justice.
45 Sex Discrimination Act 1975, s. 74; Sex Discrimination (Questions and Replies) Order 1975, SI 1975 No 2048.
46 See *Oxford* v *DHSS* [1977] IRLR 225.
47 For a general discussion of discovery, see *Science Research Council* v *Nasse* [1980] AC 1028.
48 *Williams* v *Thomas and Dyfed County Council* (1986) *Equal Opportunities Review* 8, p. 29.
49 [1980] IRLR 193.
50 Ibid, p. 195.
51 [1981] ICR 653.
52 Ibid, p. 658–9.
53 Sex Discrimination Act 1975, s. 1(1)(*b*).
54 *Clarke* v *Eley (IMI) Kynoch Ltd* [1982] IRLR 482, 485.
55 *Watches of Switzerland* v *Savell* [1983] IRLR 141.
56 *Home Office* v *Holmes* [1985] 1 WLR 71, 75.
57 [1983] ICR 428.
58 Pannick, D., *Sex Discrimination Law*, Oxford University Press, 1985, p. 43.
59 [1985] 1 WLR 71.
60 Ch. 4, pp. 61–62.
61 [1989] IRLR 241.
62 Ibid, p. 36.
63 [1985] 1 WLR 71, 77.
64 (1989) *Equal Opportunities Review* 25, p. 34, *see* p. 36.
65 Ibid, p. 247.
66 *Price* v *Civil Service Commission* [1977] IRLR 291, 293.
67 See the account of the changing judicial attitude to statistics given in Byre, A., *Indirect Discrimination*, Equal Opportunities Commission, 1987, pp. 30–7.
68 [1985] IRLR 190.
69 Ibid, p. 195.
70 Ibid, p. 191.
71 [1982] IRLR 482.

72 [1985] IRLR 190, 196.
73 See, for example, *Hayward* v *Cammell Laird Shipbuilders Ltd* [1988] ICR 464 (equal pay case).
74 *Steel* v *Union of Post Office Workers* [1978] ICR 181.
75 [1982] ICR 661.
76 Ibid, p. 668.
77 170/84 [1987] ICR 110.
78 [1987] IRLR 26.
79 Ellis, E., *Sex Discrimination Law*, Gower, 1988, p. 89.
80 [1989] IRLR 69. The Court of Appeal's decision was reversed by the House of Lords [1990] 2 All ER 513 but on a different point.
81 Ibid, p. 75.
82 Ibid, p. 75.
83 See *Turner* v *Labour Party* [1987] IRLR 101.
84 [1977] IRLR 291.
85 Dex, S., and Shaw, L., *British and American Women at Work*, Macmillan, 1986, p. 22.
86 In *Horsey* v *Dyfed County Council* [1982] IRLR 395 the refusal to let a woman attend a course in London on the basis that, since her husband was there, she would not return, constituted unlawful discrimination.
87 This case is noted in Collinson, D., above, n. 6, p. 2.
88 *FTATU* v *Modgill* [1980] IRLR 142.
89 Unreported. See Ellis, E., op cit, p. 95. Cf. *Saunders* v *Richmond upon Thames BC* [1977] IRLR 362.
90 [1986] IRLR 134.
91 Ibid, p. 138.
92 [1990] IRLR 3.
93 [1986] IRLR 103.
94 Ibid, p. 107. The applicant was in fact unsuccessful in this particular case.
95 [1987] IRLR 397.
96 Sex Discrimination Act 1975, s. 41.
97 [1987] IRLR 401.
98 [1983] IRLR 141.
99 Ibid, p. 145.
100 [1985] ICR 703.
101 *Turley* v *Allders Department Stores Ltd* [1980] IRLR 4.
102 For an example of a successful claim, see the account given of *Curl* v *Air UK Ltd* in (1988) *Equal Opportunities Review* 22, p. 44.
103 [1981] IRLR 208.
104 In Industrial Tribunal Statistics (1989) *Employment Gazette* 257, 691 sex discrimination cases are recorded for the period April 1987–March 1988.
105 See, for example, its decisions in *Bilka-Kaufhaus GmbH* v *Weber von Hartz* 170/84 [1987] ICR 110; *Rinner-Kühn* v *FWW Spezial-Gebaudereinigung GmbH & Co KG* [1989] IRLR 493.
106 The European Community has proposed a Directive on parental leave. The United Kingdom has, however, consistently blocked such a move. See 'Parental and family leave' (1989) *Equal Opportunities Review* 27, p. 8.

107 Sex Discrimination Act 1975, s. 2(2); Equal Treatment Directive, Article 2(3).
108 Employment Protection (Consolidation) Act 1978, s. 33(3)(*b*).
109 Ch. 4, pp. 61–64.
110 Employment Protection (Consolidation) Act 1978, s. 60(1)(*a*) and (*b*).
111 Ibid, s. 60(2).
112 *Elegbede* v *The Wellcome Foundation Ltd* [1977] IRLR 383.
113 [1987] IRLR 438.
114 Employment Protection (Consolidation) Act 1978, s. 57(3).
115 *Martin* v *BSC Footwear (Supplies) Ltd* [1978] IRLR 95.
116 [1988] IRLR 230.
117 *The Times*, 9 October 1989.
118 Employment Protection (Consolidation) Act 1978, ss. 33, 47.
119 *Lavery* v *Plessey Telecommunications Ltd* [1983] ICR 534.
120 For a survey of such occupational benefits see Maternity Leave and Childcare, IDS Study, 425, January 1989.
121 Employment Protection (Consolidation) Act 1978, s. 48.
122 [1978] ICR 934.
123 Employment Protection (Consolidation) Act 1978, s. 56A(2), (3).
124 Ibid, s. 45(3).
125 [1986] IRLR 203.
126 For an account of some of those difficulties see O'Grady, F., and Wakefield, H., *Women, Work and Maternity: The Inside Story*, Maternity Alliance, 1989.
127 See *Gregory* v *Tudsbury* [1982] IRLR 267.
128 Ch. 7, pp. 145–152.
129 For an account of the Draft Directive on Parental Leave – which the United Kingdom has consistently opposed – as well as some indication of employer practice, see 'Parental and family leave' (1989) *Equal Opportunities Review* 27, p. 8.
130 Stang Dahl, T., *Women's Law*, Norwegian University Press, 1987, p. 76.

Chapter six Women's wages

1 See Ch. 5, pp. 82–89.
2 See for examples, Phelps Brown, H., *The Inequality of Pay*, Oxford University Press, 1977, p. 148; Meehan, E. M., *Women's Rights at Work*, Macmillan, 1985, pp. 15–18; Yeandle, S., *Women's Working Lives: Patterns and Strategies*, Tavistock, 1984, p. 129.
3 See Ch. 5, pp. 73–76. Meehan, E. M., above, n. 2, p. 20.
4 Barron, R.D., and Norris, G. M., 'Sexual divisions and the dual labour market', in Barker, D., and Allen, S. (eds), *Dependence and Exploitation in Work and Marriage*, Longman, 1976.
5 Meehan, E. M., above, n. 2, p. 22.
6 Phelps Brown, H., above, n. 2.
7 The Act is wider than its title would suggest; it covers all contractual terms and conditions: Equal Pay Act 1970, s. 1(2).
8 *Civilian War Claimants Association Ltd* v *R* [1932] AC 14, at p. 26.

9 *Defrenne* v *Sabena* 43/74 [1976] ICR 547 ECJ.

10 [1987] ICR 867 CA, affirmed [1988] ICR 697 HL.

11 Above, n. 9.

12 Below pp. 123–125 and see *Commission of EC* v *United Kingdom of Great Britain and Northern Ireland* 61/81 [1982] ICR 578 ECJ; Equal Pay (Amendment) Regulations 1983, SI 1983, No 1794, amending Equal Pay Act 1970, as from 1.1.84.

13 152/84 [1986] ICR 335.

14 *Van Duyn* v *Home Office* 41/74 [1975] Ch 358.

15 *Foster* v *British Gas plc* [1988] IRLR 354, [1990] IRLR 353 ECJ.

16 [1988] ICR 697.

17 *Litster* v *Forth Dry Dock & Engineering Co Ltd* [1989] ICR 341, per Lord Oliver at p. 371.

18 *Defrenne* v *Sabena*, above, n. 9 at p. 565.

19 The relevance of the provisions relating to pensions must now be seen in the light of *Barber* v *Guardian Royal Exchange Assurance Group* [1990] IRLR 240 ECJ. See below, p. 115 and Ch. 7.

20 *Defrenne* v *Sabena*, above, n. 9; *Macarthys Ltd* v *Smith* 129/79 [1980] ICR 672 ECJ; *Worringham and Humphreys* v *Lloyds Bank Ltd* 69/80 [1981] ICR 558 ECJ; *Jenkins* v *Kingsgate (Clothing Productions) Ltd* 96/80 [1981] ICR 592 ECJ.

21 ECJ in *Jenkins*, ibid, at p. 614 and see *O'Brien* v *Sim-Chem Ltd* [1980] ICR 429 CA: Art. 119 was inapplicable to a case relying on a job evaluation scheme because it involved hidden discrimination. Reversed on different grounds, [1980] ICR 573, HL.

22 *Pickstone* v *Freemans plc* [1988] ICR 697 at p. 723.

23 For example, in *Macarthys Ltd* v *Smith* 129/79; *Worringham and Humphreys* v *Lloyds Bank Ltd* 69/80, above, n. 20.

24 For example, *O'Brien* v *Sim-Chem Ltd* [1980] ICR 429 CA.

25 *Commission of EC* v *UK* 61/81 [1982] ICR 578 ECJ.

26 See Ch. 5 for discussion of indirect discrimination in the context of the Sex Discrimination Act 1975.

27 *Bilka-Kaufhaus GmbH* v *Weber von Hartz* 170/84 [1987] ICR 110 ECJ and see below p. 131. *Rinner-Kühn* v *FWW Spezial-Gebaudereinigung GmbH & Co KG* [1989] IRLR 493 ECJ.

28 See below pp. 114–116. See also *Burton* v *British Railways Board* 19/81 [1982] ICR 329 ECJ; *Hammersmith & Queen Charlotte's Special Health Authority* v *Cato* [1988] ICR 132.

29 *Hugh-Jones* v *St John's College, Cambridge* [1979] ICR 848; *Barber* v *Guardian Royal Exchange Assurance Group* [1983]; *Roberts* v *Tate & Lyle Food Distribution Ltd* [1983] ICR 521.

30 *Marshall* v *Southampton and South-West Hampshire Area Health Authority (Teaching)* 152/84 [1986] ICR 335 ECJ.

31 Sex Discrimination Act 1986, section 2.

32 See Pannick, D., *Sex Discrimination Law*, Oxford University Press, 1985, pp. 137–41.

33 Cf. the Sex Discrimination Act 1975.

34 69/80 [1981] ICR 558 ECJ.

35 See Sex Discrimination Act 1975, s. 6, as amended.
36 The ECJ did not decide whether pension benefits constitute pay. See now *Bilka-Kaufhaus GmbH* v *Weber von Hartz*, above, n. 27 and *Barber* v *Guardian Royal Exchange Assurance Group*, above n. 19.
37 192/85 [1988] ICR 332 ECJ.
38 [1990] IRLR 240 ECJ. The court did not refer to *Newstead*, though the Advocate General did attempt to distinguish that case on the basis that in *Newstead* the discrepancy arose from the fact that the employer was required by law to withhold a contribution to the widows' fund in order for the scheme to qualify as a contracted-out scheme. *Barber* was said to be analogous to *Bilka-Kaufhaus*, above n. 27, since the matter was purely contractual: ibid, p. 247. See Ch. 7.
39 *Bilka-Kaufhaus GmbH* v *Weber von Hartz* 170/84 [1987] ICR 110 ECJ.
40 12/81 [1982] ICR 420 ECJ, [1982] ICR 420 HL.
41 Employment Protection (Consolidation) Act 1978, Part VI.
42 [1988] ICR 132.
43 Above, n. 40.
44 [1989] IRLR 469.
45 Employment Protection (Consolidation) Act 1978, s. 106.
46 [1989] IRLR 493 ECJ.
47 See Ch. 5 and Employment Protection (Consolidation) Act 1978, Sched. 13.
48 Cf. *Hayward* v *Cammell Laird Shipbuilders Ltd* [1987] ICR 682, reversed [1988] ICR 464 HL where the Court of Appeal used the wider interpretation to defeat a claim.
49 The Equal Pay Act 1970 does not apply to Northern Ireland: s. 11.
50 Cf. for example, Employment Protection (Consolidation) Act 1978; Social Security Act 1986.
51 Equal Pay Act 1970, s. 1(6)(*a*).
52 Sex Discrimination Act 1975, s. 82(1).
53 *Quinnen* v *Hovells* [1984] ICR 525. Certain categories of crown employees are covered: s. 1(8), (10). Armed forces are excluded, s. 1(9), but see s. 7. Those employed abroad are excluded, s. 1, but cf. s. 1(12): territorial waters.
54 Sex Discrimination Act 1975, s. 1.
55 129/79 [1980] ICR 672 ECJ.
56 She was not allowed to use a hypothetical male because that would involve 'hidden' discrimination. Further, the ECJ refused to comment on the direct applicability of the Equal Pay Directive.
57 *Albion Shipping Agency* v *Arnold* [1982] ICR 22.
58 Equal Pay Act 1970, s. 1(6).
59 Ibid, s. 1(6)(*c*).
60 Establishment is not defined but the term has been judicially considered in other contexts: *Barratt Developments (Bradford) Ltd* v *UCATT* [1977] IRLR 403.
61 [1989] ICR 33 HL.
62 [1977] ICR 83.
63 [1977] ICR 48.
64 Case remitted to an industrial tribunal. Equal pay was eventually awarded to most of the applicants: [1977] IRLR 160.

65 See below p. 125.
66 Also the frequency, nature and extent of differences: Equal Pay Act 1970, s. 1(4) and *Redland Roof Tiles Ltd* v *Harper* [1977] ICR 349.
67 *Coomes (Holdings) Ltd* v *Shields* [1978] ICR 1159 and see *Electrolux Ltd* v *Hutchinson* [1976] IRLR 410.
68 [1978] IRLR 462.
69 [1977] ICR 272.
70 [1977] ICR 266.
71 Waddington could now claim under Equal Pay Act 1970, s. 1(2)(*c*). The fact that her work was of greater value would not be a bar: *Murphy* v *Bord Telcomm Eireann 157/86* [1988] ICR 445 ECJ.
72 See Equal Pay Act 1970, s. 1(3), below p. 125.
73 [1977] ICR 48.
74 [1978] ICR 700. Cf. *Thomas* v *NCB* [1987] ICR 757.
75 [1978] ICR 700, at p. 704.
76 See, for example, Rubenstein, M., *Equal Pay for Work of Equal Value*, Macmillan, 1984.
77 See, for example, comments of the Advocate General in *Commission of EC* v *UK* 61/81 [1982] ICR 578, at p. 585.
78 *Eaton Ltd* v *Nuttall* [1977] ICR 272 at p. 277.
79 *Bromley* v *H. & J. Quick Ltd* [1988] ICR 623.
80 *Eaton Ltd* v *Nuttall*, above, n. 78, at p. 278.
81 *Rummler* v *Dato-Druck GmbH* 237/85 [1987] ICR 774 ECJ. See also *Bilka-Kaufhaus GmbH* v *Weber von Hartz* 170/84 [1987] ICR 110 ECJ. Recognising the difficulty for an applicant in proving that a job evaluation scheme is discriminatory when the employer has all the information, the EOC proposes that it should assist the applicant under Sex Discrimination Act 1975, s. 75 (see Ch. 8) or that legal aid be made available in equal value cases.
82 *Green* v *Broxtowe District Council* [1977] ICR 241.
83 [1980] ICR 573.
84 In *Arnold* v *Beecham Group Ltd* [1982] ICR 744, the EAT tried to narrow this by requiring acceptance of the job evaluation scheme by the employer and union, a decision which seems unduly restrictive and difficult to reconcile with *O'Brien*.
85 SI 1983 No.1794.
86 *Commission of EC* v *UK* 61/81 [1982] ICR 578 ECJ.
87 Under Article 119.
88 [1987] ICR 867 CA; [1988] ICR 697.
89 Applying the test in *Worringham*, above, n. 20: Art. 119 is directly applicable where the court can establish all the necessary facts.
90 Industrial Tribunal (Rules of Procedure) Regulations 1985, SI 1985 No.16.
91 An EOC report on independent experts calls for better pay and better channels of communication: Bowey, A., *Evaluation of the Role of Independent Experts in Equal Value Cases in Britain 1984-88*, EOC, 1988. The EOC in its Consultative Document, *Review of the Equal Pay Legislation*, 1989, puts forward a number of possible reforms in relation to the role of the independent expert: these include arbitration in place of the industrial

tribunal, dispensing with the expert, changing the role of the expert or retaining but improving the current system.

92 Equal Pay Act 1970, s. 1(2)(*c*).

93 Cf. s. 1(5), ibid.

94 See Beddoe, R., 'Independent experts?' (1986) *Equal Opportunities Review* 6, p. 13.

95 Industrial Tribunal (Rules of Procedure) Regulations 1985, SI 1985 No. 16 Sched. 2, Rule 12(2A).

96 Equal Pay Act 1970, s. 2A(1)(*a*). The industrial tribunal must at least hear the claim before deciding: cf. *Dennehy* v *Sealink UK Ltd* [1987] IRLR 120. In its *Review of the Equal Pay Legislation*, the EOC recommends that the no reasonable grounds hearing should be replaced by a hearing simply to determine the issues.

97 Equal Pay Act 1970, s. 2A(2)(*b*); s. 2A(3). Cf. *Neil* v *Ford Motor Co.* [1984] IRLR 339.

98 Industrial Tribunal (Rules of Procedure) Regulations 1985, SI 1985 No. 16 Sched. 2, Rule 8(2E). The EOC argues that an employer should be able to present the defence only once: (1989) Consultative Document, *Review of the Equal Pay Legislation*, EOC.

99 *Forex Neptune (Overseas) Ltd* v *Miller* [1987] ICR 170. *McGregor* v *GMBATU* [1987] ICR 505.

100 Rules 7A(1)(4). Forty-six cases were referred in 1984–88; reports were completed in twenty-eight: Angela Bowey, op cit, n. 91. See also Ch. 8.

101 *Tennants Textile Colours Ltd* v *Todd* [1989] IRLR 3.

102 On a balance of probabilities: *National Vulcan Engineering Insurance Group Ltd* v *Wade* [1978] ICR 800.

103 Equal Pay Act 1970, s. 1(3)(*a*).

104 Ibid, s. 1(3)(*b*).

105 *McGregor* v *GMBATU*, above, n. 99: greater experience.

106 *NAAFI* v *Varley* [1977] ICR 11, 1976 IRLR 408.

107 *Leverton* v *Clwyd CC* [1989] ICR 33.

108 For example, in relation to motherhood, *Coyne* v *Exports Credits Guarantee Department* [1981] IRLR 51.

109 For example, in *Coomes* v *Shields*, above, n. 67, there was no genuine material difference as the man had no real role in deterrence.

110 [1979] 1 All ER 474; [1978] IRLR 361 per Lord Denning.

111 *Rainey* v *Greater Glasgow Health Board* [1987] ICR 129.

112 In so concluding, reliance was placed on European Community law and in particular *Jenkins* v *Kingsgate* 96/80 [1981] ICR 592 ECJ and *Bilka-Kaufhaus GmbH* v *Weber von Hartz* 170/84 [1987] ICR 110 ECJ.

113 *Clark* v *Bexley Health Authority and Secretary of State for Health* (1989), *Enderby* v *Frenchay Health Authority and Secretary of State for Health* (1989), unreported. For a discussion see (1989) *Equal Opportunities Review* 24, p. 42.

114 *Waddington* v *Leicester Council for Voluntary Services* [1977] ICR 266.

115 *Pointon* v *University of Sussex* [1979] IRLR 119.

116 *Electrolux Ltd* v *Hutchinson* [1976] IRLR 410.

117 [1988] ICR 391.
118 *Handels-og Kontorfunktionaerernes Forbund I Danmark* v *Dansk Arbejdsgiverforening (acting for Danfoss)* [1989] IRLR 532.
119 170/84 [1987] ICR 110 ECJ.
120 [1989] IRLR 122
121 *Snoxell and Davies* v *Vauxhall Motors Ltd* [1978] QB 11; *United Biscuits* v *Young* [1978] IRLR 15.
122 Women in segregated jobs would need to claim work of equal value. Additionally, job evaluation studies are unlikely to favour part-timers.
123 *Handley* v *Mono Ltd* [1979] ICR 147.
124 [1981] ICR 715.
125 But is not *per se* unlawful under Article 119.
126 170/84 [1987] ICR 110, at p. 126.
127 *McGregor* v *GMBATU* [1987] ICR 505. The EOC recommends that s.1(3) should revert to its original form: Consultative Document, *Review of the Equal Pay Legislation*, EOC, 1989.
128 *Atkinson* v *Tress Engineering Co Ltd* [1976] IRLR 245.
129 [1986] IRLR 287, p. 291 per Popplewell J.
130 [1986] ICR 862, [1986] IRLR 287 EAT; [1987] ICR 682, [1987] IRLR 186 CA; [1988] ICR 464, [1988] IRLR 257 HL.
131 This approach was supported by the ECJ in *Barber* v *Guardian Royal Exchange Assurance Group* [1990] IRLR 240 ECJ.
132 *Reed Packaging Ltd* v *Boozer* [1988] ICR 391.
133 'At the very least for s. 1(3) to operate it would have to be shown that the unfavourable character of the term in the woman's contract was in fact due to the difference in the opposite sense in the other term and that the difference was not due to the reason of sex.'
134 See Ch. 4.
135 Wages Councils Acts 1945–1979.
136 In 1987 the number of underpaid workers was 9,129. In 1986 it was 15,533: figures supplied by Secretary of State for Employment in Parliament, 17 March 1988: *Employment Gazette* (1988) 96, No. 4, p. 253.
137 *Who Needs the Wages Councils?* Low Pay Unit 1983, p. 11.
138 Another criticism was the length and complexity of Wages Councils Orders: *Consultative Paper on Wages Councils*, Department of Employment, 1985.
139 For a general survey of government and TUC criticism, see Keevash, S., 'Wages Councils: an examination of trade union and Conservative government misconceptions about the effect of statutory wage fixing' (1985) *Industrial Law Journal* 14, p. 217.
140 Wages Act 1986, s. 13.
141 Ibid, s. 12.
142 For a contrary view, see, e.g., Makeham, P., *Youth Unemployment*, Department of Employment Research Paper No. 10, HMSO, 1980; *Report on Employment Perspectives and the Distributive Trades*, NEDO, 1985.
143 Employment Protection Act 1975.
144 Wages Act 1986, s. 14.

145 Ibid, s. 14(6)(*a*).
146 Nine employers were prosecuted in the twelve months ending 31 January 1988: above, n. 136.
147 *Report of the Committee on Social Insurance and Allied Services*, Cmnd 6404, HMSO, 1942, Beveridge Report.
148 Especially Directives 76/207, 79/7, above pp. 111–112.
149 See, for example, O'Donovan, K., *Sexual Divisions in Law*, Weidenfeld & Nicolson, 1985, pp. 142–8; O'Donovan, K., and Szyszczak, E., *Equality and Sex Discrimination Law*, Blackwell, 1988.
150 This excludes child benefit and one parent benefit.
151 1990–91: lower earnings limit is £46. Married women no longer have the option of paying reduced contributions: Social Security Act 1975.

Chapter seven   Financial implications of work

1 See, for example, Rawls, J., *A Theory of Justice*, Oxford University Press, 1973.
2 Nozick, R., *Anarchy, State and Utopia*, Oxford University Press, 1974. For a criticism of his stance on this issue, see Hart, H. L. A., *Essays in Jurisprudence and Philosophy*, Oxford University Press, 1983, p. 206.
3 This figure which is for 1990–91 is fixed annually by the Secretary of State and is roughly equivalent to the basic state pension.
4 It may be an attractive economic proposition for employers to pay their part-time employees below the threshold for national insurance contributions, since above this limit the employer has to make a contribution as well as the employee. In Martin, J., and Roberts, C., *Women and Employment*, HMSO, 1984, a survey suggested that one-third of the part-time employees studied did not qualify for benefits.
5 *Equality for Women*, HMSO, Cmnd 5724, 1974, para 77.
6 Holdsworth, W., *A History of English Law*, Vol. III, 4th ed., Methuen, 1935, pp. 520–33.
7 Married Women's Property Acts 1870, 1882.
8 For an analysis of the figures see Rimmer, L., 'The intra-family distribution of paid work, 1968–81', in Hunt, A. (ed.), *Women and Paid Work*, Macmillan, 1988, p. 52.
9 Hills, J., *Changing Tax*, CPAG, 1988, p. 17.
10 For the tax year 1989–90 this allowance amounts to £2,785.
11 For the tax year 1989–90 this allowance amounts to £4,375.
12 Such as the Child Poverty Action Group. See also the criticisms in Hills, J., op cit, p. 25.
13 Income Taxation and Equal Treatment for Men and Women.
14 Finance Act 1988, ss. 32, 33, 34.
15 Ibid, s. 32.
16 Ibid, s. 33.
17 Ibid, s. 33.
18 Ibid, s. 33. Any unused portion of this allowance can be transferred to a wife.
19 Local Government Finance Act 1988, s. 16.

20 *Sunday Times*, 20 August 1989, p. D10.
21 Currently this is set at £46.
22 Ogus, A., and Barendt, E., *The Law of Social Security*, 3rd ed., Butterworths, 1988, p. 57.
23 Ibid, p. 52.
24 Social Security (Contributions) Regulations 1979, S1 1979 No 591, Part VIII.
25 Social Security Act 1975, Sched. 3.
26 Bates, J. D. N., 'Gender, social security and pensions: the myth of the "everyday housewife"?', in McLean, S., and Burrows, N. (eds), *The Legal Relevance of Gender*, Macmillan, 1988, Ch. 7, p. 124.
27 Ogus, A., and Barendt, E., op cit, p. 227.
28 Social Security Act 1986, ss. 46-50.
29 Ibid, s. 46(2).
30 The 'qualifying week' is the week immediately preceding the fourteenth week before the expected week of confinement. Social Security Act 1986, s. 46.
31 Social Security Act 1975, s. 22, as amended by the Social Security Act 1986, Sched. 4, Part II, para 13. Note that SMP and SMA are mutually exclusive. For a more detailed description of both benefits, see Ogus, A., and Barendt, E., op cit, pp. 227–33.
32 Social Security Act 1975, Sched. 3, Part I, para 3.
33 Social Security (Maternity Allowance) Regulations 1987, SI 1987 No 416, Reg 2(1)(*c*).
34 When Beveridge devised his plan for national insurance he relied on the 1931 census for his data regarding married women. He ignored the increasing numbers of women who had entered paid employment during the course of the Second World War, since he did not regard this as a permanent feature.
35 Ch. 6, pp. 110–112.
36 McLean, S., and Burrows, N., op cit, pp. 123–4.
37 Ch. 6, pp. 133–139.
38 In order to claim income support, for example, the claimant must be available for work. Should a couple with children wish to claim then the likelihood is that the partner without child care responsibilities will do so. In most cases this will be the man. There are exceptions to the available for work rule. Single parents may be treated as a special case.
39 Hills, J., op cit, Ch. 10.
40 Sick Pay Schemes, IDS Study 430, March 1989.
41 *Behind the Fringe: Unequal Access to Employee Benefits*, survey conducted by Monks Partnership for the Equal Opportunities Commission.
42 Because of women's shorter service records and propensity to work part-time.
43 Social Security Act 1989, Sched. 3, para 2(3).
44 [1989] IRLR 493.
45 If the benefit in question falls within this Article's extended definition of pay. See Ch. 6, pp. 114–116.
46 If some benefit not connected with pay is at issue. This Directive is directly applicable only so far as employees of the state are concerned.

47 Currently the lower earnings threshold which is £46.
48 Ogus, A., and Barendt, E., op cit, pp. 205–6.
49 Ibid, p. 206.
50 Social Security Pensions Act 1975, Part III, subsequently amended by the Social Security Act 1986.
51 Social Security Act 1986, ss. 1-5.
52 Under the terms of the Social Security Act 1986 occupational pension schemes which are contracted out must provide a guaranteed minimum pension to surviving spouses of both sexes. This is not the case with other schemes such as the state scheme. A Draft Directive is in preparation by the European Community which would require the elimination of discrimination in the provision of survivors' benefits.
53 [1981] ICR 558.
54 Ibid, p. 588.
55 [1988] IRLR 66.
56 [1987] ICR 110.
57 [1990] IRLR 240. A case raising a similar point has been referred to the ECJ: *Clarke* v *Cray Precision Engineering* (1989) *Equal Opportunities Review* 27, p. 20.
58 It amends s. 6(4), Sex Discrimination Act 1975 which specifically excludes 'provision in relation to death or retirement'. See Social Security Act 1989, Sched. 5, para 14.
59 Social Security Act 1989, Sched. 5, paras 2(4)(a)(i), 12. The exception allowed for actuarial differences is to cease by 30 July 1990.
60 Ibid, para 2(4)(a).
61 Ibid, para 2(4)(e).
62 [1990] IRLR 240, 259 where the court states that its decision overrides certain provisions in Directive 86/378.
63 Ogus, A., and Barendt, E., op cit, pp. 180–1.
64 Currently a Draft Directive on the equalisation of pensionable ages is being considered by the European Community. For its terms see (1989) *Equal Opportunities Review* 27, p. 15.
65 [1986] ICR 335.
66 Sex Discrimination Act 1986, s. 3.
67 [1990] 2 All ER 607.
68 Ballard, B., 'Women part-time workers: evidence from the 1980 Women and Employment Survey', *Employment Gazette* (1984) 92, No. 9, p. 409, *see* p. 413.
69 Child Benefit Act 1975. Receipt of benefit for a child over sixteen can continue in certain circumstances, for example if that child is receiving full-time education.
70 Ogus, A., and Barendt, E., op cit, p. 392. The additional benefit paid to one-parent families has been increased.
71 Moss, P., *Childcare and Equality of Opportunity in the EEC*, HMSO, 1988.
72 By such organisations as Childcare Now!. The government's response is to urge the use of schools out of school hours as child care centres, though it has not offered to finance such a scheme.

73 Metcalf, H., *Retaining Women Workers*, Institute of Manpower Studies, 1990.

Chapter eight   The mechanics of equality

1 Gregory, J., *Sex, Race and the Law*, Sage, 1987.
2 See especially Pannick, D., *Sex Discrimination Law*, Oxford University Press, 1985, Ch. 10: 'The EOC and class actions'. Also Lockley, A., 'Regulating group actions' (1989) *New Law Journal* 139, p. 798.
3 Equal pay cases resemble contractual claims. Cases under the Employment Protection (Consolidation) Act 1978, e.g. in relation to maternity rights, are governed by that Act. The usual remedy is compensation but in appropriate cases the tribunal may order re-employment. See Smith, I. T., and Wood, J. C., *Industrial Law*, Butterworths, 4th ed., 1989, Chs 3 and 6.
4 Legum, M., *The Times*, 17 August 1977, quoted in Gregory, J., op cit, p. 73.
5 See especially Leonard, A. M., *Judging Inequality: The Effectiveness of the Industrial Tribunal System in Sex Discrimination and Equal Pay Cases*, London, Cobden Trust, 1987; *Pyrrhic Victories: Winning Sex Discrimination and Equal Pay Cases in the Industrial Tribunals 1980–84*, London, HMSO, 1987. Gregory, J., 'Equal pay and sex discrimination: why women are giving up the fight' (1982) *Feminist Review* 10, pp. 75–89.
6 Even small businesses represent an accumulation of resources in terms of access to advice and expertise.
7 In the case of denial of maternity rights and pregnancy dismissals, remedies are contained in the Employment Protection (Consolidation) Act 1978 and are part of general employment protection rights.
8 Race Relations Acts 1965 and 1968.
9 Industrial Training Act 1964, to hear appeals against training board levies.
10 *Industrial Tribunals*, A Report by Justice, London, 1987.
11 Leonard, A., *Judging Inequality* and *Pyrrhic Victories*, see above, n. 5.
12 Above, n. 5.
13 Cf. Scotland, where discrimination and equal pay cases are assigned to a defined number of Chairs.
14 Above, n. 10 at p. 36.
15 Such a requirement is proposed by Justice, above, n. 10., para. 3.23.
16 See Leonard, A. M., *Judging Inequality*, above, n. 5. Success rates generally were higher with full-time chairmen. Ellis, E., *Sex Discrimination Law*, Gower, 1988, at p. 39, gives figures from Central Office of Industrial Tribunals relating to 1987, also indicating that of sixty-six full-time chairpersons (*sic*), six were women and of 122 part-time chairpersons, nine were women.
17 This would leave untouched the problems in the appeals system where women judges are even rarer and where the attitude of the judiciary has tended to be unsympathetic and trivialising, see O'Donovan, K., and Szyszczak, E., *Equality and Sex Discrimination Law*, Blackwell, 1988, p. 84.
18 Above, n. 10, at para. 3.18 (*e*).

19 A proposal made by Justice, and also by the EOC, in *Equal Treatment for Men and Women: Strengthening the Acts*, EOC, 1988. The latter also recommends efforts to recruit more women, in order to include one in the panel for all equality cases.

20 In 1987–88, there were 1,043 equal pay cases, of which 719 represented a multiple application: *Employment Gazette* (1989) 97, No. 5, p. 258.

21 There were 691 claims in 1987-88 as compared to 24,916 unfair dismissal claims: *Employment Gazette*, above, n. 20.

22 Leonard, A. M., *Pyrrhic Victories: Winning Sex Discrimination and Equal Pay Cases in the Industrial Tribunals, 1980–84*, London, HMSO, 1987.

23 Leonard, A. M., *Judging Inequality: The Effectiveness of the Tribunal System in Sex Discrimination and Equal Pay Cases*, London, Cobden Trust, 1987.

24 Ibid, at p. 48.

25 See the Justice Report, above, n. 10, at para 2.7.

26 Leonard, A., *The First Eight Years: A Profile of Applicants to the Industrial Tribunals under the Sex Discrimination Act 1975 and the Equal Pay Act 1970*, EOC, 1986.

27 Justice Report, above, n. 10, para. 2.8.

28 Royal Commission on Legal Services, 1979, Cmnd 7648.

29 Legal Aid Act 1988 (Part III). The Scheme covers preliminary advice and assistance, including advice, writing letters and the preparation of a tribunal case, but not representation in the tribunal. See *Legal Aid Handbook*, HMSO, 1989.

30 *Legal Aid Handbook*, HMSO, 1989, p. 2.

31 See, for example, Leonard's findings in *Pyrrhic Victories*, above, n. 22.

32 See now Industrial Tribunals (Rules of Procedure) Regulations 1985, SI 1985 No. 16, Sched. 1, para. 11.

33 Ibid, n. 32, Sched. 1, para. 6.

34 Graham, C., and Lewis, N., *The Role of ACAS Conciliation in Equal Pay and Sex Discrimination Cases*, EOC, 1985.

35 *Pyrrhic Victories*, above, n. 22, at p. 47.

36 Gregory, J., 'Equal pay and sex discrimination: why women are giving up the fight' (1982) *Feminist Review* 10, pp. 75–89.

37 Dickens, L., Hart, M., Jones, M., and Weekes, B., *Dismissed: A Study of Unfair Dismissal and the Industrial Tribunal System*, Oxford, Blackwell, 1985.

38 For example, Franks Committee Report 1957, Cmnd 218.

39 Justice Report, above, n. 10, paras 2.2, 2.3.

40 *Pyrrhic Victories*, above, n. 22, at p. 47.

41 Employment Protection (Consolidation) Act 1978, s. 60. See above pp. 96–98.

42 *Oxford* v *DHSS* [1977] ICR 884.

43 But the courts are inconsistent. Compare *London Borough of Barking* v *Camera* [1988] IRLR 373 EAT and *Noone* v *North West Thames Regional Health Authority* [1988] IRLR 195 CA.

44 *Equal Treatment for Men and Women: Strengthening the Acts*, EOC, 1988.

45 The CBI fears that reversal of the burden of proof would result in more

cases being brought. A Select Committee of the House of Lords reported that the objective is admirable but not practicable: *Financial Times*, 10 August 1989.

46 *West Midlands Passenger Transport Executive* v *Singh* [1988] ICR 614.
47 No similar procedure applies under the Equal Pay Act 1970.
48 Industrial Tribunals (Rules of Procedure) Regulations 1985 SI 1985 No. 16, Rule 4; County Court Rules 1981, Order 14.
49 [1979] IRLR 465 at p. 468 per Lord Wilberforce.
50 Ibid, at p. 468.
51 Equal Pay (Amendment) Regulations 1983 SI 1983 No. 1794. See Ch. 6.
52 Information taken from 'Equal value update' (1989) *Equal Opportunities Review* 26, p. 10. Note that many are multiple applications relating to the šame complaint.
53 See (1989) *Equal Opportunities Review* 26, p. 10.
54 The Employment Appeal Tribunal has described the present procedure as giving rise to delays 'which are properly described as scandalous and to amount to a denial of justice to women seeking remedy through the judicial process': *Aldridge* v *British Telecommunications plc* [1990] IRLR 10, at p. 14. Wood J suggested that independent experts should be used purely in an advisory capacity, leaving it to the Industrial Tribunal to determine the issue on the basis of evidence submitted by each side.
55 In 1987–88, there were seven successful equal pay cases and sixty-one successful sex discrimination cases. In the same period, there were 2,392 successful unfair dismissal cases. *Employment Gazette* (1989) 97, No. 5, p. 259.
56 See Ch. 6, p. 132.
57 For example, *British Railways Board* v *Paul* [1988] IRLR 20.
58 The EOC recommends that Industrial Tribunals should be able to hear representative actions, *Review of the Equal Pay Legislation*, Consultative Document, EOC, 1989.
59 Sex Discrimination Act 1975, s. 65.
60 Gregory, J., *Sex, Race and the Law*, Sage, 1987. In 1987–88 there were forty-six successful sex discrimination cases, forty-one of which attracted an award of compensation. This compares with twenty-eight out of forty-eight in 1986-87: *Employment Gazette* (1989) 97, No. 5, pp. 259–60.
61 Sex Discrimination Act 1975, s. 65(2). There is no maximum in non-employment cases: ibid, s. 66(2). The limit is reviewed annually. The figure is correct for 1989–90.
62 *Pyrrhic Victories*, above, n. 22 at p. 14.
63 (1988) *Equal Opportunities Review* 19, p. 7. In 1987-88, over half the awards of compensation were under £1,000. *Employment Gazette* (1989) 97, No. 5, p. 260.
64 [1988] IRLR 325.
65 *Von Colson and Kamann* v *Land Nordrhein-Westfalen* 14/83 (1984) ECR 1891.
66 *Southampton and South-West Hampshire Area Health Authority (Teaching)* v *Marshall (No. 2)* [1989] IRLR 459. But see now the Industrial Tribunals (Interest) Order 1990 SI 1990 No. 479.

67 Sex Discrimination Act 1975, s. 66(4) and see below p. 177.
68 Sex Discrimination Act 1975, s. 66(1). Note *Hurley* v *Mustoe* (No. 2) [1983] ICR 422. See also *Alexander* v *Home Office* [1988] ICR 685, below, n. 79 and *City of Bradford Metropolitan Council* v *Arora* [1989] IRLR 442, below, n. 85.
69 Cf. *Prestcold Ltd* v *Irvine* [1981] ICR 777.
70 Sex Discrimination Act 1975, s. 66(3).
71 Race Relations Act 1976, s. 57(3)
72 Ellis, E., *Sex Discrimination Law*, Gower, 1988, pp. 147–8.
73 [1989] IRLR 318 CA, [1990] 2 AUER 607 HL.
74 *Equal Treatment for Men and Women: Strengthening the Acts*, EOC, 1988.
75 Sex Discrimination Act 1975, s. 66(4).
76 *Hurley* v *Mustoe* (No. 2) [1983] ICR 422. The Industrial Tribunal had awarded 50 pence.
77 *Wileman* v *Minilec* [1988] IRLR 144 EAT, referring to the Industrial Tribunal.
78 [1987] ICR 719.
79 *Alexander* v *Home Office* [1988] ICR 685.
80 (1988) *Equal Opportunities Review* 19, p. 7.
81 Also, in 1989, an advertising director who resigned because of sexual harassment settled her High Court action for breach of contract and assault and battery for £25,000. Another woman accepted £6,000 from her employers: (1989) *Equal Opportunities Review* 25, p. 2. Cf. *Bracebridge Engineering Ltd* v *Darby* [1990] IRLR 3, in which a woman who successfully complained of unfair dismissal after a particularly unpleasant incident of sexual harassment was awarded only £150 in respect of her complaint under the Sex Discrimination Act.
82 [1988] IRLR 195.
83 Though the EOC Annual Report 1988 notes a marked rise in compensation indicating a 'changing climate of opinion'.
84 Above, n. 78.
85 See *Rookes* v *Barnard* [1964] 1 All ER 367 and *Cassell & Co* v *Broome* [1972] AC 1027.
86 [1989] IRLR 442.
87 Above, n. 79.
88 Above, n. 74.
89 Sex Discrimination Act 1975, s. 65(2).
90 See *Southampton and South-West Hampshire Area Health Authority (Teaching)* v *Marshall (No. 2)* [1989] IRLR 459, above, p. 175.
91 [1988] IRLR 195.
92 Above, n. 22.
93 *Equal Treatment for Men and Women: Strengthening the Acts*, EOC, 1988.
94 Sex Discrimination Act 1975, s. 4(1).
95 *Pyrrhic Victories*, above, n. 22.
96 *Equal Treatment for Men and Women: Strengthening the Acts*, EOC, 1988. See now the Industrial Tribunals (Interest) Order 1990 SI 1990 No. 479.
97 Sex Discrimination Act 1975, s. 65(3).

98 Subject to the contributory conduct of the applicant: Employment Protection (Consolidation) Act 1978, s. 73.

99 Cmnd 5724, 1974.

100 Sex Discrimination Act 1975, s. 53(1).

101 Pannick, D., *Sex Discrimination Law*, Oxford University Press, 1985, at p. 272, n. 3, suggests this means only the elimination of discrimination made unlawful by the Sex Discrimination Act 1975 and Equal Pay Act 1970, citing *Home Office* v *CRE* [1982] QB 385, 395–6.

102 Ibid at pp. 396–7.

103 Sex Discrimination Act 1975, s. 75.

104 For example, *Science Research Council* v *Nasse* [1978] IRLR 352, 355, per Lord Denning MR.

105 [1982] AC 779 HL.

106 [1984] ICR 473.

107 In *Equal Treatment for Men and Women: Strengthening the Acts*, EOC, 1988, para 4.7.

108 [1984] ICR 473.

109 See above, n. 107 at para 4.8.

110 See above, n. 107 at para 4.12.

111 Sex Discrimination Act 1975, s. 59. This applies only to 'belief' investigations, not to exploratory investigations.

112 *R* v *CRE ex parte London Borough of Hillingdon* [1982] QB 276 CA per Lord Denning at p. 286.

113 Sex Discrimination Act 1975, s. 60(2). There are no rules as to when it must be published. Information given to EOC during a formal investigation is confidential and disclosure is an offence: Sex Discrimination Act 1975, s. 61.

114 Ibid, s. 60(1)(*b*).

115 Also covers discriminatory practices, discriminatory advertisements, instructing another to discriminate and putting pressure on another to discriminate: ibid, s. 67.

116 Especially, Sex Discrimination (Formal Investigations) (Amendment) Regulations 1977, SI 1977 No. 843.

117 Sex Discrimination Act 1975, s. 67(3).

118 The EOC wishes the right to make representations against the notice abolished: *Equal Treatment for Men and Women: Strengthening the Acts*, EOC, 1988.

119 Sex Discrimination Act 1975, s. 68.

120 [1982] ICR 304.

121 Ibid, at p. 313.

122 Ellis, E., *Sex Discrimination Law*, Gower, 1988, p. 255.

123 Sex Discrimination Act 1975, s. 70.

124 Ibid, s. 71. Also applies to circumstances where a court or tribunal has previously found a person guilty of unlawful discrimination.

125 Ibid, s. 71(2).

126 *R* v *CRE ex parte London Borough of Hillingdon* [1982] QB 276, CA, p. 287.

127 *R* v *CRE ex parte London Borough of Hillingdon* [1982] AC 779, HL, p. 788.

128 Though the EOC has proposed that it should be able to require the cessation of specific practices: *Equal Treatment for Men and Women: Strengthening the Acts*, EOC, 1988.

129 The EOC has proposed that individuals should be entitled to present a claim to an Industrial Tribunal or County Court as appropriate. Above, n. 116.

130 Appleby, G., and Ellis, E., 'Formal investigations: the CRE and EOC as law enforcement agencies' (1984) *Public Law* 236. Ellis, E., *Sex Discrimination Law*, Gower, 1988, pp. 259–69. Gregory, J., *Sex, Race and the Law*, Sage, 1987, Ch. 6.

131 See Sex Discrimination Act 1975, ss. 37–40, 53–56, 71. See Sacks, V., 'The EOC ten years on' (1986) *Modern Law Review* 49, p. 560.

132 Examples: *Hayward* v *Cammell Laird Shipbuilders Ltd* [1988] ICR 464; *Pickstone* v *Freemans plc* [1988] ICR 697; *Marshall* v *Southampton and South-West Hampshire Area Health Authority (Teaching)* 152/84 [1986] ICR 335 ECJ.

133 See Meehan, E. M., *Women's Rights at Work*, Penguin, 1985.

134 All the chairmen have, so far, been women.

135 Sex Discrimination Act 1975, Sched. 3, para 2.

136 Ibid, Sched. 3, para 14.

137 The Charter was presented to the 1979 TUC Conference by Bill Keys, whose union SOGAT had been the subject of one of the few Formal Investigations by the EOC. In 1985, when women formed half of SOGAT's membership, it sent six women out of a delegation of forty-two to the TUC Conference: Boston, S., *Women Workers and the Trade Unions*, Lawrence & Wishart, 1988, p. 330.

138 TUC Report 1988, cited in (1988) *Equal Opportunities Review* 22, p. 4; also, 'South Eastern Region TUC Women's Committee: still moving towards equality' (1989) *Equal Opportunities Review* 24, p. 4.

139 Rule changes at the 1989 TUC resulted in a doubling of the reserved seats for women on the General Council. Of the fifty-three members of the General Council, fifteen are women.

140 For example, in the machinists' dispute at Fords. See Gregory, op cit, n. 1, at pp. 7–8.

141 For example, the speech therapists were backed by the Manufacturing, Science and Finance Union.

142 See (1988) *Equal Opportunities Review* 22, p. 9, 'Equal value, a union update'.

143 Dickens, L., Townley, B., and Winchester, D., *Tackling Sex Discrimination through Collective Bargaining: The Impact of Section 6 of the Sex Discrimination Act 1986*, London: HMSO, 1988.

144 *Commission of European Communities* v *UK* 165/82 [1984] ICR 192 ECJ.

145 Also employers' rules, trade union rules, employers' association rules, rules of professional organisations and qualifying bodies.

146 As to whether this means anything in practice, see 'Advertising equality' (1988) *Equal Opportunities Review* 22, p. 15.

147 Local authorities have reported that they find the monitoring of equality policies to be difficult: (1988) 'Survey by Association of Metropolitan Authorities', *Equal Opportunities Review* 22, p. 3. But see also Harris, H.

'Practical ethnic and sex monitoring – the Calderdale experience', *Employment Gazette* (1989) 97, No. 2, p. 94.
148 Local Government Act 1988, s. 17. See *R.* v *London Borough of Islington ex parte Building Employers Confederation* [1989] IRLR 382.
149 Race Relations Act 1976, s. 71, and Local Government Act, 1988, s. 18.

Chapter nine   Conclusions

1 Smart, C., *Feminism and the Power of Law*, Routledge, 1989.
2 For examples of the 'liberal' approach, see Pannick, D., *Sex Discrimination Law*, Oxford University Press, 1985, and Ellis, E., *Sex Discrimination Law*, Gower, 1988.
3 Op cit, n. 1.
4 Ibid, p. 3.
5 Ibid, p. 5.
6 Ibid, p. 138.
7 Ibid, pp. 138–9.
8 Ibid, p. 139.
9 [1988] ICR 697.
10 [1988] ICR 464.
11 [1985] IRLR 367.
12 [1989] IRLR 241.
13 [1989] IRLR 381 in the CA. See [1990] 2 All ER 607.
14 [1988] ICR 391.
15 On this point we agree with Smart, who notes in the context of abortion that 'the law may concede a right, but if the state refuses to fund abortions or abortion clinics it is an empty right', op cit, n. 1, at p. 144.

Bibliography

Allott, A. (1980) *The Limits of Law*, London: Butterworths.

Appleby, G. and Ellis, E. (1984) 'Formal investigations: the CRE and EOC as law enforcement agencies', *Public Law* 236.

Aristotle, *Nichomachean Ethics*, translated by H. Rackham (1962), London: Heinemann.

Baldwin, R. and Houghton, J. (1986) 'Circular arguments: the status and legitimacy of administrative rules', *Public Law* 239.

Ballard, B. (1984) 'Women part-time workers: evidence from the Women and Employment Survey', *Employment Gazette* 92, No. 9.

Barron, R. D. and Norris, G. M. (1976) 'Sexual divisions and the dual labour market', in D. Barker and S. Allen (eds) *Dependence and Exploitation in Work and Marriage*, London: Longman.

Bates, J. D. N. (1988) 'Gender, social security and pensions: the myth of the "everyday housewife"?', in S. McLean and N. Burrows (eds) *The Legal Relevance of Gender*, London: Macmillan.

Bedau, H. (1975) 'Inequality, how much and why?', *Journal of Social Philosophy* 6: 25.

Beddoe, R. (1986) 'Independent experts?', *Equal Opportunities Review* 6: 13.

Beechey, V. (1987) *A Matter of Hours: Women, Part-Time Work and the Labour Market*, London: Polity Press.

Beechey, V. (1987) *Unequal Work*, London: Verso.

Beveridge Report (1942) *Report of the Committee on Social Insurance and Allied Services*, Cmnd 6404, London: HMSO.

Boston, S. (1988) *Women Workers and the Trade Unions*, London: Lawrence & Wishart.

Bowers, J. (1990) *A Practical Approach to Employment Law*, 3rd ed, London: Blackstone Press.

Bowey, A. (1988) *Evaluation of the Role of Independent Experts in Equal Value Cases in Britain 1984–1988*, EOC.

Breugel, I. (1979) 'Women as a reserve army of labour', *Feminist Review* 12.

Byre, A. (1987) *Indirect Discrimination*, EOC.

Cain, M. and Hunt, A. (1979) *Marx and Engels on Law*, London: Academic Press.

Campbell, T. (1983) *The Left and Rights: A Conceptual Analysis of the Idea of Socialist Rights*, London: Routledge & Kegan Paul.

Collins, H. (1984) *Marxism and Law*, Oxford University Press.

Collinson, D. (1988) *Barriers to Fair Selection*, EOC.

Coyle, A. (1985) 'Going private' *Feminist Review* 6.

Coyle, A. (1988) 'Continuity and change: women in paid work', in A. Coyle and J. Skinner (eds) *Women and Work*, London: Macmillan.

Creighton, W. B. (1979) *Working Women and the Law*, London: Mansell.

Cretney, S. M. (1987) *Elements of Family Law*, London: Sweet & Maxwell.

Cross, R. (1977) *Precedent in English Law*, 3rd ed., Oxford: Clarendon Press.

Curran, M. (1985) *Stereotypes and Selection*, EOC.

Daniel, W. W. (1980) *Maternity Rights: The Experience of Women*, Report No. 588, Policy Studies Institute.

Daniel, W. W. (1981) *Maternity Rights: The Experience of Employers*, Report No. 596, Policy Studies Institute.

Daniels, N. (ed.) (1975) *Reading Rawls*, Oxford: Blackwell.

David, M. and Land H. (1983) 'Sex and social policy', in H. Glennerster (ed.) *The Future of the Welfare State*, London: Heinemann.

Devlin, P. (1968) *The Enforcement of Morals*, Oxford University Press.

Dex, S. (1987) *Women's Occupational Mobility*, London: Macmillan.

Dex, S. and Shaw, L. (1986) *British and American Women at Work*, London: Macmillan.

Dicey, A. V. (1885) *An Introduction to the Study of the Law of the Constitution*, 10th ed., London: Macmillan.

Dickens, L., Hart, M., Jones, M., and Weekes, B. (1985) *Dismissed: A Study of Unfair Dismissal and the Industrial Tribunal System*, Oxford: Blackwell.

Dickens, L., Townley, B., and Winchester, D. (1988) *Tackling Sex Discrimination through Collective Bargaining: The Impact of Section 6 of the Sex Discrimination Act 1986*, London: HMSO.

Disney, R. and Szyszczak, E. (1989) 'Part-time work: reply to Catherine Hakim', *Industrial Law Journal* 18: 223–8.

Dworkin, G. (1971) 'Paternalism', in R. Wasserstrom (ed.), *Morality and the Law*, Wadsworth, USA.

Dworkin, R. (1978) *Taking Rights Seriously*, London: Duckworth.

Dworkin, R. (1986) *Law's Empire*, London: Fontana.

Edwards, J. (1987) *Positive Discrimination*, London: Tavistock.

Elias, P. and Main, B. (1982) *Women's Working Lives: Evidence from the National Training Survey*, University of Warwick: Institute for Employment Research.

Ellis, E. (1988) *Sex Discrimination Law*, London: Gower.

Employment Gazette, Department of Employment.

Engels, F. (1884) *The Origins of the Family, Private Property and the State*.

Equal in the Law (1988) The Law Society.

Equal Opportunities Review (1985): 'Harassment at work', 4: 8.

Equal Opportunities Review (1987): 'Achieving equal opportunity through positive action', 14: 13.

Equal Opportunities Review (1989): 'Age discrimination: over the hill at 45?', 25: 10; 'Advertising equality', 22: 15.

Equal Opportunities Review (1989): 'Parental and family leave', 27: 8; 'Equal value update' 26: 10.

Equal Treatment for Men and Women: Strengthening the Acts (1988) EOC.

Equality for Women (1974), London: HMSO, Cmnd 5724.

Finnis, J. (1980) *Natural Law and Natural Rights*, Oxford: Clarendon Press.

Fuller, L. (1958) 'Positivism and fidelity to law – a reply to Professor Hart', *Harvard Law Review* 71: 630–72.

Fuller, L. (1979) *The Morality of Law*, Yale University Press.

Goldstein, L. (1987) *Precedent in Law*, Oxford: Clarendon Press.

Graham, C. and Lewis, N. (1985) *The Role of ACAS Conciliation in Equal Pay and Sex Discrimination Cases*, EOC.

Gregory, J. (1982) 'Why women are giving up the fight', *Feminist Review* 10: 75–89.

Gregory, J. (1987) *Sex, Race and the Law*, London: Sage.

Griffith, J. A. (1985) *Politics of the Judiciary*, 3rd ed., London: Fontana.

Hakim, C. (1979) *Occupational Segregation*, Department of Employment Research Paper No. 9, London: HMSO.

Hakim, C. (1987) *Home-Based Work in Britain*, Department of Employment Research Paper No. 60, London: HMSO.

Hakim, C. (1989) 'Employment rights: a comparison of part-time and full-time employees', *Industrial Law Journal* 18: 69–83.

Hakim, C. (1989) 'Employment rights: a comparison of part-time and full-time employees', *Industrial Law Journal* 18: 228–9.

Harris, H. (1989) 'Practical ethnic and sex monitoring – the Calderdale Experience', *Employment Gazette* 97, No. 2.

Hart, H. L. A. (1958) 'Positivism and the separation of laws and morals', *Harvard Law Review* 71: 593–629.

Hart, H. L. A. (1961) *The Concept of Law*, Oxford University Press.

Hart, H. L. A. (1968) *Law, Liberty and Morality*, Oxford University Press.

Hart, H. L. A. (1983) *Essays in Jurisprudence and Philosophy*, Oxford University Press.

Hills, J. (1988) *Changing Tax*, CPAG.

Holdsworth, W. (1935) *A History of English Law*, Vol III, 4th ed., London: Methuen.

Incomes Data Services (1988) Study 402, London: Data Services.

Incomes Data Services (1989) Study 425, London: Data Services.

Industrial Tribunals, A Report by Justice (1987) London.

Keevash, S. (1985) 'Wages Councils: an examination of trade union and Conservative government misconceptions about the effect of statutory wage fixing', *Industrial Law Journal* 14: 217.

Legislating for Change (1986), EOC.

Leonard, A. (1986) *The First Eight Years: A Profile of Applicants to the Industrial Tribunals under the Sex Discrimination Act 1975 and the Equal Pay Act 1970*, EOC.

Leonard, A. (1987) *Judging Inequality: The Effectiveness of the Industrial Tribunal System in Sex Discrimination and Equal Pay Cases*, London: Cobden Trust.

Leonard, A. (1987) *Pyrrhic Victories: Winning Sex Discrimination and Equal Pay Cases in the Industrial Tribunals 1980–84*, London: HMSO.

Lewis, R. (ed.) (1986) *Labour Law in Britain*, Oxford: Blackwell.

Lloyd, D., Baron Lloyd of Hampstead and Freeman, M. D. A. (1985) *Lloyd's Introduction to Jurisprudence*, 5th ed., London: Stevens.

Lockley, A. (1989) 'Regulating group actions' *New Law Journal* 139: 798.

Lukes, S. (1982) 'Marxism, morality and justice', in G. H. R. Parkinson (ed.) *Marx and Marxisms*, Cambridge University Press.

McCluskey, J. H. (1987) *Law Justice and Democracy*, London: Sweet & Maxwell.

McCrudden, C. (ed.) (1987) *Women, Employment and Equality Law*, London: Eclipse.

Makeham, P. (1980) *Youth Unemployment*, Department of Employment Research Paper No. 10.

Martin, J. and Roberts, C. (1984) *Women and Employment: A Lifetime Perspective*, London: HMSO.

Martin, J. and Roberts, C. (1984) 'Evidence from the Women and Employment Survey', *Employment Gazette* 92, No. 5.

Meehan, E. M. (1985) *Women's Rights at Work*, London: Macmillan.

Mill, J. S. (1859) *On Liberty*, Harmondsworth: Penguin, 1983.

Mill, J. S. (1869) 'The subjection of women', in J. S. and H. T. Mill *Essays on Sex Equality*, University of Chicago Press, 1970.

Moss, P. (1988) *Childcare and Equality of Opportunity in the EEC*, London: HMSO.

Nozick, R. (1974) *Anarchy, State and Utopia*, Oxford University Press.

O'Donovan, K. (1985) *Sexual Divisions in Law*, London: Weidenfeld & Nicolson.

O'Donovan, K. and Szyszczak, E. (1988) *Equality and Sex Discrimination Law*, Oxford: Blackwell.

O'Grady F. and Wakefield, H. (1989) *Women, Work and Maternity: The Inside Story*, Maternity Alliance.

Ogus, A. and Barendt, E. (1988) *The Law of Social Security*, 3rd ed., London: Butterworths.

Pannick, D. (1985) *Sex Discrimination Law*, Oxford University Press.

Pascall, G. (1986) *Social Policy: A Feminist Analysis*, London: Tavistock.

Phelps Brown, H. (1977) *The Inequality of Pay*, Oxford University Press.

Rawls, J. (1973) *A Theory of Justice*, Oxford University Press.

Rimmer, L. (1988) 'The intra-family distribution of paid work, 1968–81', in A. Hunt (ed.) *Women and Paid Work*, London: Macmillan.

Robbins, D. (1986) *Wanted: Railmen*, EOC.

Roberts, S. (1979) *Order and Dispute: An Introduction to Legal Anthropology*, Harmondsworth: Penguin.

Rubenstein, M. (1984) *Equal Pay for Work of Equal Value*, London: Macmillan.

Sacks, V., 'The EOC ten years on' (1986) *Modern Law Review* 49, p. 560.

Smart, C.(1989) *Feminism and the Power of Law*, London: Routledge.

Smith, I. T. and Wood, J. C. (1989) *Industrial Law*, 4th ed, London: Butterworths.

Stang Dahl, T. (1987) *Women's Law*, Norwegian University Press.

Stephen, J. F. (1874) *Liberty, Equality and Fraternity*, London.

Taub, N. and Schneider, E. (1982) 'Perspectives on women's subordination and the role of law', in D. Kairys (ed.) *The Politics of Law*, New York: Partheon.

Warrington, R. (1983) 'Pashukanis and the commodity form theory', in D. Sugarman (ed.) *Legality, Ideology and the State*, London: Academic Press.

Wedderburn, K. W. (1986) *The Worker and the Law*, Harmondsworth: Penguin.

Women and Employment Survey (1980) Department of Employment and Office of Population Census and Surveys.

Women and Men in Britain 1987 (1988) EOC, London: HMSO.

Women and Men in Britain 1989 (1989) EOC, London: HMSO.

Women and Unemployment (1989) Employment Institute Economic Report, Vol. 4, No. 5.

Yeandle, S. (1984) *Women's Working Lives: Patterns and Strategies*, London: Tavistock.

Index